EVERYMAN, I will go with thee,

and be thy guide,

In thy most need to go by thy side

JOHN KEATS

Born Finsbury, 31st October 1795. At John Clarke's school, Enfield, 1803–11. Father died and mother remarried, 1804. Mother died, guardians appointed, 1810. Apprenticed 1811 to Thomas Hammond, a surgeon at Edmonton. Entered Guy's Hospital as a medical student in October 1815. Became a dresser in March 1816; in July pased examination making him Licentiate of the Society of Apothecaries; gave up medicine for poetry in December. Began *Endymion* at Shanklin and Margate, 1817. In 1818 toured Lakes and Scotland with Charles Brown (June–August); in the autumn met Fanny Brawne; nursed younger brother Tom, who died in December; went to live with Brown in Hampstead. Shanklin and Winchester with Brown, June–July 1819. First haemorrhage, February 1820; sailed for Italy with Severn in September; reached Naples in October, and Rome in November. Died in Rome, 23rd February 1821.

RICHARD MONCKTON MILNES,
LORD HOUGHTON

Social leader and politician, author and minor poet. Born London, 1809; educated at Trinity College, Cambridge; travelled in Germany, Italy, Greece and Egypt; married Annabel Crewe, 1851 (their son became Marquess of Crewe in 1911); created Baron Houghton, 1863. Died at Vichy, 1885.

LORD HOUGHTON

The Life & Letters
of John Keats

INTRODUCTION BY
SYLVA NORMAN

DENT: LONDON
EVERYMAN'S LIBRARY
DUTTON: NEW YORK

© Introduction and Notes,
J. M. Dent & Sons Ltd, 1969

NO. 801

SBN: 460 00801 3

INTRODUCTION

AT AN hour when illness and despair had laid their hold on him
Keats called for the epitaph that now stands carved indelibly
on his tombstone: 'Here lies one whose name was writ in water.'
Perhaps Joseph Severn should not have paid attention; Keats
knew, deep in his own nature, that he would be numbered hereafter among the English poets. He was aware of the brief time
given him to stake his claim: 'When I have fears that I may
cease to be . . .'; and he remains the shortest lived to attain
such immortality.

The life span of the five major Romantic poets presents a
statistical anomaly: like a planetary system, each one's orbit
lies within the other. Wordsworth, the first-born, is the last to
quit—as hoary as the outer planet Saturn. Coleridge, born soon
after him, dies many years before, but attains his sixties. Then
at both ends there is a gap until we reach the birth of Byron,
who dies ten years before Coleridge at thirty-six. Shelley comes
after Byron and dies before him on the verge of thirty. Lastly
John Keats sets up his tiny inner orbit, like the planet Mercury
half lost in sun-rays, and is gone a long year before Shelley.

Leaving aside the Elder Statesmen in their dignified orbits,
we find a further oddity touching Keats alone. Why was he left
so long without a memoir? Byron, a world figure whether as
rebel or hero, evoked memoirs, conversations, portraits from
nearly all who crossed his path. Shelley, less spectacular, was
yet subjected to memorial poems, admonitions, prefatory
memoirs to pirated volumes; later to biographies from his
personal friends. But Keats, apart from a brief sketch in Leigh
Hunt's *Lord Byron and Some of his Contemporaries*, might
indeed have had his name obliterated by the moving waters.
And this although he left a number of living and articulate
friends.

When at last, twenty-seven years after his death, a *Life and
Letters* appeared, it was the work of an admiring stranger who
had been a schoolboy when his subject died. It is true that the

young Richard Monckton Milnes had, as a Cambridge under-graduate, paid tribute. A member of that exclusive literary group, the 'Apostles', he had helped to produce the first London edition (1829) of Shelley's elegy on Keats, the *Adonais*. He had since talked in Rome with Joseph Severn, who could tell him much about the poet's last illness, and led him to reflect on that prodigious promise cut short so early by disease and death.

The decisive factor was his meeting with Charles Armitage Brown at Landor's villa in Fiesole. Milnes, now steeped in 'Keatsiana', was impressed by Brown's report of extensive manuscript material that he meant to publish. Called to New Zealand Brown 'confided to my care' his whole collection, together with his Life of Keats.

So much we learn from Milnes, but there is more to it. The truth is not that Keats's friends were negligent, but that too many of them were anxious to perform, and, as so often happens, their ideas and opinions were incompatible. First in the field was Keats's publisher John Taylor, who fancied him-self as a literary man—a poet, even—and saw his obligation. Within a month of Keats's death he was writing to a relative: 'I believe I shall try to write his life—it is the Wish of his Friends, and was Keats's Wish also.' Later he announced and advertised this memoir in the Press. Bailey and Reynolds obediently handed him their manuscript material; Woodhouse, the firm's literary adviser, was inclined to do the same until he saw that the matter was not progressing. All knew that Charles Brown had a rival project. Severn sent Taylor genial wishes, but his valuable papers went to Brown.

Quietly Taylor had withdrawn; but Brown, left in possession, came up against a mammoth-sized obstacle of his own construc-ting. For him the villain of the entire tragedy was Keats's younger brother George (Milnes unaccountably writes George down as the eldest). Brown believed, and yelled it on the house tops, that George, on his second departure for America, had taken with him money from the family inheritance that belonged by right to John. After brooding darkly on the facts and figures he acquired the fanatical certainty that is born of prejudice. Charles Dilke supported George's claim to be innocent and benevolent. To restrain Brown from a public libel George laid an injunction on the copyright poems he held. Without them Brown was hamstrung. George, however, meant to take his place, writing to Dilke in 1836 of his intention to do a worthy biography of his brother based on his letters and memories.

George too dropped out, withdrew his injunction and left a clear field to Brown. But now, in 1841, Brown had yielded to his son's persuasion to follow him as an emigrant to New Zealand. In deciding to hand over his Keats material he by-passed the whole circle and offered it, Life and all, to Richard Monckton Milnes, hoping no doubt that an outsider would support his views.

Now it was up to Milnes to magnetize manuscripts from their several owners. A man of tact, charm and discrimination, he was almost totally successful. Today we have the privilege of being able to *watch* him at it. The publication of *The Keats Circle* (see Bibliography, page xiv) brought together all the correspondence relating to Keats that Milnes had amassed, and that is now in the Harvard Library. It gives us the whole background to the *Life and Letters*. Milnes himself, in Volume II, has become a central figure. For three years—1845–8—he was cajoling, collecting, persuading the reluctant, gently flattering the amenable. Charles Cowden Clarke sent in a wad of reminiscences; Severn (who believed himself part author) supplemented what Milnes already had from him through Brown. The artist B. R. Haydon leapt to his assistance. Dilke was still hostile—hostile, that is, to Brown's memory, for Brown had not long survived his emigration. Of the original *Life* he had written to Severn, 'in truth it is no Memoir of Keats, but a memoir of Brown in his intercourse with Keats—or rather, a dream on the subject'. Brown's Life, the basic germ of Milne's book, is on view entire in *The Keats Circle*. It must be admitted that Dilke has a case. The piece is anything but impartial; all the scenes wherein Brown is a participant are written up strongly in his favour. Apart from this *Brown*ing the account is coloured only by the incorporated letters from Keats and Severn.

With all this original material spread out, we can observe the destined biographer employing his arts of tact and compromise in the effort to please his worthy helpers. (He notes, by the way, that there is no response from Benjamin Bailey—vanished without trace. Chancing his arm he writes that Bailey, poor thing, shared Keats's fate by dying soon after him. That news was to call forth enormous letters from the *ghost* of Bailey which has wafted itself to Ceylon and functions as Archdeacon of Colombo.)

Milnes was undoubtedly aware of eyes and ears all round him. He would have to walk delicately to avoid offending one friend or another. Two factors were distinctly helpful: one, that half his book was already written for him by Keats in those incomparable letters. Here, except for some transcribing slips, it was impossible to go wrong.

The second factor was a negative one. In October 1845—the year Milnes seriously began assembling material—Severn wrote giving him 'the real tragedy of [Keats's] death'; the anguish of the fatal symptoms 'when he was about to be married to a most lovely and accomplished girl . . . this Lady was a Miss Brawn [sic]'. It would be the first time Milnes had heard the name. In 1833 she had married Louis Lindon and lived mainly out of England. The existence of Keats's stormy letters to her was known to few, and Milnes was not among them. Severn alone dissented from the need for secrecy.

Fanny was living; the Victorian age with its façade of prim morality had clamped down on the social scene. It was unthinkable that her identity should be hinted at. So strong were the seismic, evangelical shudders that not only could poor Fanny have been ruined but the book as well. It was still a Victorian world when Harry Buxton Forman boldly published the letters to Fanny in 1878. They brought the expected outcry from the 'country parsonage'. Today, apart from a school that would judge each work of art as a monolith in a desert, opinion is that all available facets of the generating spirit should be brought to bear on it—with an emphasis, thanks to Freudian analysis, on sex. Evidence that each creator lives in his creation leans with particular force on the Romantics; but the artist has to educate his public, and so loses the votes of untaught generations. The citizen of the 1840s put more faith in ethics than in natural laws. Since Milnes's aim was to substitute for the milksop myth a vigorous, manly, pugilistic hero he could not have exposed this other aspect even had the letters been in his hands. It was fortunate for him to have been spared the problem.

Yet he did have some awkward balances to negotiate. By far the most delicate was that financial jeremiad of Brown's against George Keats and Dilke. Brown had been immovably convinced that George was guilty. The accused, from far Kentucky, sent a number of rational, defensive arguments home to Dilke with a backing of hard figures and a considerable air of honesty. It was for Milnes to make his own decision. George Keats had died at the end of 1841, Brown in the following year. The other friends and helpers—some supporting Brown, some George—were, together with Dilke, alive and watching.

Milnes can be seen displaying the celebrated tact. He could not with decency condemn the man whose invitation was responsible for his present task. Yet he was not convinced that George was a soulless hypocrite. It was a case for compromise. Brown's indignation sprang from loyalty to a suffering friend left so impoverished. ('Didn't he make Keats pay for his lodging?' the enemies of Brown rejoined.) But George's perceptive devotion to his brother almost served as circumstantial evidence. In the event, Milnes chose to cut himself in half: deplore the destitute state that John was left in, and defend George as having been unconscious of it. The whole financial puzzle goes back to a parental lawsuit, and a sum in Chancery left to the Keats children by the wills of their maternal grandparents. A recent piece of close research into the documents has established almost beyond doubt that George Keats did not go off with a penny of John's inheritance.[1] Dilke remained unappeasable. His copy of Milnes's *Life and Letters* is festooned with marginal comments in a half-illegible hand. The angriest were aimed at Brown, whom he still saw at the base of Milnes's edifice.

For a biographer to be so copiously advised can be both asset and liability, when he cannot check on his advisers' facts. An outstanding instance is the tale of the 'Bright Star' sonnet as being Keats's final poem, composed on shipboard as he sailed from England. The delusion, which was to travel some way down the years, is not to be blamed on Milnes. He had it direct from the one observer. Did not Severn watch Keats write it in his copy of Shakespeare's poems? Had the artist been himself a poet he would have known that even a sonnet does not work in the mind so fast. Keats *recalled* it, possibly

[1] It established, too, the poignant fact that a separate legacy payable to each Keats child by the court was not applied for because no one, during Keats's lifetime, knew of its existence (see Robert Gittings, *The Keats Inheritance*, 1964).

from memory, in order to give Severn a memento. 'Bright Star' is commonly dated 1819, addressed, though namelessly, to Fanny Brawne.

For another poetical error Milnes must once again be spared the lash. Keats had written in a letter to his brothers of 16th February 1818: 'The Wednesday before last, Shelley, Hunt and I each wrote a sonnet on the river Nile.' Having quoted the letter Milnes presents the sonnets: the first by Keats, the second by Hunt, the third—not Shelley's 'To the Nile' but 'Ozymandias'! The three sonnets were composed on 4th February; Hunt had published 'Ozymandias' in the January *Examiner*. But Shelley was not cheating at the contest; he did write a sonnet 'To the Nile' on 4th February, beginning, 'Month after month the gathered rains descend . . .' It was found among Hunt's papers (to which Milnes was denied access) and published in the *St James's Magazine* for March 1876. Seeking the sonnet, Milnes took the nearest he could find in date and setting. Nobody, bar Hunt, could have corrected him.

In view of Milnes's activities as Member of Parliament he can hardly have spared time to test and verify all his information. By 'killing' Bailey he missed one delightful touch that reached him afterwards, in a letter with much clerical phraseology about 'poor Keats': 'If you placed your hand upon his head, the silken curls felt like the rich plumage of a bird.' This tactile portrait suggests a poetic vein in Bailey. Reverting to himself, he *did* send Milnes, not poetry, but a doggerel quatrain:

Dicky Milnes—Dicky Milnes! Why what the deuce could ail ye
When you wrote the life of Keats—to write the death of Bailey—
The poet sleeps—oh! let him sleep—within the silent tomb-o
But Parson Bailey lives and kicks—Archdeacon of Colombo.

However, Milnes's concern was with the sleeping poet, not the kicking parson. Nor has the poet slept unregarded. In the more-than-century since the *Life and Letters* appeared Keats has come up to us more closely. His letters, in greater numbers and more accurate transcriptions, illuminate the poetical mind as never before; his personality retains its primary colours. Again, only biographers of our scientific era have gauged the influence of Keats's medical training. Milnes had only some remarks of Brown's and the account sent by a fellow student.

Henry Stephens chose to depict him as immersed in poetry, careless of study, using his technical notebooks for an alien purpose.

It is now recognized that Keats was a hard worker, enjoyed much of his hospital training, and came through tough examinations that his seniors failed in. As a surgeon's dresser he performed all but the gravest operations, dealt with emergency cases, steeled himself to sights that would appal the squeamish. Even with half his mind on literature, the other half was strong enough to see him through the test that made him a Licentiate of the Society of Apothecaries, qualified to practise.

The other Romantics took their university course in arts and classics; Keats's apprenticeship to life was in a more material school. It taught him the realism that drives iron into his Olympic deities; it taught him to look with an expert's certainty on his own death sign when it came. As doctor, his handicap lay in too great a sympathy with human suffering. He could not cultivate the cold indifference needed to cut into the flesh and organs of an unanaesthetized patient when a false twist of the instrument could cause harm.

It is only this inverted view of the surgeon Keats that Milnes is able to bring out. 'Back to your gallipots,' the reviewers had taunted, having heard a whisper as to his calling when they damned *Endymion*. It was not such a bad shot, but that Keats's natural ambition, even in that discarded field, leapt higher than gallipots; if poetry would not pay, he thought of signing on as a ship's surgeon, bound for the East Indies.

John Keats was to sail no farther east than Italy, himself the patient. Yet this twenty-five year life in a minimal orbit has been expanding, filling and intensifying ever since its end. The biography of 1848 stands out, and always must, as the initial broadening of the boundaries. Milnes himself still looked on the poetical works as immature harbingers; no more than— to adapt a phrase from Shelley—shadows of Beauty unbeheld. It might even have surprised him to have known that twentieth-century critics would find the beauty visible and immortal.

No matter if Milnes did understate the genius; no matter if his aspiring last-page peroration was obscured by a smoking clash of images. What matters is that he has given us Keats —in the words of his letters, from the memories of his friends, through the biographer's ability to deduce and sympathize.

He has given us a Keats of many angles and much argument, neither classical deity nor cockney weakling, but a rather unusually complete human, whether grave or gay. Hence, the biography is a key work and an epoch-maker that merits a permanent place in the history of his reputation.

SYLVA NORMAN.

London, 1969.

SELECT BIBLIOGRAPHY

POETICAL WORKS. Lifetime Publications: *Poems*, 1817; *Endymion*, 1818; *Lamia, Isabella, The Eve of St Agnes, and Other Poems*, 1820.
Posthumous Publications: *The Poetical Works of Coleridge, Shelley and Keats*, Paris, 1829; *The Poetical Works of John Keats*, ed. R. Monckton Milnes, 1854; *The Poems of John Keats*, ed. E. de Selincourt, 5th ed., 1926; *The Poetical Works of John Keats*, ed. H. W. Garrod, 1939; revised, 1958.

LETTERS. *The Letters of John Keats to Fanny Brawne*, ed. H. Buxton Forman, 1878; *The Letters of John Keats*, ed. M. Buxton Forman, 1931; *Letters of Fanny Brawne to Fanny Keats*, ed. Fred Edgcumbe, 1936; *The Keats Circle, Letters and Papers 1816–1878*, ed. H. E. Rollins, 2 vols., Cambridge, Mass., 1948; *The Letters of John Keats*, ed. H. E. Rollins, 2 vols., Cambridge, Mass., 1958.

BIOGRAPHY. Sir Sidney Colvin, *John Keats: His Life and Poetry, His Friends and After-Fame*, 1917; Amy Lowell, *John Keats*, 2 vols., New York and Boston, 1925; Dorothy Hewlett, *A Life of John Keats* (formerly *Adonais*), 1950; Aileen Ward, *John Keats: the Making of a Poet*, New York, 1963; Walter Jackson Bate, *John Keats*, Cambridge, Mass., 1963; Robert Gittings, *The Keats Inheritance*, 1964; Robert Gittings, *John Keats*, 1968.

CRITICAL WORKS. John Middleton Murry, *Keats and Shakespeare*, 1925; M. R. Ridley, *Keats's Craftsmanship*, 1933; Claude Lee Finney, *The Evolution of Keats's Poetry*, 2 vols., Cambridge, Mass., 1936; Earl R. Wasserman, *The Finer Tone: Keats's Major Poems*, Baltimore, 1953; Robert Gittings, *John Keats: The Living Year*, 1954.

KEATS'S CORRESPONDENTS

THE following is a brief account of Keats's correspondents and friends.

His family: both parents being dead by 1810 it consisted, for the present purpose, of the poet (the eldest son); his brothers, George born 1797 and Thomas born 1799; also a sister, Fanny, born in 1803. In addition to these we have to notice George's wife Georgiana Augusta, whom he married in 1818, and her mother, Mrs Wylie.

Keats's first publisher was Ollier (who published all Shelley's works), but *Endymion* and the 1820 volume were brought out by Taylor & Hessey, a firm distinguished for its associations with authors and artists. Keats had a happy relationship with both partners, and Taylor helped financially to make his Italian journey possible.

Richard Woodhouse (1788–1834), a lawyer, was literary and legal adviser to Taylor & Hessey. He believed in Keats's genius to the extent of transcribing all verse and prose manuscripts he could come by. His collection of Keatsiana is now invaluable to scholars and students.

Charles Armitage Brown (1786–1842), close friend and housemate of Keats, was a merchant until 1810, when he inherited enough money to enable him to give up trade. In 1814 he had a comic opera produced at Drury Lane, and in 1818 collaborated with Keats in the writing of *Otho the Great*. After Keats's death he lived for several years in Italy, and in 1841 emigrated to New Zealand, where he died.

John Hamilton Reynolds (1794–1852) met Keats at Leigh Hunt's Hampstead cottage in 1816, by which time he had already published a good deal of verse. He entered the legal profession in 1818, but kept up his interest in literature, writing regularly for periodicals.

Charles Wentworth Dilke (1789–1864), essayist and critic, made the acquaintance of Keats in 1817. He owned and edited the *Athenaeum* from 1830 to 1846 and is chiefly remembered for *Papers of a Critic*, edited by his grandson, Sir Charles Dilke.

Joseph Severn (1793–1879), the painter, accompanied Keats to Italy and was with him at his death. Afterwards he won the Royal Academy's travelling scholarship, spent much of his life in Rome, was British Consul there, 1861–72, died in Rome in 1789 and was buried beside Keats.

James Henry Leigh Hunt (1784–1859). As Keats remained largely outside the orbits of such men as Shelley, Wordsworth, Coleridge, and Byron, Hunt was the most prominent man of letters with whom he came into close contact. In some ways this was unfortunate. It was Hunt, however, who brought about the meeting of Keats and Shelley, and it was he who, in *Lord Byron and some of his Contemporaries* (1828), wrote the earliest account of Keats.

Benjamin Robert Haydon (1786–1846), the painter, met Keats in autumn 1816. For his tragic career, which ended in suicide, see his *Autobiography and Memoirs* edited by Tom Taylor (new edition with introduction by Aldous Huxley, 1926).

William Haslam (1795–1851) is said to have known Keats when the latter was a medical student. As a business man, he was not concerned with literature otherwise than as a friend of the poet and his circle. He helped substantially towards Keats's journey to Rome.

Benjamin Bailey (1791–1853) was an undergraduate at Oxford when Keats first met him. He entered the Church and eventually became Archdeacon of Colombo. He published a volume of verse and books on religious subjects.

Charles Cowden Clarke (1787–1877) was the son of John Clarke, at whose school he was an usher when Keats was educated there .It was Clarke who introduced Keats to Leigh Hunt. He and his wife Mary collaborated in *Recollections of Writers*, containing much about Keats.

James Rice, a lawyer and a wit of whom little is known, was introduced by Reynolds to Keats in 1817. Later Rice and Reynolds in partnership mismanaged the affairs of Fanny and George Keats; but George, Dilke, and Reynolds paid generous tributes on his death in 1833.

The name of Fanny Brawne is not to be found in Lord Houghton's book, but her presence there is so disturbing that even Keats's letters to her (which were not published until 1878), though they throw a strong light on the story as it is here told, can add little to its poignancy. Thus we find Keats writing from Naples, when he was close to his death and felt by anticipation the sting of it: "I can bear to die—I cannot bear to leave her."

Fanny Brawne was born in 1800 and was just eighteen when Keats first met her. She has not always been charitably judged, but since the publication, in 1936, of her letters to Fanny Keats, it has hardly been possible to question the reality of her affection for the poet, or to find fault, considering all the circumstances, with her conduct. She married twelve years after Keats's death, and lived until 1865.

FRANCIS JEFFREY,

DEAR LORD JEFFREY,

It is with great pleasure that I dedicate to you these late memorials and relics of a man, whose early genius you did much to rescue from the alternative of obloquy or oblivion.

The merits which your generous sagacity perceived under so many disadvantages, are now recognised by every student and lover of poetry in this country, and have acquired a still brighter fame in that other and wider England beyond the Atlantic, whose national youth is, perhaps, more keenly susceptible of poetic impressions and delights, than the maturer and more conscious fatherland.

I think that the poetical portion of this volume will confirm the opinions you hazarded at the time, when such views were hazardous even to a critical reputation so well-founded as your own: and I believe that you will find in the clear transcript of the poet's mind, conveyed in these familiar letters, more than a vindication of all the interest you took in a character, whose moral purity and nobleness is as significant as its intellectual excellence.

It has no doubt frequently amused you to have outlived literary reputations, whose sound and glitter you foresaw would not stand the tests of time and altered circumstance; but it is a far deeper source of satisfaction to have received the ratification by public opinion of judgments, once doubted or derided, and thus to have anticipated the tardy justice which a great work of art frequently obtains, when the hand of the artist is cold, and the heart, that palpitated under neglect, is still for ever.

This composition, or rather compilation, has been indeed a labour of love, and I rejoice to prefix to it a name not dearer to public esteem than to private friendship—not less worthy of gratitude and of affection than of high professional honours and wide intellectual fame.

I remain, dear Lord Jeffrey,

Yours with respect and regard,

R. MONCKTON MILNES.

PALL MALL,
  1 *August,* 1848.

AUTHOR'S PREFACE

It is now fifteen years ago that I met, at the villa of my distinguished friend Mr. Landor, on the beautiful hill-side of Fiesole, Mr. Charles Brown, a retired Russia-merchant, with whose name I was already familiar as the generous protector and devoted friend of the Poet Keats. Mr. Severn the artist, whom I had known at Rome, had already satisfied much of my curiosity respecting a man, whom the gods had favoured with great genius and early death, but had added to one gift the consciousness of public disregard, and to the other the trial of severe physical suffering. With the works of Keats I had always felt a strong poetical sympathy, accompanied by a ceaseless wonder at their wealth of diction and of imagery, which was increased by the consciousness that all that he had produced was rather a promise than an accomplishment; he had ever seemed to me to have done more at school in poetry than almost any other man who had made it the object of a mature life. This adolescent character had given me an especial interest in the moral history of this Marcellus of the empire of English song, and when my imagination measured what he might have become by what he was, it stood astounded at the result.

Therefore the circumstances of his life and writings appeared to me of a high literary interest, and I looked on whatever unpublished productions of his that fell in my way with feelings perhaps not in all cases warranted by their intrinsic merits. Few of these remains had escaped the affectionate care of Mr. Brown, and he told me that he only deferred their publication till his return to England. This took place two or three years afterwards, and the preliminary arrangements for giving them to the world were actually in progress, when the accident of attending a meeting on the subject of the colonisation of New Zealand altered all Mr. Brown's plans, and determined him to transfer his fortunes and the closing years of his life to the Antipodes. Before he left this country he confided to my care all his collections of Keats's writings, accompanied with a biographical notice, and I engaged to use them to the best of my ability for the purpose of vindicating the character and advancing the fame of his honoured friend.

As soon as my intention was made known, I received from the friends and acquaintances of the poet the kindest assistance. His earliest guide and companion in literature, Mr. Cowden Clarke, and his comrades in youthful study, Mr. Holmes and Mr. Felton Mathew, supplied me with all their recollections of his boyhood; Mr. Reynolds, whom Mr. Leigh Hunt, in the *Examiner* of 1816, associated with Shelley and Keats as the three poets of promise whom time was ripening, contributed the rich store of correspondence which began with Keats's introduction into literary society, and never halted to the last; Mr. Haslam and Mr. Dilke aided me with letters and remembrances, and many persons who casually heard of my project forwarded me information that circumstances had placed in their way. To the enlightened publishers, Messrs. Taylor and Hessey, and to Mr. Ollier, I am also indebted for willing co-operation.

Mr. Leigh Hunt had already laid his offering on the shrine of his beloved brother in the trials and triumphs of genius, and could only encourage me by his interest and sympathy.

I have already mentioned Mr. Severn, without whom I should probably have never thought of undertaking the task, and who now offered me the additional inducement of an excellent portrait of his friend to prefix to the book: he has also in his possession a small full-length of Keats sitting reading, which is considered a striking and characteristic resemblance.

But perhaps the most valuable, as the most confidential communication I received, was from the gentleman who has married the widow of George Keats, and who placed at my disposal, with the consent of the family, the letters George received from his brother after he emigrated to America. I have taken the liberty of omitting some few

unimportant passages which referred exclusively to in-
dividuals or transitory circumstances, regarding this part
of the correspondence as of a more private character than
any other that has fallen into my hands.

I am not, indeed, unprepared for the charge, that I have
published in this volume much that might well have
been omitted, both for its own irrelevancy, and from the
decent reverence that should always veil, more or less,
the intimate family concerns and the deep internal life
of those that are no more. Never has such remonstrance
been more ably expressed than in the following passage
from Mr. Wordsworth's "Letter to a friend of Robert
Burns," [1] which, on account of the rarity of the pamphlet,
I here transcribe:

Biography, though differing in some essentials from works
of fiction, is nevertheless like them an art—an art, the laws of
which are determined by the imperfections of our nature and
the constitution of society. Truth is not here, as in the sciences
and in natural philosophy, to be sought without scruple, and
promulgated for its own sake upon the mere chance of its
being serviceable, but only for obviously justifying purposes,
moral or intellectual. Silence is a privilege of the grave, a
right of the departed; let him therefore, who infringes that
right by speaking publicly of, for, or against those who cannot
speak for themselves, take heed that he open not his mouth
without a sufficient sanction. . . . The general obligation
upon which I have insisted is especially binding upon those
who undertake the biography of *authors*. Assuredly there is
no cause why the lives of that class of men should be pried
into with diligent curiosity, and laid open with the same disregard of reserve which may sometimes be expedient in composing the history of men who have borne an active part in
the world. Such thorough knowledge of the good and bad
qualities of these latter, as can only be obtained by a scrutiny
of their private bias, conduces to explain, not only their own
public conduct, but that of those with whom they have acted.
Nothing of this applies to authors, considered merely as
authors. Our business is with their books, to understand and
to enjoy them. And of poets more especially it is true, that if
their works be good, they contain within themselves all that

[1] Published 1816.

is necessary to their being comprehended and relished. It should seem that the ancients thought in this manner, for of the eminent Greek and Roman poets, few and scanty memorials were, I believe, ever prepared, and fewer still are preserved. It is delightful to read what, in the happy exercise of his own genius, Horace chooses to communicate of himself and his friends; but I confess I am not so much a lover of knowledge independent of its quality, as to make it likely that it would much rejoice me were I to hear that records of the Sabine poet and his contemporaries, composed upon the Boswellian plan, had been unearthed among the ruins of Herculaneum.

With this earnest warning before me, I hesitated some time as to the application of my materials. It was easy for me to construct out of them a signal monument of the worth and genius of Keats; by selecting the circumstances and the passages that illustrated the extent of his abilities, the purity of his objects and the nobleness of his nature, I might have presented to the world a monography, apparently perfect, and at least as real as those which the affection or pride of the relatives or dependants of remarkable personages generally prefix to their works. But I could not be unconscious that, if I were able to present to public view the true personality of a man of genius, without either wounding the feelings of mourning friends or detracting from his existing reputation, I should be doing a much better thing in itself, and one much more becoming that office of biographer, which I, a personal stranger to the individual, had consented to undertake. For, if I left the memorials of Keats to tell their own tale, they would in truth be the book, and my business would be almost limited to their collection and arrangement; whereas, if I only regarded them as the materials of my own work, the general effect would chiefly depend on my ability of construction, and the temptation to render the facts of the story subservient to the excellence of the work of art would never have been absent.

I had else to consider which procedure was most likely to raise the character of Keats in the estimation of those most capable of judging it. I saw how grievously he was misapprehended even by many who wished to see in him only what was best. I perceived that many, who heartily admired his poetry, looked on it as the production of a wayward, erratic genius, self-indulgent in conceits, disrespectful of the rules and limitations of Art, not only unlearned but careless of knowledge, not only exaggerated but despising proportion. I knew that his moral disposition was assumed to be weak, gluttonous of sensual excitement, querulous of severe judgment, fantastical in its tastes, and lackadaisical in its sentiments. He was all but universally believed to have been killed by a stupid, savage article in a review, and to the compassion generated by his untoward fate he was held to owe a certain personal interest, which his poetic reputation hardly justified.

When, then, I found, from the undeniable documentary evidence of his inmost life, that nothing could be farther from the truth than this opinion, it seemed to me that a portrait, so dissimilar from the general assumption, would hardly obtain credit, and might rather look like the production of a paradoxical partiality than the result of conscientious inquiry. I had to show that Keats, in his intellectual character, reverenced simplicity and truth above all things, and abhorred whatever was merely strange and strong—that he was ever learning and ever growing more conscious of his own ignorance—that his models were always the highest and the purest, and that his earnestness in aiming at their excellence was only equal to the humble estimation of his own efforts—that his poetical course was one of distinct and positive progress, exhibiting a self-command and self-direction which enabled him to understand and avoid the faults even of the writers he was most naturally inclined to esteem, and to liberate himself at once, not only from the fetters of literary partisanship, but even from the subtler influences and associations of the accidental literary spirit of his own time. I had also to exhibit the moral peculiarities of Keats as the effects of a strong will, passionate temperament, indomitable courage, and a somewhat contemptuous disregard of other men—to represent him as unflinchingly meeting all criticism of his writings, and caring for the article, which was supposed to have had such homicidal success, just so far as it was an evidence of the little power he had as yet acquired over the sympathies of mankind, and no more. I had to make prominent the brave front he opposed to poverty and pain—to show how love of pleasure was in him continually subordinate to higher aspirations notwithstanding the sharp zest of enjoyment which his mercurial nature conferred on him; and above all, I had to illustrate how little he abused his full possession of that imaginative faculty, which enables the poet to vivify the phantoms of the hour, and to purify the objects of sense, beyond what the moralist may sanction, or the mere practical man can understand.

I thus came to the conclusion that it was best to act simply as editor of the Life which was, as it were, already written. I had not the right, which many men yet living might claim from personal knowledge, of analysing motives of action and explaining courses of conduct; I could tell no more than was told to me, and that I have done as faithfully as I was able: and I now leave the result in the hands of the few whose habits of thought incline them to such subjects, not, indeed, in the hope that their task will be as agreeable as mine has been, but in the belief that they will find in it much that is not mine to appreciate and enjoy: a previous admiration of the works of Keats which have been already published is the test of their authority to approve or condemn these supplementary memorials, and I admit no other.

LIFE AND LETTERS OF JOHN KEATS

To the Poet, if to any man, it may justly be conceded to be estimated by what he has written rather than by what he has done, and to be judged by the productions of his genius rather than by the circumstances of his outward life. For although the choice and treatment of a subject may enable us to contemplate the mind of the Historian, the Novelist, or the Philosopher, yet our observation will be more or less limited and obscured by the sequence of events, the forms of manners, or the exigencies of theory, and the personality of the writer must be frequently lost; while the Poet, if his utterances be deep and true, can hardly hide himself even beneath the epic or dramatic veil, and often makes of the rough public ear a confessional into which to pour the richest treasures and holiest secrets of his soul. His Life is in his writings, and his Poems are his works indeed.

The biography, therefore, of a poet can be little better than a comment on his Poems, even when itself of long duration, and chequered with strange and various adventures: but these pages concern one whose whole story may be summed up in the composition of three small volumes of verse, some earnest friendships, one passion, and a premature death. As men die, so they walk among posterity; and our impression of Keats can only be that of a noble nature perseveringly testing its own powers, of a manly heart bravely surmounting its first hard experience, and of an imagination ready to inundate the world, yet learning to flow within regulated channels and abating its violence without lessening its strength.

It is thus no more than the beginning of a Life which can here be written, and nothing but a conviction of the singularity and greatness of the fragment would justify anyone in attempting to draw general attention to its shape and substance. The interest, indeed, of the Poems of Keats has already had much of a personal character: and his early end, like that of Chatterton (of whom he ever speaks with a sort of prescient sympathy), has, in some degree, stood him in stead of a fulfilled poetical existence. Ever improving in his art, he gave no reason to believe that his marvellous faculty had anything in common with that lyrical facility which many men have manifested in boyhood or in youth, but which has grown torpid or disappeared altogether with the advance of mature life; in him no one doubts that a true genius was suddenly arrested, and they who will not allow him to have won his place in the first ranks of English poets will not deny the promise of his candidature. When a man has had a fair field of existence before him and free scope for the exhibition of his energies, it becomes a superfluous and, generally, an unprofitable task to collect together the unimportant incidents of his career and hoard up the scattered remnants of his mind, most of which he would probably have himself wished to be forgotten. But in the instance of Keats, it is a natural feeling in those who knew and loved, and not an extravagant one in those who merely admire, him to desire, as far as may be, to repair the injustice of destiny, and to glean whatever relics they may find of a harvest of which so few full sheaves were permitted to be garnered.

The interest which attaches to the family of every remarkable individual has failed to discover in that of Keats anything more than that the influences with which his childhood was surrounded were virtuous and honourable. His father, who was employed in the establishment of Mr. Jennings, the proprietor of large livery-stables on the Pavement in Moorfields, nearly opposite the entrance into Finsbury Circus, became his master's son-in-law, and is still remembered as a man of excellent natural sense, lively and energetic countenance, and entire freedom from any vulgarity or assumption on account of his prosperous alliance. He was killed by a fall from his horse in 1804, at the early age of thirty-six. The mother, a lively intelligent woman, was supposed to have prematurely hastened the birth of John by her passionate love of amusement, though his constitution gave no signs of the peculiar debility of a seven months child. He was born on 29 October, 1795.[1] He had two brothers, George, older than himself, Thomas, younger, and a sister much younger; John resembled his father in feature, stature and manners, while the two brothers were more like their mother, who was tall, had a large oval face, and a somewhat saturnine demeanour. She succeeded, however, in inspiring her children with the profoundest affection, and especially John, who, when on an occasion of illness the doctor ordered her not to be disturbed for some time, kept sentinel at her door for above three hours with an old sword he had picked up, and allowed no one to enter the room. At this time he was between four and five years old, and later he was sent, with his brothers, to Mr. Clarke's school at Enfield, which was then in high repute. Harrow had been at first proposed but was found to be too expensive.

A maternal uncle of the young Keatses had been an officer in Duncan's ship in the action off Camperdown and had distinguished himself there both by his signal bravery and by his peculiarly lofty stature, which made him a mark for the enemy's shot; the Dutch admiral said as much to him after the battle. This sailor-uncle was the ideal of the boys, and filled their imagination when they went to school with the notion of keeping up the family's reputation for courage. This was manifested in the elder brother by a passive manliness, but in John and Tom by the fiercest pugnacity. John was always fighting; he chose his favourites among his schoolfellows from those that fought the most readily and pertinaciously, nor were the brothers loath to exercise their mettle even on one another. This disposition, however, in all of them, seems to have been combined with much tenderness, and, in John, with a passionate sensibility, which exhibited itself in the strongest contrasts. Convulsions of laughter and of tears were equally frequent with him, and he would pass from one to the other almost without an interval. He gave vent to his impulses with

[1] This point, which has been disputed (Mr. Leigh Hunt making him a year younger), is decided by the proceedings in Chancery, on the administration of his effects, where he is said to have come of age in October 1816. *Rawlings* v. *Jennings*, 3 June, 1825.

no regard for consequences; he violently attacked an usher who had boxed his brother's ears, and on the occasion of his mother's death, which occurred suddenly in 1810 (though she had lingered for some years in a consumption), he hid himself in a nook under the master's desk for several days, in a long agony of grief, and would take no consolation from master or from friend. The sense of humour, which almost universally accompanies a deep sensibility, and is perhaps but the reverse of the medal, abounded in him; from the first, he took infinite delight in any grotesque originality or novel prank of his companions, and, after the exhibition of physical courage, appeared to prize these above all other qualifications. His indifference to be thought well of as "a good boy" was as remarkable as his facility in getting through the daily tasks of the school, which never seemed to occupy his attention, but in which he was never behind the others. His skill in all manly exercises and the perfect generosity of his disposition, made him extremely popular: "he combined," writes one of his schoolfellows, "a terrier-like resoluteness of character, with the most noble placability"; and another mentions that his extraordinary energy, animation and ability impressed them all with a conviction of his future greatness, "but rather in a military or some such active sphere of life, than in the peaceful arena of literature." [1] This impression was no doubt unconsciously aided by a rare vivacity of countenance and very beautiful features. His eyes, then, as ever, were large and sensitive, flashing with strong emotions or suffused with tender sympathies, and more distinctly reflected the varying impulses of his nature than when under the self-control of maturer years: his hair hung in thick brown ringlets round a head diminutive for the breadth of the shoulders below it, while the smallness of the lower limbs, which in later life marred the proportion of his person, was not then apparent, any more than the undue prominence of the lower lip, which afterwards gave his face too pugnacious a character to be entirely pleasing, but at that time only completed such an impression as the ancients had of Achilles—joyous and glorious youth, everlastingly striving.

[1] Mr. E. Holmes, author of the *Life of Mozart*, etc.

After remaining some time at school his intellectual ambition suddenly developed itself: he determined to carry off all the first prizes in literature, and he succeeded: but the object was only obtained by a total sacrifice of his amusements and favourite exercises. Even on the half-holidays, when the school was all out at play, he remained at home translating his Virgil or his Fenelon: it had frequently occurred to the master to force him out into the open air for his health, and then he would walk in the garden with a book in his hand. The quantity of translations on paper he made during the last two years of his stay at Enfield was surprising. The twelve books of the Æneid were a portion of it, but he does not appear to have been familiar with much other and more difficult Latin poetry, nor to have even commenced learning the Greek language. Yet Tooke's *Pantheon*, Spence's *Polymetis*, and Lemprière's *Dictionary* were sufficient fully to introduce his imagination to the enchanted world of old mythology; with this, at once, he became intimately acquainted, and a natural consanguinity, so to say, of intellect, soon domesticated him with the ancient ideal life, so that his scanty scholarship supplied him with a clear perception of classic beauty, and led the way to that wonderful reconstruction of Grecian feeling and fancy, of which his mind became afterwards capable. He does not seem to have been a sedulous reader of other books, but *Robinson Crusoe* and Marmontel's *Incas of Peru* impressed him strongly, and he must have met with Shakespeare, for he told a schoolfellow considerably younger than himself "that he thought no one could dare to read *Macbeth* alone in a house, at two o'clock in the morning."

On the death of their remaining parent, the young Keatses were consigned to the guardianship of Mr. Abbey, a merchant. About eight thousand pounds were left to be equally divided among the four children. It does not appear whether the wishes of John, as to his destination in life, were at all consulted, but on leaving school in the summer of 1810, he was apprenticed, for five years, to Mr. Hammond, a surgeon of some eminence at Edmonton. The vicinity to Enfield enabled him to keep up his connection with the family of Mr. Clarke, where he was always received with familiar kindness. His talents and energy had strongly recommended him to his preceptor, and his affectionate disposition endeared him to his son. In Charles Cowden Clarke, Keats found a friend capable of sympathising with all his highest tastes and finest sentiments, and in this genial atmosphere his powers gradually expanded. He was always borrowing books, which he devoured rather than read. Yet so little expectation was formed of the direction his ability would take, that when, in the beginning of 1812, he asked for the loan of Spenser's *Faerie Queene*, Mr. Clarke remembers that it was supposed in the family that he merely desired, from a boyish ambition, to study an illustrious production of literature. The effect, however, produced on him by that great work of ideality was electrical: he was in the habit of walking over to Enfield at least once a week, to talk over his reading with his friend, and he would now speak of nothing but Spenser. A new world of delight seemed revealed to him: "he ramped through the scenes of the romance," writes Mr. Clarke, "like a young horse turned into a spring meadow": he revelled in the gorgeousness of the imagery, as in the pleasures of a sense fresh-found: the force and felicity of an epithet (such, for example, as—"the sea-shouldering whale") would light up his countenance with ecstasy, and some fine touch of description would seem to strike on the secret chords of his soul and generate countless harmonies. This, in fact, was not only his open presentation at the Court of the Muses (for the lines in imitation of Spenser,

> Now Morning from her orient chamber came,
> And her first footsteps touched a verdant hill, etc.

are the earliest known verses of his composition), but it was the great impulse of his poetic life, and the stream of his inspiration remained long coloured by the rich soil over which it first had flowed. Nor will the just critic of the maturer poems of Keats fail to trace to the influence of the study of Spenser much that at first appears forced and fantastical both in idea and in expression, and discover that precisely those defects which are commonly attributed to an extravagant originality may be distinguished as proceeding from a too indiscriminate reverence for a great

but unequal model. In the scanty records which are left
of the adolescent years in which Keats became a poet, a
Sonnet on Spenser, the date of which I have not been able
to trace, itself illustrates this view:

> Spenser! a jealous honourer of thine,
> A forester deep in thy midmost trees,
> Did, last eve, ask my promise to refine
> Some English, that might strive thine ear to please.
> But, Elfin-poet! 'tis impossible
> For an inhabitant of wintry earth
> To rise, like Phœbus, with a golden quill,
> Fire-winged, and make a morning in his mirth.
> It is impossible to 'scape from toil
> O' the sudden, and receive thy spiriting:
> The flower must drink the nature of the soil
> Before it can put forth its blossoming:
> Be with me in the summer days and I
> Will for thine honour and his pleasure try.

A few memorials remain of his other studies. Chaucer
evidently gave him the greatest pleasure: he afterwards
complained of the diction as "annoyingly mixed up with
Gallicisms," but at the time when he wrote the Sonnet, at
the end of the tale of *The Flower and the Leaf*, he felt
nothing but the pure breath of Nature in the morning of
English literature. His friend Clarke, tired with a long
walk, had fallen asleep on the sofa with the book in his
hand, and when he woke, the volume was enriched with
this addition:

> This pleasant tale is like a little copse: etc.[1]

The strange tragedy of the fate of Chatterton, "the
marvellous Boy, the sleepless soul that perished in its
pride," so disgraceful to the age in which it occurred and
so awful a warning to all others of the cruel evils which
the mere apathy and ignorance of the world can inflict
on genius, is a frequent subject of allusion and interest in
Keats's letters and poems, and some lines of the following
invocation bear a mournful anticipatory analogy to the
close of the beautiful elegy which Shelley hung over
another early grave:

> O Chatterton! how very sad thy fate!
> Dear child of sorrow—son of misery!
> How soon the film of death obscured that eye,
> Whence Genius mildly flashed, and high debate.

[1] See the *Literary Remains*.

C 801

> How soon that voice, majestic and elate,
> Melted in dying numbers! Oh! how nigh
> Was night to thy fair morning. Thou didst die
> A half-blown flow'ret which cold blasts amate.[1]
> But this is past: thou art among the stars
> Of highest Heaven: to the rolling spheres
> Thou sweetly singest: nought thy hymning mars,
> Above the ingrate world and human fears.
> On earth the good man base detraction bars
> From thy fair name, and waters it with tears.

Not long before this, Keats had become familiar with the works of Lord Byron, and indited a Sonnet, of little merit, to him in December 1814:

> Byron! how sweetly sad thy melody!
> Attuning still the soul to tenderness,
> As if soft Pity, with unusual stress,
> Had touched her plaintive lute, and thou, being by,
> Hadst caught the tones, nor suffered them to die.
> O'ershading sorrow doth not make thee less
> Delightful: thou thy griefs dost dress
> With a bright halo, shining beamily,
> As when a cloud the golden moon doth veil,
> Its sides are tinged with a resplendent glow,
> Through the dark robe oft amber rays prevail,
> And like fair veins in sable marble flow;
> Still warble, dying swan! still tell the tale,
> The enchanting tale, the tale of pleasing woe.

Confused as are the imagery and diction of these lines, their feeling suggests a painful contrast with the harsh judgment and late remorse of their object, the proud and successful poet, who never heard of this imperfect utterance of boyish sympathy and respect.

The impressible nature of Keats would naturally incline him to erotic composition, but his early love-verses are remarkably deficient in beauty and even in passion. Some which remain in manuscript are without any interest, and those published in the little volume of 1817 are the worst pieces in it. The world of personal emotion was then far less familiar to him than that of fancy, and indeed it seems to have been long before he descended from the ideal atmosphere in which he dwelt so happily, into the troubled realities of human love. Not, however, that the creatures even of his young imagination were unimbued with natural affections; so far from it, it may be reasonably conjectured that it was the interfusion of ideal and sensual

---

[1] Amate.—*Affright.* Chaucer.

life which rendered the Grecian mythology so peculiarly congenial to the mind of Keats, and when the *Endymion* comes to be critically considered, it will be found that its excellence consists in its clear comprehension of that ancient spirit of beauty, to which all outward perceptions so excellently ministered, and which undertook to ennoble and purify, as far as was consistent with their retention, the instinctive desires of mankind.

Friendship, generally ardent in youth, would not remain without its impression in the early poems of Keats, and a congeniality of literary dispositions appears to have been the chief impulse to these relations. With Mr. Felton Mathew, to whom his first published Epistle was addressed, he appears to have enjoyed a high intellectual sympathy. This friend had introduced him to agreeable society, both of books and men, and those verses were written just at the time when Keats became fully aware that he had no real interest in the profession he was sedulously pursuing, and was already in the midst of that sad conflict between the outer and inner worlds, which is too often, perhaps always in some degree, the Poet's heritage in life. That freedom from the bonds of conventional phraseology which so clearly designates true genius, but which, if unwatched and unchastened, will continually outrage the perfect form that can alone embalm the beautiful idea and preserve it for ever, is there already manifest, and the presence of Spenser shows itself not only by quaint expressions and curious adaptations of rhyme, but by the introduction of the words, "and make a sun-shine in a shady place," applied to the power of the Muse. Mr. Mathew retains his impression that at that time "the eye of Keats was more critical than tender, and so was his mind: he admired more the external decorations than felt the deep emotions of the Muse. He delighted in leading you through the mazes of elaborate description, but was less conscious of the sublime and the pathetic. He used to spend many evenings in reading to me, but I never observed the tears in his eyes nor the broken voice which are indicative of extreme sensibility." This modification of a nature at first passionately susceptible, and the growing preponderance of the imagination, is a frequent phenomenon in poetical psychology.

To his brother George, then a clerk in Mr. Abbey's house, his next Epistle is addressed, and Spenser is there too. But by this time the delightful complacency of conscious genius had already dawned upon his mind and gives the poem an especial interest. After a brilliant sketch of the present happiness of the Poet, "his proud eye looks through the film of death"; he thinks of leaving behind him lays

> of such a dear delight,
> That maids will sing them on their bridal night;

he foresees that the patriot will thunder out his numbers,

> To startle princes from their easy slumbers;

and while he checks himself in what he calls "this mad ambition," yet he owns he has felt

> relief from pain,
> When some bright thought has darted through my brain—
> Through all the day, I've felt a greater pleasure
> Than if I'd brought to light a hidden treasure.

Although this foretaste of fame is in most cases a delusion (as the fame itself may be a greater delusion still), yet it is the best and purest drop in the cup of intellectual ambition. It is enjoyed, thank God, by thousands, who soon learn to estimate their own capacities aright and tranquilly submit to the obscure and transitory condition of their existence: it is felt by many, who look back on it in after years with a smiling pity to think they were so deceived, but who, nevertheless, recognise in that aspiration the spring of their future energies and usefulness in other and far different fields of action; and the few in whom the prophecy is accomplished—who become what they have believed—will often turn away with uneasy satiety from present satisfaction to the memory of those happy hopes, to the thought of the dear delight they then derived from one single leaf of those laurels that now crowd in at the window, and which the hand is half inclined to push away to let in the fresh air of heaven.

The lines

> As to my Sonnets—though none else should heed them,
> I feel delighted still that you should read them,

occur in this Epistle, and several of these have been preserved, besides those published or already mentioned.

Some, indeed, are mere experiments in this difficult but attractive form of composition, and others evidently refer to forgotten details of daily life and are unmeaning without them. A few of unequal power and illustrative of the progress of genius should not be forgotten, while those contained in the first volume of his Poems are perhaps the most remarkable pieces in it. They are as noble in thought, rich in expression, and harmonious in rhythm as any in the language, and among the best may be ranked that "On first looking into Chapman's Homer." Unable as he was to read the original Greek, Homer had as yet been to him a name of solemn significance, and nothing more. His friend and literary counsellor, Mr. Clarke, happened to borrow Chapman's translation, and having invited Keats to read it with him one evening, they continued their study till daylight. He describes Keats's delight as intense, even to shouting aloud, as some passage of especial energy struck his imagination. It was fortunate that he was introduced to that heroic company through an interpretation which preserves so much of the ancient simplicity, and in a metre that, after all various attempts, including that of the hexameter, still appears the best adapted, from its pauses and its length, to represent in English the Greek epic verse. An accomplished scholar may perhaps be unwilling, or unable, to understand how thoroughly the imaginative reader can fill up the necessary defects of any translation which adheres, as far as it may, to the tone and spirit of the original, and does not introduce fresh elements of thought, incongruous ornaments, or cumbrous additions; be it bald and tame, he can clothe and colour it—be it harsh and ill-jointed, he can perceive the smoothness and completeness that has been lost; only let it not be like Pope's Homer, a new work with an old name—a portrait, itself of considerable power and beauty, but in which the features of the individual are scarcely to be recognised. The Sonnet in which these his first impressions are concentrated, was left the following day on Mr. Clarke's table, realising the idea of that form of verse expressed by Keats himself in his third Epistle, as—

swelling loudly
Up to its climax, and then dying proudly.

This Epistle is written in a bolder and freer strain than the others; the Poet in excusing himself for not having addressed his Muse to Mr. Clarke before, on account of his inferiority to the great masters of song, implies that he is growing conscious of a possible brotherhood with them; and his terse and true description of the various orders of verse, with which his friend has familiarised his mind— the Sonnet, as above cited—the Ode,

> Growing, like Atlas, stronger from its load,

the Epic,

> of all the king,
> Round, vast, and spanning all, like Saturn's ring,

and last,

> The sharp, the rapier-pointed Epigram,—

betokens the justness of perception generally allied with redundant fancy.

These notices have anticipated the period of the termination of Keats's apprenticeship and his removal to London, for the purpose of walking the hospitals. He lodged in the Poultry, and having been introduced by Mr. Clarke to some literary friends, soon found himself in a circle of minds which appreciated his genius and stimulated him to exertion. One of his first acquaintances, at that time eminent for his poetical originality and his political persecutions, was Mr. Leigh Hunt, who was regarded by some with admiration, by others with ridicule, as the master of a school of poets, though in truth he was only their encourager, sympathiser, and friend; while the unpopularity of his liberal and cosmopolite politics was visited with indiscriminating injustice on all who had the happiness of his friendship or even the gratification of his society. In those days of hard opinion, which we of a freer and worthier time look upon with indignation and surprise, Mr. Hunt had been imprisoned for the publication of phrases which, at the most, were indecorous expressions of public feeling, and became a traitor or a martyr according to the temper of the spectator. The heart of Keats leaped towards him in human and poetic brotherhood, and the earnest Sonnet on the day he left his prison riveted the connexion. They read and walked together, and wrote verses in competition on a given subject. "No imaginative pleasure," character-istically observes Mr. Hunt, "was left unnoticed by us or unenjoyed, from the recollection of the bards and patriots of old, to the luxury of a summer rain at our windows, or the clicking of the coal in winter time." Thus he became intimate with Hazlitt, Shelley, Haydon, and Godwin, with Mr. Basil Montague and his distinguished family, and with Mr. Ollier, a young publisher, himself a poet, who, out of sheer admiration, offered to publish a volume of his pro-ductions. The poem with which it commences was suggested to Keats by a delightful summer's day, as he stood beside the gate that leads from the Battery, on Hampstead Heath, into a field by Caen Wood; and the last, *Sleep and Poetry*, was occasioned by his sleeping in Mr. Hunt's pretty cottage, in the Vale of Health, in the same quarter. These two pieces, being of considerable length, tested the strength of the young poet's fancy, and it did not fail. For the masters of song will not only rise lark-like with quivering wings in the sunlight, but must train their powers to sustain a calm and protracted flight, and pass, as if poised in air, over the heads of mankind. Yet it was to be expected that the apparent faults of Keats's style would be here more manifest than in his shorter efforts; poetry to him was not yet an Art; the irregularities of his own and other verse were no more to him than the inequalities of that nature of which he regarded himself as the interpreter:

> For what has made the sage or poet write,
> But the fair paradise of Nature's light?
> In the calm grandeur of a sober line
> We see the waving of the mountain pine,
> And when a tale is beautifully staid,
> We feel the safety of a hawthorn glade.

He had yet to learn that Art should purify and elevate the Nature that it comprehends, and that the ideal loses nothing of its truth by aiming at perfection of form as well as of idea. Neither did he like to regard poetry as a matter of study and anxiety, or as a representative of the struggles and troubles of the mind and heart of men. He said most exquisitely, that:

> a drainless shower
> Of light is Poesy—'tis the supreme of power;
> 'Tis Might half-slumbering on its own right arm.

He thought that:

> strength alone, though of the Muses born,
> Is like a fallen angel—trees uptorn,
> Darkness and worms and shrouds and sepulchres
> Delight it—for it feeds upon the burrs
> And thorns of life, forgetting the great end
> Of Poesy, that it should be a friend
> To soothe the cares and lift the thoughts of men.

And yet Keats did not escape the charge of sacrificing beauty to supposed intensity, and of merging the abiding grace of his song in the passionate fantasies of the moment. Words, indeed, seem to have been often selected by him rather for their force and their harmony, than according to any just rules of diction; if he met with a word anywhere in an old writer that took his fancy he inserted it in his verse on the first opportunity; and one has a kind of impression that he must have thought aloud as he was writing, so that many an ungainly phrase has acquired its place by its assonance or harmony, or capability to rhyme (for he took great pleasure in fresh and original rhymes), rather than for its grammatical correctness or even justness of expression. And when to this is added the example set him by his great master Spenser, of whom a noted man of letters has been heard irreverently to assert "that every Englishman might be thankful that Spenser's gibberish had never become part and parcel of the language," the wonder is rather that he sloughed off so fast so many of his offending peculiarities, and in his third volume attained so great a purity and concinnity of phraseology, that little was left to designate either his poetical education or his literary associates.

At the completion of the matter for this first volume he gave a striking proof of his facility in composition; he was engaged with a lively circle of friends when the last proof-sheet was brought in, and he was requested by the printer to send the Dedication directly, if he intended to have one: he went to a side-table, and while all around were noisily conversing, he sat down and wrote the sonnet:

> Glory and loveliness have passed away, etc.,

which, but for the insertion of one epithet of doubtful taste, is excellent in itself, and curious, as showing how he already had possessed himself with the images of Pagan beauty, and was either mourning over their decay and extinction, or attempting, in his own way, to bid them live again. For in him was realised the mediaeval legend of the Venus-worshipper, without its melancholy moral; and while the old Gods rewarded him for his love with powers and perceptions that a Greek might have envied, he kept his affections high and pure above these sensuous influences, and led a temperate and honest life in an ideal world that knows nothing of duty and repels all images that do not please.

This little book, the beloved first-born of so great a genius, scarcely touched the public attention. If, indeed, it had become notable, it would only have been to the literary formalist the sign of the existence of a new Cockney poet whom he was bound to criticise and annihilate, and to the political bigot the production of a fresh member of a revolutionary propaganda to be hunted down with ridicule or obloquy, as the case might require. But these honours were reserved for maturer labours; beyond the circle of ardent friends and admirers, which comprised most of the most remarkable minds of the period, it had hardly a purchaser; and the contrast between the admiration he had, perhaps in excess, enjoyed among his immediate acquaintances, and the entire apathy of mankind without, must have been a hard lesson to his sensitive spirit. It is not surprising, therefore, that he atrributed his want of success to the favourite scapegoat of unhappy authors, an inactive publisher, and incurred the additional affliction of a breach of his friendship with Mr. Ollier.

Mr. Haydon, Mr. Dilke, Mr. Reynolds, Mr. Woodhouse, Mr. Rice, Mr. Taylor, Mr. Hessey, Mr. Bailey, and Mr. Haslam, were his chief companions and correspondents at this period. The first name of this list now excites the most painful associations: it recalls a life of long struggle without a prize, of persevering hope stranded on despair; high talents laboriously applied earning the same catastrophe as waits on abilities vainly wasted; frugality, self-denial, and simple habits, leading to the penalties of profligacy and the death of distraction; an independent genius starving on the crumbs of ungenial patronage, and even these failing him at the last! It might be that Haydon did not so realise his conceptions as to make them to other men what they were to himself; it might be that he over-estimated his own æsthetic powers, and underrated those provinces of art in which some of his contemporaries excelled; but surely a man should not have been so left to perish, whose passion for lofty art, notwithstanding all discouragements, must have made him dear to artists, and whose capabilities were such as in any other country would have assured him at least competence and reputation—perhaps wealth and fame.

But at this time the destiny of Haydon seemed to be spread out very differently before him; if ever stern presentiments came across his soul, Art and Youth had then colours bright enough to chase them all away. His society seems to have been both agreeable and instructive to Keats. It is easy to conceive what a revelation of greatness the Elgin Marbles must have been to the young poet's mind, when he saw them for the first time, in March 1817. The following Sonnets on the occasion were written directly after, and published in the *Examiner*. With more polish they might have been worthy of the theme, but as it is, the diction, of the first especially, is obscure though vigorous, and the thought does not come out in the clear unity becoming the Sonnet, and attained by Keats so successfully on many other subjects.

ON SEEING THE ELGIN MARBLES

My spirit is too weak; mortality
Weighs heavily on me like unwilling sleep,
And each imagined pinnacle and steep
Of godlike hardship tells me I must die
Like a sick eagle looking at the sky.
Yet 'tis a gentle luxury to weep,
That I have not the cloudy winds to keep
Fresh for the opening of the morning's eye.
Such dim-conceived glories of the brain,
Bring round the heart an indescribable feud;
So do these wonders a most dizzy pain,
That mingles Grecian grandeur with the rude
Wasting of old Time—with a billowy main
A sun, a shadow of a magnitude.

The image of the "Eagle" is beautiful in itself, and interesting in its application.

TO HAYDON

(WITH THE ABOVE)

Haydon! forgive me that I cannot speak
Definitively of these mighty things;
Forgive me, that I have not eagle's wings,
That what I want I know not where to seek.
And think that I would not be over-meek,
In rolling out upfollowed thunderings,
Even to the steep of Heliconian springs,
Were I of ample strength for such a freak.
Think, too, that all these numbers should be thine;
Whose else? In this who touch thy vesture's hem?
For, when men stared at what was most divine
With brainless idiotism and o'erwise phlegm,
Thou hadst beheld the full Hesperian shine
Of their star in the east, and gone to worship them!

In the previous autumn Keats was in the habit of frequently passing the evening in his friend's painting-room, where many men of genius were wont to meet, and, sitting before some picture on which he was engaged, criticise, argue, defend, attack, and quote their favourite writers. Keats used to call it "Making us wings for the night." The morning after one of these innocent and happy symposia, Haydon received a note enclosing the picturesque Sonnet

> Great Spirits now on Earth are sojourning, etc.

Keats adding, that the preceding evening had wrought him up, and he could not forbear sending it. Haydon in his acknowledgment suggested the omission of part of it; and also mentioned that he would forward it to Wordsworth; he received this reply:

My Dear Sir,

Your letter has filled me with a proud pleasure, and shall be kept by me as a stimulus to exertion. I begin to fix my eyes on an horizon. My feelings entirely fall in with yours with regard to the ellipsis, and I glory in it. The idea of your sending it to Wordsworth puts me out of breath—you know with what reverence I would send my well-wishes to him.

Yours sincerely,

JOHN KEATS.

It should here be remembered that Wordsworth was not then what he is now, that he was confounded with much that was thought ridiculous and unmanly in the new school, and that it was something for so young a student to have torn away the veil of prejudice then hanging over that now-honoured name, and to have proclaimed his reverence in such earnest words, while so many men of letters could only scorn or jeer.

The uncongenial profession to which Keats had attached himself now became every day more repulsive. A book of very careful annotations, preserved by Mr. Dilke, attests his diligence, although a fellow-student,[1] who lodged in the same house, describes him at the lectures as scribbling doggerel rhymes among the notes, particularly if he got hold of another student's syllabus. Of course, his peculiar tastes did not find much sympathy in that society. Whenever he showed his graver poetry to his companions, it was pretty sure to be ridiculed and severely handled. They were therefore surprised when, on presenting himself for examination at Apothecaries' Hall, he passed his examination with considerable credit. When, however, he entered on the practical part of his business, although successful in all his operations, he found his mind so oppressed during the task with an overwrought apprehension of the possibility of doing harm, that he came to the determined conviction that he was unfit for the line of life on which he had expended so many years of his study and a considerable part of his property. "My dexterity," he said, "used to seem to me a miracle, and I resolved never to take up a surgical instrument again," and thus he found himself on his first entrance into manhood thrown on the world almost without the means of daily subsistence, but with many friends interested in his fortunes, and with the faith in the future which generally accompanies the highest genius. Mr. Haydon seems to have been to him a wise and prudent counsellor, and to have encouraged him to brace his powers by undistracted study, while he advised him to leave London for awhile, and take more care of his health. The following note, written in March, shows that Keats did as he was recommended:

My Dear Reynolds,

My brothers are anxious that I should go by myself into the country; they have always been extremely fond of me, and

[1] Mr. H. Stephens.

now that Haydon has pointed out how necessary it is that I should be alone to improve myself, they give up the temporary pleasure of being with me continually for a great good which I hope will follow; so I shall soon be out of town. You must soon bring all your present troubles to a close, and so must I, but we must, like the Fox, prepare for a fresh swarm of flies. Banish money—Banish sofas—Banish wine—Banish music; but right Jack Health, honest Jack Health, true Jack Health. Banish Health and banish all the world.

Your sincere friend,
JOHN KEATS.

During his absence he wrote the following letters. The correspondence with Mr. Reynolds will form so considerable a portion of this volume, and will so distinctly enunciate the invaluable worth of his friendship to Keats, that one can only regret that both portions of it are not preserved.[1]

CARISBROOKE,
17 April, 1817.

MY DEAR REYNOLDS,

Ever since I wrote to my brother from Southampton, I have been in a taking, and at this moment I am about to become settled, for I have unpacked my books, put them into a snug corner, pinned up Haydon, Mary Queen [of] Scots, and Milton with his daughters in a row. In the passage I found a head of Shakespeare, which I had not before seen. It is most likely the same that George spoke so well of, for I like it extremely. Well, this head I have hung over my books, just above the three in a row, having first discarded a French Ambassador; now this alone is a good morning's work. Yesterday I went to Shanklin, which occasioned a great debate in my mind whether I should live there or at Carisbrooke. Shanklin is a most beautiful place; sloping wood and meadow ground reach round the Chine, which is a cleft between the cliffs, of the depth of nearly three hundred feet at least. This cleft is filled with trees and bushes in the narrow part; and as it widens becomes bare, if it were not for primroses on one

[1] It is also to be lamented that Mr. Reynolds's own remarkable verse is not better known. Lord Byron speaks with praise of several pieces, and attributes some to Moore. *The Fancy*, published under the name of Peter Corcoran, and *The Garden of Florence*, under that of John Hamilton, are full of merit, especially the former, to which is prefixed one of the liveliest specimens of fictitious biography I know.

side, which spread to the very verge of the sea, and some fishermen's huts on the other, perched midway in the balustrades of beautiful green hedges along the steps down to the sands. But the sea, Jack, the sea, the little waterfall, then the white cliff, then St. Catherine's Hill, "the sheep in the meadows, the cows in the corn." Then why are you at Carisbrooke ? say you. Because, in the first place, I should be at twice the expense, and three times the inconvenience; next, that from here I can see your continent from a little hill close by, the whole north angle of the Isle of Wight, with the water between us; in the third place, I see Carisbrooke Castle from my window, and have found several delightful wood alleys, and copses, and quiet freshes; as for primroses, the Island ought to be called Primrose Island, that is, if the nation of Cowslips agree thereto, of which there are divers clans just beginning to lift up their heads. Another reason of my fixing is, that I am more in reach of the places around me. I intend to walk over the Island, east, west, north, south. I have not seen many specimens of ruins. I don't think, however, I shall ever see one to surpass Carisbrooke Castle. The trench is overgrown with the smoothest turf, and the walls with ivy. The Keep within side is one bower of ivy; a colony of jackdaws have been there for many years. I dare say I have seen many a descendant of some old cawer who peeped through the bars at Charles the First, when he was there in confinement. On the road from Cowes to Newport I saw some extensive Barracks, which disgusted me extremely with the Government for placing such a nest of debauchery in so beautiful a place. I asked a man on the coach about this, and he said that the people had been spoiled. In the room where I slept at Newport, I found this on the window—"O Isle spoilt by the milatary!"

The wind is in a sulky fit, and I feel that it would be no bad thing to be the favourite of some Fairy, who would give one the power of seeing how our friends got on at a distance. I should like, of all loves, a sketch of you, and Tom, and George in ink: which Haydon will do if you tell him how I want them. From want of regular rest I have been rather *narvus*, and the passage in *Lear*, "Do you not hear the sea!" has haunted me intensely.

It keeps eternal whisperings around, etc.[1]

---

[1] See the *Literary Remains*.

I'll tell you what—on the 23rd was Shakespeare born. Now if I should receive a letter from you, and another from my brother on that day, 'twould be a parlous good thing. Whenever you write, say a word or two on some passage in Shakespeare that may have come rather new to you, which must be continually happening, notwithstanding that we read the same play forty times—for instance, the following from the *Tempest* never struck me so forcibly as at present:

> Urchins
> Shall, for that vast of night that they may work,
> All exercise on thee.

How can I help bringing to your mind the line—

> In the dark backward and abysm of time.

I find I cannot exist without Poetry—without eternal Poetry, half the day will not do the whole of it. I began with a little, but habit has made me a leviathan. I had become all in a tremble from not having written anything of late: the Sonnet over-leaf (i.e. on the preceding page) did me good; I slept the better last night for it; this morning, however, I am nearly as bad again. Just now I opened Spenser, and the first lines I saw were these—

> The noble heart that harbours virtuous thought,
> And is with child of glorious great intent,
> Can never rest until it forth have brought
> Th' eternal brood of glory excellent.

Let me know particularly about Haydon, ask him to write to me about Hunt, if it be only ten lines. I hope all is well. I shall forthwith begin my *Endymion*, which I hope I shall have got some way with before you come, when we will read our verses in a delightful place, I have set my heart upon, near the Castle. Give my love to your sisters severally.

> Your sincere friend,
>
> JOHN KEATS.

(Without date, but written early in May 1817.)

MARGATE.

MY DEAR HAYDON,

> Let Fame, that all pant after in their lives,
> Live registered upon our brazen tombs,
> And so grace us in the disguise of death;
> When, spite of cormorant devouring Time,
> The endeavour of this present breath may bring
> That honour which shall bate his scythe's keen edge,
> And make us heirs of all eternity.

To think that I have no right to couple myself with you in this speech would be death to me, so I have e'en written it, and I pray God that our "brazen tombs" be nigh neighbours.[1] It cannot be long first; the "endeavour of this present breath" will soon be over, and yet it is as well to breathe freely during our sojourn—it is as well if you have not been teased with that money affair, that bill-pestilence. However, I must think that difficulties nerve the spirit of a man; they make our prime objects a refuge as well as a passion; the trumpet of Fame is as a tower of strength, the ambitious bloweth it, and is safe. I suppose, by your telling me not to give way to forebodings, George has been telling you what I have lately said in my letters to him; truth is, I have been in such a state of mind as to read over my lines and to hate them. I am one that "gathereth samphire, dreadful trade"; the cliff of Poetry towers above me; yet when my brother reads some of Pope's *Homer*, or Plutarch's *Lives*, they seem like music to mine. I read and write about eight hours a-day. There is an old saying, "Well begun is half done"; 'tis a bad one; I would use instead, "Not begun at all till half done"; so, according to that, I have not begun my Poem, and consequently, *a priori*, can say nothing about it; thank God, I do begin ardently, when I leave off, notwithstanding my occasional depressions, and I hope for the support of a high power while I climb this little eminence, and especially in my years of more momentous labour. I remember your saying that you had notions of a good Genius presiding over you. I have lately had the same thought, for things which, done half at random, are afterwards confirmed by my judgment in a dozen features of propriety. Is it too daring to fancy Shakespeare this presider? when in the Isle of Wight I met with a Shakespeare in the passage of the house at which I lodged. It comes nearer to my idea of him than any I have seen; I was but there a week, yet the old woman made me take it with me, though I went off in a hurry. Do you not think this ominous of good? I am glad you say every man of great views is at times tormented as I am.

(Sunday after.) This morning I received a letter from George, by which it appears that money troubles are to follow up for some time to come—perhaps for always: those vexations

---

[1] To the copy of this letter, given me by Mr. Haydon on 14 May, 1846, a note was affixed at this place, in the words "Perhaps they may be."—Alas! no.

are a great hindrance to one; they are not, like envy and
detraction, stimulants to further exertion, as being immediately relative and reflected on at the same time with the prime
object; but rather like a nettle-leaf or two in your bed. So
now I revoke my promise of finishing my Poem by autumn,
which I should have done had I gone on as I have done. But
I cannot write while my spirit is fevered in a contrary direction,
and I am now sure of having plenty of it this summer; at this
moment I am in no enviable situation. I feel that I am not in
a mood to write any to-day, and it appears that the loss of it
is the beginning of all sorts of irregularities. I am extremely
glad that a time must come when everything will leave not
a wrack behind. You tell me never to despair. I wish it was
as easy for me to observe this saying: truth is, I have a horrid
morbidity of temperament, which has shown itself at intervals;
it is, I have no doubt, the greatest stumbling-block I have to
fear; I may surer say, it is likely to be the cause of my disappointment. However, every ill has its share of good; this,
my bane, would at any time enable me to look with an obstinate
eye on the very devil himself; or, to be as proud to be the
lowest of the human race, as Alfred would be in being of the
highest. I am very sure that you do love me as your very
brother. I have seen it in your continual anxiety for me, and
I assure you that your welfare and fame is, and will be, a chief
pleasure to me all my life. I know no one but you who can be
fully aware of the turmoil and anxiety, the sacrifice of all that
is called comfort, the readiness to measure time by what is
done, and to die in six hours, could plans be brought to conclusions; the looking on the sun, the moon, the stars, the earth,
and its contents, as materials to form greater things, that is
to say, ethereal things—but here I am talking like a madman
—greater things than our Creator Himself made.

I wrote to —— yesterday: scarcely know what I said in it;
I could not talk about poetry in the way I should have liked,
for I was not in humour with either his or mine. There is no
greater sin, after the seven deadly, than to flatter one's self
into the idea of being a great poet, or one of those beings who
are privileged to wear out their lives in the pursuit of honour.
How comfortable a thing it is to feel that such a crime must
bring its heavy penalty, that if one be a self-deluder, accounts
must be balanced! I am glad you are hard at work; it will
now soon be done. I long to see Wordsworth's, as well as to

have mine in; but I would rather not show my face in town till the end of the year, if that would be time enough; if not, I shall be disappointed if you do not write me ever when you think best. I never quite despair, and I read Shakespeare—indeed, I shall, I think, never read any other book much; now this might lead me into a very long confab, but I desist. I am very near agreeing with Hazlitt, that Shakespeare is enough for us. By-the-bye, what a tremendous Southean article this last was. I wish he had left out "grey hairs." It was very gratifying to meet your remarks on the manuscript. I was reading *Antony and Cleopatra* when I got the paper, and there are several passages applicable to the events you commentate. You say that he arrived by degrees, and not by any single struggle, to the height of his ambition, and that his life had been as common in particular as other men's. Shakespeare makes Enobarbus say,

> Where's Antony?
> *Eros.* He's walking in the garden, and *spurns*
> *The rush before* him; cries, *Fool, Lepidus.*

In the same scene we find:

> Let determined things
> To destiny hold unbewailed their way.

Dolabella says of Antony's messenger,

> An argument that he is plucked, when hither
> He sends so poor a pinion of his wing.

Then again Enobarbus:

> men's judgments are
> A parcel of their fortunes; and things outward
> Do draw the inward quality after them,
> To suffer all alike.

The following applies well to Bertrand:

> Yet he that can endure
> To follow with allegiance a fallen Lord,
> Does conquer him, that did his master conquer,
> And earns a place i' the story.

'Tis good, too, that the Duke of Wellington has a good word or so in the *Examiner*; a man ought to have the fame he deserves; and I begin to think that detracting from him is the same thing as from Wordsworth. I wish he (Wordsworth) had a little more taste, and did not in that respect "deal in Lieutenantry." You should have heard from me before this; but, in the first place, I did not like to do so, before I had got

a little way in the first Book, and in the next, as G. told me
you were going to write, I delayed till I heard from you. So
now in the name of Shakespeare, Raphael, and all our Saints,
I commend you to the care of Heaven.

Your everlasting friend,

JOHN KEATS.

In the early part of May, it appears from the following
extract of a letter to Mr. Hunt,[1] written from Margate,
that the sojourn in the Isle of Wight had not answered
his expectations: the solitude, or rather the company
of self, was too much for him.

I went to the Isle of Wight, thought so much about poetry,
so long together, that I could not get to sleep at night; and
moreover, I know not how it is, I could not get wholesome
food. By this means, in a week or so, I became not over capable
in my upper stories, and set off pell-mell for Margate, at least
a hundred and fifty miles, because, forsooth, I fancied I should
like my old lodgings here, and could continue to do without
trees. Another thing, I was too much in solitude, and consequently was obliged to be in continual burning of thought as
an only resource. However, Tom is with me at present, and
we are very comfortable. We intend, though, to get among
some trees. How have you got on among them? How are the
nymphs?—I suppose they have led you a fine dance. Where
are you now?

I have asked myself so often why I should be a Poet more
than other men, seeing how great a thing it is, how great things
are to be gained by it, what a thing to be in the mouth of Fame,
that at last the idea has grown so monstrously beyond my
seeming power of attainment, that the other day I nearly
consented with myself to drop into a Phaeton. Yet 'tis a
disgrace to fail even in a huge attempt, and at this moment
I drive the thought from me. I begun my poem about a fortnight since, and have done some every day, except travelling
ones. Perhaps I may have done a good deal for the time, but
it appears such a pin's point to me, that I will not copy any
out. When I consider that so many of these pin-points go to
form a bodkin-point (God send I end not my life with a bare
bodkin, in its modern sense), and that it requires a thousand

[1] Given entire in the first volume of *Lord Byron and some of his
Contemporaries.*

bodkins to make a spear bright enough to throw any light to posterity, I see nothing but continual up-hill journeying. Nor is there anything more unpleasant (it may come among the thousand and one) than to be so journeying and to miss the goal at last. But I intend to whistle all these cogitations into the sea, where I hope they will breed storms violent enough to block up all exit from Russia.

Does Shelley go on telling "strange stories of the deaths of kings"? [1] Tell him there are strange stories of the death of poets. Some have died before they were conceived. "How do you make that out, Master Vellum?"

This letter is signed "John Keats *alias* Junkets," an appellation given him in play upon his name, and in allusion to his friends of Fairyland.

The poem here begun was *Endymion*. In the first poem of the early volume some lines occur showing that the idea had long been germinating in his fancy; and how suggestive of a multitude of images is one such legend to an earnest and constructive mind!

> He was a poet, sure a lover too,
> Who stood on Latmos' top, what time there blew
> Soft breezes from the myrtle vale below;
> And brought, in faintness, solemn, sweet, and slow
> A hymn from Dian's temple—while upswelling,
> The incense went to her own starry dwelling.—
> But, though her face was clear as infants' eyes,
> Though she stood smiling o'er the sacrifice,
> The Poet wept at her so piteous fate,
> Wept that such beauty should be desolate:
> So, in fine wrath, some golden sounds he won,
> And gave meek Cynthia her Endymion.

And the description of the effect of the union of the Poet and the Goddess on universal nature is equal in

[1] Mr. Hunt mentions that Shelley was fond of quoting the passage in Shakespeare, and of applying it in an unexpected manner. Travelling with him once to town in the Hampstead stage, in which their only companion was an old lady, who sat silent and stiff, after the English fashion, Shelley startled her into a look of the most ludicrous astonishment by saying abruptly:

> "Hist!
> For God's sake, let us sit upon the ground,
> And tell strange stories of the deaths of kings."

The old lady looked on the coach floor, expecting them to take their seats accordingly.

vivacity and tenderness to anything in the maturer work.

> The evening weather was so bright and clear
> That men of health were of unusual cheer,
> Stepping like Homer at the trumpet's call,
> Or young Apollo on the pedestal;
> And lovely woman there is fair and warm,
> As Venus looking sideways in alarm.
> The breezes were ethereal and pure,
> And crept through half-closed lattices, to cure
> The languid sick; it cooled their fevered sleep,
> And soothed them into slumbers full and deep.
> Soon they awoke, clear-eyed, nor burnt with thirsting,
> Nor with hot fingers, nor with temples bursting,
> And springing up they met the wond'ring sight
> Of their dear friends, nigh foolish with delight,
> Who feel their arms and breasts, and kiss and stare,
> And on their placid foreheads part the hair.
> Young men and maidens at each other gazed
> With hands held back and motionless, amazed
> To see the brightness in each other's eyes;
> And so they stood, filled with a sweet surprise,
> Until their tongues were loosed in poesy:
> Therefore no lover did of anguish die,
> But the soft numbers, in that moment spoken,
> Made silken ties, that never may be broken.

George Keats had now for some time left the counting-house of Mr. Abbey, his guardian, on account of the conduct of a younger partner towards him, and had taken lodgings with his two brothers. Mr. Abbey entertained a high opinion of his practical abilities and energies, which experience shortly verified. Tom, the youngest, had more of the poetic and sensitive temperament, and the bad state of health into which he fell, on entering manhood, absolutely precluded him from active occupation. He was soon compelled to retire to Devonshire, as his only chance for life, and George accompanied him. John, in the meantime, was advancing with his poem, and had come to an arrangement with Messrs. Taylor and Hessey (who seem to have cordially appreciated his genius) respecting its publication. The following letters indicate that they gave him tangible proofs of their interest in his welfare, and his reliance on their generosity was, probably, only equal to his trust in his own abundant powers of repayment. The physical symptoms he alludes to had nothing dangerous about them and merely suggested some prudence in his mental labours. Nor had he then experienced the harsh

repulse of ungenial criticism, but, although never unconscious of his own deficiencies, nor blind to the jealousies
and spites of others, believed himself to be, on the whole,
accompanied on his path to fame by the sympathies and
congratulations of all the fellow-men he cared for: and
they were many.

MARGATE,
16 *May*, 1817.

MY DEAR SIR,

I am extremely indebted to you for your liberality in the
shape of manufactured rag, value £20, and shall immediately
proceed to destroy some of the minor heads of that hydra
the Dun; to conquer which the knight need have no sword,
shield, cuirass, cuisses, herbadgeon, spear, casque, greaves,
paldrons, spurs, chevron, or any other scaly commodity, but
he need only take the Bank-note of Faith and Cash of Salvation,
and set out against the monster, invoking the aid of no Archi-
mago or Urganda, but finger me the paper, light as the Sybil's
leaves in Virgil, whereat the fiend skulks off with his tail
between his legs. Touch him with this enchanted paper, and
he whips you his head away as fast as a snail's horn; but then
the horrid propensity he has to put it up again has discouraged
many very valiant knights. He is such a never-ending, still-
beginning, sort of a body, like my landlady of the Bell. I think
I could make a nice little allegorical poem, called "The Dun,"
where we would have the Castle of Carelessness, the Draw-
bridge of Credit, Sir Novelty Fashion's expedition against
the City of Tailors, etc. etc. I went day by day at my poem
for a month; at the end of which time, the other day, I found
my brain so overwrought, that I had neither rhyme nor reason
in it, so was obliged to give up for a few days. I hope soon to
be able to resume my work. I have endeavoured to do so once
or twice; but to no purpose. Instead of poetry, I have a
swimming in my head, and feel all the effects of a mental
debauch, lowness of spirits, anxiety to go on, without the power
to do so, which does not at all tend to my ultimate progression.
However, to-morrow I will begin my next month. This evening
I go to Canterbury, having got tired of Margate; I was not
right in my head when I came. At Canterbury I hope the
remembrance of Chaucer will set me forward like a billiard
ball. I have some idea of seeing the Continent some time
this summer.

In repeating how sensible I am of your kindness, I remain your obedient servant and friend,

JOHN KEATS.

I shall be happy to hear any little intelligence in the literary or friendly way when you have time to scribble.

10 *July*, 1817.

MY DEAR SIR,

A couple of Duns that I thought would be silent till the beginning, at least, of next month (when I am certain to be on my legs, for certain sure), have opened upon me with a cry most "untunable"; never did you hear such "ungallant chiding." Now, you must know, I am not desolate, but have, thank God, twenty-five good notes in my fob. But then, you know, I laid them by to write with, and would stand at bay a fortnight ere they should quit me. In a month's time I must pay, but it would relieve my mind if I owed you, instead of these pelican duns.

I am afraid you will say I have "wound about with circumstance," when I should have asked plainly. However, as I said, I am a little maidenish or so, and I feel my virginity come strong upon me, the while I request the loan of a £20 and a £10, which, if you would enclose to me, I would acknowledge and save myself a hot forehead. I am sure you are confident of my responsibility, and in the sense of squareness that is always in me.

Your obliged friend,

JOHN KEATS.

In September he visited his friend Bailey at Oxford, and wrote thus:

Believe me, my dear ——, it is a great happiness to see that you are, in this finest part of the year, winning a little enjoyment from the hard world. In truth, the great Elements we know of, are no mean comforters: the open sky sits upon our senses like a sapphire crown; the air is our robe of state; the earth is our throne; and the sea a mighty minstrel playing before it—able, like David's harp, to make such a one as you forget almost the tempest cares of life. I have found in the ocean's music—varying (the self-same) more than the passion of Timotheus, an enjoyment not to be put into words; and, "though inland far I be," I now hear the voice most audibly while pleasing myself in the idea of your sensations.

—— is getting well apace, and if you have a few trees, and a little harvesting about you, I'll snap my fingers in Lucifer's eye. I hope you bathe too; if you do not, I earnestly recommend it. Bathe thrice a week, and let us have no more sitting up next winter. Which is the best of Shakespeare's plays? I mean in what mood and with what accompaniment do you like the sea best? It is very fine in the morning, when the sun,

> Opening on Neptune with fair blessed beams,
> Turns into yellow gold his salt sea streams;

and superb when

> The Sun from meridian height
> Illumines the depth of the sea,
> And the fishes, beginning to sweat,
> Cry d—— it! how hot we shall be;

and gorgeous, when the fair planet hastens

> To his home
> Within the Western foam.

But don't you think there is something extremely fine after sunset, when there are a few white clouds about, and a few stars blinking; when the waters are ebbing, and the horizon a mystery? This state of things has been so fulfilling to me that I am anxious to hear whether it is a favourite with you. So when you and —— club your letter to me put in a word or two about it. Tell Dilke that it would be perhaps as well if he left a pheasant or partridge alive here and there to keep up a supply of game for next season; tell him to rein in, if possible, all the Nimrod of his disposition, he being a mighty hunter before the Lord of the Manor. Tell him to shoot fair, and not to have at the poor devils in a furrow: when they are flying, he may fire, and nobody will be the wiser.

Give my sincerest respects to Mrs. Dilke, saying that I have not forgiven myself for not having got her the little box of medicine I promised, and that, had I remained at Hampstead, I would have made precious havoc with her house and furniture —drawn a great harrow over her garden—poisoned Boxer —eaten her clothes-pegs—fried her cabbages—fricaseed (how is it spelt?) her radishes—ragouted her onions—belaboured her *beat*-root—outstripped her scarlet-runners—*parlez-vous'd* with her french-beans—devoured her mignon or mignonette

—metamorphosed her bell-handles—splintered her looking-glasses—bullocked at her cups and saucers—agonised her decanters—put old P—— to pickle in the brine-tub—disorganised her piano—dislocated her candlesticks—emptied her wine-bins in a fit of despair—turned out her maid to grass—and astonished B——; whose letter to her on these events I would rather see than the original copy of the Book of Genesis.

Poor Bailey, scarcely ever well, has gone to bed, pleased that I am writing to you. To your brother John (whom henceforth I shall consider as mine) and to you, my dear friends, I shall ever feel grateful for having made known to me so real a fellow as Bailey. He delights me in the selfish, and (please God) the disinterested part of my disposition. If the old Poets have any pleasure in looking down at the enjoyers of their works, their eyes must bend with a double satisfaction upon him. I sit as at a feast when he is over them, and pray that if, after my death, any of my labours should be worth saving, they may have so "honest a chronicler" as Bailey. Out of this, his enthusiasm in his own pursuit and for all good things is of an exalted kind—worthy a more healthful frame and an untorn spirit. He must have happy years to come—"he shall not die, by God."

A letter from John the other day was a chief happiness to me. I made a little mistake, when, just now, I talked of being far inland. How can that be when *Endymion* and I are at the bottom of the sea ? whence I hope to bring him in safety before you leave the sea-side; and, if I can so contrive it, you shall be greeted by him upon the sea-sands, and he shall tell you all his adventures, which having finished, he shall thus proceed: —"My dear Ladies, favourites of my gentle mistress, however my friend Keats may have teased and vexed you, believe me he loves you not the less—for instance, I am deep in his favour, and yet he has been hauling me through the earth and sea with unrelenting perseverance. I know for all this that he is mighty fond of me, by his contriving me all sorts of pleasures. Nor is this the least, fair ladies, this one of meeting you on the desert shore, and greeting you in his name. He sends you moreover this little scroll." My dear girls, I send you, per favour of *Endymion*, the assurance of my esteem for you, and my utmost wishes for your health and pleasure, being ever,

Your affectionate brother,

JOHN KEATS.

This is of about the same date:

Oxford,
Sunday Morning

My Dear Reynolds,

So you are determined to be my mortal foe—draw a sword at me, and I will forgive—put a bullet in my brain, and I will shake it out as a dew-drop from the lion's mane—put me on a gridiron and I will fry with great complacency—but—oh, horror! to come upon me in the shape of a dun!—send me bills! As I say to my tailor, send me bills and I'll never employ you more. However, needs must, when the devil drives: and for fear of "before and behind Mr. Honeycomb," I'll proceed. I have not time to elucidate the forms and shapes of the grass and trees; for, rot it! I forgot to bring my mathematical case with me, which unfortunately contained my triangular prisms; so that the hues of the grass cannot be dissected for you.

For these last five or six days we have had regularly a boat on the Isis, and explored all the streams about, which are more in number than your eye-lashes. We sometimes skim into a bed of rushes, and there become naturalised river-folks. There is one particularly nice nest, which we have christened "Reynolds' Cove," in which we have read Wordsworth, and talked as may be.

. . . Failings I am always rather rejoiced to find in a man than sorry for; they bring us to a level. —— has them, but then his makes-up are very good. —— agrees with the Northern Poet in this, "He is not one of those who much delight to season their fire-side with personal talk." I must confess, however, having a little itch that way, and at this present moment I have a few neighbourly remarks to make. The world, and especially our England, has, within the last thirty years, been vexed and teased by a set of devils, whom I detest so much that I almost hunger after an Acherontic promotion to a Torturer, purposely for their accommodation. These devils are a set of women, who having taken a snack or luncheon of literary scraps, set themselves up for towers of Babel in languages, Sapphos in poetry, Euclids in geometry, and everything in nothing. The thing has made a very uncomfortable impression on me. I had longed for some real feminine modesty in these things, and was therefore gladdened in the extreme, on opening, the other day, one of Bailey's books— a book of poetry written by one beautiful Mrs. Philips, a friend of Jeremy Taylor's, and called "The Matchless Orinda." You must have heard of her, and most likely read her poetry.—I wish you have not, that I may have the pleasure of treating you with a few stanzas. I do it at a venture. You will not regret reading them once more. The following, to her friend Mrs. M. A., at parting, you will judge of.

> I have examined and do find,
>   Of all that favour me,
> There's none I grieve to leave behind,
>   But only, only thee:
> To part with thee I needs must die,
> Could parting sep'rate thee and I.
>
> But neither chance nor compliment
>   Did element our love;
> 'Twas sacred sympathy was lent
>   Us from the Quire above.
> That friendship Fortune did create
> Still fears a wound from Time or Fate.
>
> Our chang'd and mingled souls are grown
>   To such acquaintance now,
> That, if each would resume her own,
>   Alas! we know not how,
> We have each other so engrost
> That each is in the union lost.
>
> And thus we can no absence know,
>   Nor shall we be confined;
> Our active souls will daily go
>   To learn each other's mind.
> Nay, should we never meet to sense
> Our souls would hold intelligence.
>
> Inspired with a flame divine,
>   I scorn to court a stay;
> For from that noble soul of thine
>   I ne'er can be away.
> But I shall weep when thou dost grieve.
> Nor can I die whilst thou dost live.
>
> By my own temper I shall guess
>   At thy felicity,
> And only like my happiness,
>   Because it pleaseth thee.
> Our hearts at any time will tell
> If thou or I be sick or well.
>
> All honour sure I must pretend,
>   All that is good or great;
> She that would be Rosannia's friend,
>   Must be at least compleat; [1]
> If I have any bravery,
> 'Tis 'cause I have so much of thee.

---

[1] "A compleat friend"—this line sounded very oddly to me at first.

Thy lieger soul in me shall lie,
  And all thy thoughts reveal,
Then back again with mine shall flie,
  And thence to me shall steal,
Thus still to one another tend:
Such is the sacred name of friend.

Thus our twin souls in one shall grow,
  And teach the world new love,
Redeem the age and sex, and show
  A flame Fate dares not move:
And courting Death to be our friend,
Our lives together too shall end.

A dew shall dwell upon our tomb
  Of such a quality,
That fighting armies thither come
  Shall reconcilèd be.
We'll ask no epitaph, but say,
Orinda and Rosannia.

In other of her poems there is a most delicate fancy of the Fletcher kind—which we will con over together.

So Haydon is in town. I had a letter from him yesterday. We will contrive as the winter comes on—but that is neither here nor there. Have you heard from Rice? Has Martin met with the Cumberland Beggar, or been wondering at the old Leech-gatherer? Has he a turn for fossils? that is, is he capable of sinking up to his middle in a morass? How is Hazlitt? We were reading his Table (*Round Table*) last night. I know he thinks himself not estimated by ten people in the world. I wish he knew he is. I am getting on famous with my third Book—have written eight hundred lines thereof, and hope to finish it next week. Bailey likes what I have done very much. Believe me, my dear Reynolds, one of my chief layings-up is the pleasure I shall have in showing it to you, I may now say, in a few days.

I have heard twice from my brothers; they are going on very well, and send their remembrances to you. We expected to have had notices from Little Hampton this morning—we must wait till Tuesday. I am glad of their days with the Dilkes. You are, I know, very much teased in that precious London, and want all the rest possible; so [I] shall be contented with as brief a scrawl—a word or two, till there comes a pat hour.

Send us a few of your stanzas to read in "Reynolds' Cove." Give my love and respects to your mother, and remember me kindly to all at home.

Yours faithfully,

JOHN KEATS.

I have left the doublings for Bailey, who is going to say that he will write to you to-morrow.

From a Letter to Haydon.

You will be glad to hear that within these last three weeks I have written 1000 lines, which are the third book of my Poem. My ideas of it, I assure you, are very low, and I would write the subject thoroughly again, but I am tired of it, and think the time would be better spent in writing a new romance, which I have in my eye for next summer. Rome was not built in a day, and all the good I expect from my employment this summer is the fruit of experience, which I hope to gather in my next Poem.

Yours eternally,

JOHN KEATS.

The first three books of *Endymion* were finished in September, and portions of the poem had come to be seen and canvassed by literary friends. With a singular anticipation of the injustice and calumny he would be subject to as belonging to "the Cockney School," Keats stood up most stoutly for the independence of all personal association with which the poem has been composed, and admiring as he did the talents and spirit of his friend Hunt, he expressed himself almost indignantly, in his correspondence, at the thought that his originality, whatever it was, should be suffered to have been marred by the assistance, influence, or counsel of Hunt, or anyone else. "I refused," he writes to Mr. Bailey (8 October), "to visit Shelley, that I might have my own unfettered scope"; and proceeds to transcribe some reflections on his undertaking, which he says he wrote to his brother George in the spring, and which are well worth the repetition.

As to what you say about my being a Poet, I can return no answer but by saying that the high idea I have of poetical fame makes me think I see it towering too high above me. At any rate I have no right to talk until *Endymion* is finished. It will be a test, a trial of my powers of imagination, and chiefly of my invention—which is a rare thing indeed—by which I must make 4000 lines of one bare circumstance, and fill them with poetry. And when I consider that this is a great task, and that when done it will take me but a dozen paces towards the Temple of Fame—it makes me say—"God forbid that I should be without such a task!" I have heard Hunt say, and [I] may be asked, *"Why endeavour after a long poem ?"* To which I should answer, "Do not the lovers of poetry like to have a little region to wander in, where they may pick and choose, and in which the images are so numerous that many are forgotten and found new in a second reading—which may be food for a week's stroll in the summer?" Do not they like this better than what they can read through before Mrs. Williams comes down stairs?—a morning's work at most.

Besides, a long poem is a test of invention, which I take to be the polar star of poetry, as Fancy is the sails, and Imagination the rudder. Did our great poets ever write short pieces? I mean, in the shape of Tales. This same invention seems indeed of late years to have been forgotten in a partial excellence. But enough of this—I put on no laurels till I shall have finished *Endymion*, and I hope Apollo is not enraged at my having made mockery of him at Hunt's.

The conclusion of this letter has now a more melancholy meaning than it had when written.

The little mercury I have taken has corrected the poison and improved my health—though I feel from my employment that I shall never again be secure in robustness. Would that you were as well as

Your sincere friend and brother,
John Keats.

"Brothers" they were in affection and in thought—brothers also in destiny. Mr. Bailey died soon after Keats.

[Postmark, 22 *November*, 1817, LEATHERHEAD.]

MY DEAR BAILEY,

I will get over the first part of this (*un*paid) letter as soon as possible, for it relates to the affairs of poor Cripps. To a man of your nature such a letter as Haydon's must have been extremely cutting. What occasions the greater part of the world's quarrels? Simply this: two minds meet, and do not understand each other time enough to prevent any shock or surprise at the conduct of either party. As soon as I had known Haydon three days, I had got enough of his character not to have been surprised at such a letter as he has hurt you with. Nor, when I knew it, was it a principle with me to drop his acquaintance; although with you it would have been an imperious feeling. I wish you knew all that I think about Genius and the Heart. And yet I think that you are thoroughly acquainted with my innermost breast in that respect, or you would not have known me even thus long, and still hold me worthy to be your dear friend. In passing, however, I must say of one thing that has pressed upon me lately, and increased my humility and capability of submission—and that is this truth—Men of genius are great as certain ethereal chemicals operating on the mass of neutral intellect—but they have not any individuality, any determined character. I would call the top and head of those who have a proper self, Men of Power.

But I am running my head into a subject which I am certain I could not do justice to under five years' study, and three vols. octavo—and moreover [I] long to be talking about the Imagination: so, my dear Bailey, do not think of this unpleasant affair, if possible do not—I defy any harm to come of it—I shall write to Cripps this week and request him to tell me all his goings-on, from time to time, by letter, wherever I may be. It will go on well—so don't, because you have discovered a coldness in Haydon, suffer yourself to be teased. Do not, my dear fellow. O! I wish I was as certain of the end of all your troubles as that of your momentary start about the authenticity of the Imagination. I am certain of nothing but of the holiness of the heart's affections, and the truth of Imagination. What the Imagination seizes as Beauty must be Truth, whether it existed before or not—for I have the same idea of all our passions as of Love: they are all, in their sublime, creative of essential Beauty. In a word, you may know my favourite speculation by my first book, and the little song I sent in my last, which is a representation from the fancy of the probable mode of operating in these matters. The Imagination may be compared to Adam's dream: he awoke and found it truth. I am more zealous in this affair, because I have never yet been able to perceive how anything can be known for truth by consecutive reasoning—and yet [so] it must be. Can it be that even the greatest philosopher ever arrived at his goal without putting aside numerous objections? However it may be, O for a life of sensations rather than of thoughts! It is "a Vision in the form of Youth," a shadow of reality to come—and this consideration has further convinced me—for it has come as auxiliary to another favourite speculation of mine—that we shall enjoy ourselves hereafter by having what we called happiness on earth repeated in a finer tone. And yet such a fate can only befall those who delight in Sensation, rather than hunger, as you do, after Truth. Adam's dream will do here, and seems to be a conviction that Imagination and its empyreal reflection is the same as human life and its spiritual repetition. But, as I was saying, the simple imaginative mind may have its rewards in the repetition of its own silent working coming continually on the spirit with a fine suddenness. To compare great things with small, have you never, by being surprised with an old melody, in a delicious place, by a delicious voice, *felt* over again your very speculations and surmises at the time it first operated on your soul ? Do you not remember forming to yourself the singer's face—more beautiful than it was possible, and yet, with the elevation of the moment, you did not think so ? Even then you were mounted on the wings of Imagination, so high that the prototype must be hereafter—that delicious face you will see. Sure this cannot be exactly the case with a complex mind —one that is imaginative, and at the same time careful of its fruits—who would exist partly on sensation, partly on thought —to whom it is necessary that "years should bring the philosophic mind " ? Such a one I consider yours, and therefore it is necessary to your eternal happiness that you not only drink this old wine of Heaven, which I shall call the redigestion of our most ethereal musings upon earth, but also increase in knowledge, and know all things.

I am glad to hear that you are in a fair way for Easter. You will soon get through your unpleasant reading, and then !— but the world is full of troubles, and I have not much reason to think myself pestered with many.

I think —— or —— has a better opinion of me than I deserve; for, really and truly, I do not think my brother's illness connected with mine. You know more of the real cause than they do; nor have I any chance of being rack'd as you have been. You perhaps, at one time, thought there was such a thing as worldly happiness to be arrived at, at certain periods of time marked out. You have of necessity, from your disposition, been thus led away. I scarcely remember counting upon any happiness. I look not for it if it be not in the present hour. Nothing startles me beyond the moment. The setting sun will always set me to rights, or if a sparrow were before my window, I take part in its existence, and pick about the gravel. The first thing that strikes me on hearing a misfortune having befallen another is this—"Well, it cannot be helped: he will have the pleasure of trying the resources of his spirit"; and I beg now, my dear Bailey, that hereafter, should you observe anything cold in me, not to put it to the account of heartlessness, but abstraction; for I assure you I sometimes feel not the influence of a passion or affection during a whole week; and so long this sometimes continues, I begin to suspect myself, and the genuineness of my feelings at other times, thinking them a few barren tragedy-tears.

My brother Tom is much improved—he is going to Devonshire—whither I shall follow him. At present, I am just arrived at Dorking, to change the scene, change the air, and give me a spur to wind up my poem, of which there are wanting 500 lines. I should have been here a day sooner, but the Reynoldses persuaded me to stop in town to meet your friend Christie. There were Rice and Martin. We talked about ghosts. I will have some talk with Taylor, and let you know, when, please God, I come down at Christmas. I will find the *Examiner*, if possible. My best regards to Gleig, my brothers, to you, and Mrs. Bentley.

Your affectionate friend,

JOHN KEATS.

I want to say much more to you—a few hints will set me going.

LEATHERHEAD,

22 *November*, 1817.

MY DEAR REYNOLDS,

There are two things which tease me here—one of them —— and the other that I cannot go with Tom into Devonshire. However, I hope to do my duty to myself in a week or so; and then I'll try what I can do for my neighbour—now, is not this virtuous? On returning to town I'll damn all idleness—indeed, in superabundance of employment, I must not be content to run here and there on little two-penny errands, but turn Rakehell, i.e. go a masking, or Bailey will think me just as great a promise-keeper as *he* thinks you; for myself I do not, and do not remember above one complaint against you for matter o' that. Bailey writes so abominable a hand, to give his letter a fair reading requires a little time, so I had not seen, when I saw you last, his invitation to Oxford at Christmas. I'll go with you. You know how poorly —— was. I do not think it was all corporeal—bodily pain was not used to keep him silent. I'll tell you what; he was hurt at what your sisters said about his joking with your mother. It will all blow over. God knows, my dear Reynolds, I should not talk any sorrow to you—you must have enough vexation, so I won't any more. If I ever start a rueful subject in a letter to you—blow me! Why don't you?—Now I was going to ask you a very silly question, [which] neither you nor anybody else could answer, under a folio, or at least a pamphlet—you shall judge. Why don't you, as I do, look unconcerned at what may be called more particularly heart-vexations? They never surprise me. Lord! a man should have the fine point of his soul taken off, to become fit for this world.

I like this place very much. There is hill and dale, and a little river. I went up Box Hill this evening after the moon—" you a' seen the moon "—came down, and wrote some lines. Whenever I am separated from you, and not engaged in a continued poem, every letter shall bring you a lyric—but I am too anxious for you to enjoy the whole to send you a particle. One of the three books I have with me is *Shakespeare's Poems*: I never found so many beauties in the Sonnets; they seem to be full of fine things said unintentionally—in the intensity of working out conceits. Is this to be borne? Hark ye!

> When lofty trees I see barren of leaves,
> Which erst from heat did canopy the head,
> And Summer's green all girded up in sheaves,
> Borne on the bier with white and bristly head.

He has left nothing to say about nothing or anything: for look at snails—you know what he says about snails—you know when he talks about "cockled snails"—well, in one of these sonnets, he says—the chap slips into—no! I lie! this is in the *Venus and Adonis*: the simile brought it to my mind.

> As the snail, whose tender horns being hit,
> Shrinks back into his shelly cave with pain,
> And there all smothered up in shade doth sit,
> Long after fearing to put forth again;
> So at his bloody view her eyes are fled,
> Into the deep dark cabins of her head.

He overwhelms a genuine lover of poetry with all manner of abuse, talking about:

> A poet's rage
> And stretched metre of an antique song.

Which, by the by, will be a capital motto for my poem, won't it? He speaks, too, of "Time's antique pen"—and "April's first-born flowers"—and "Death's eternal cold."—By the Whim-King! I'll give you a stanza, because it is not material in connection, and when I wrote it I wanted you to give your vote, pro or con.

> Chrystalline Brother of the belt of Heaven,
> Aquarius! to whom King Jove hath given
> Two liquid pulse-streams, 'stead of feather'd wings—
> Two fan-like fountains—thine illuminings
> For Dian play:
> Dissolve the frozen purity of air;
> Let thy white shoulders, silvery and bare,
> Show cold through wat'ry pinions: make more bright
> The Star-Queen's crescent on her marriage-night:
> Haste, haste away!

I see there is an advertisement in the *Chronicle* to Poets —he is so over-loaded with poems on the "late Princess." I suppose you do not lack—send me a few—lend me thy hand to laugh a little—send me a little pullet-sperm, a few finch-eggs—and remember me to each of our card-playing Club. When you die you will all be turned into dice, and be put in pawn with the devil: for cards, they crumple up like anything. I rest,

> Your affectionate friend,
>
> JOHN KEATS.

Give my love to both houses—*hinc atque illinc.*

Endymion was finished at Burford Bridge, on 28 November, 1817; so records the still existing manuscript, written fairly in a book, with many corrections of phrases and some of lines, but with few of sentences or of arrangement. It betrays the leading fault of the composition, namely, the dependence of the matter on the rhyme, but shows the confidence of the poet in his own profusion of diction, the strongest and most emphatic words being generally taken as those to which the continuing verse was to be adapted. There was no doubt a pleasure to him in this very victory over the limited harmonies of our language, and the result, when fortunate, is very impressive; yet the following criticism of his friend Mr. Leigh Hunt is also just:

He had a just contempt for the monotonous termination of every-day couplets; he broke up his lines in order to distribute the rhyme properly; but, going only upon the ground of his contempt, and not having yet settled with himself any principle of versification, the very exuberance of his ideas led him to make use of the first rhymes that offered; so that, by a new meeting of extremes, the effect was as artificial and much more obtrusive than one under the old system. Dryden modestly confessed that a rhyme had often helped him to a thought. Mr. Keats, in the tyranny of his wealth, forced his rhymes to help him, whether they would or not, and they obeyed him, in the most singular manner, with equal promptitude and ingeniousness; though occasionally in the MS., when the second line of the couplet could not be made to rhyme, the sense of the first is arbitrarily altered, and its sense cramped into a new and less appropriate form.

Keats passed the winter of 1817–18 at Hampstead gaily enough among his friends; his society was much sought after, from the delightful combination of earnestness and pleasantry which distinguished his intercourse with all men. There was no effort about him to say fine things, but he did say them most effectively, and they gained considerably by his happy transition of manner. He joked well or ill, as it happened, and with a laugh which still echoes sweetly in many ears; but at the mention of oppression or wrong, or at any calumny against those he loved, he rose into grave manliness at once, and seemed like a tall man. His habitual gentleness made his occasional looks of indignation almost terrible: on one occasion, when a gross falsehood respecting the young artist Severn was repeated and dwelt upon, he left the room, declaring "he should be ashamed to sit with men who could utter and believe such things." On another occasion, hearing of some unworthy conduct, he burst out: "Is there no human dust-hole into which we can sweep such fellows?"

Display of all kinds was especially disagreeable to him, and he complains, in a note to Haydon, that "conversation is not a search after knowledge, but an endeavour at effect —if Lord Bacon were alive, and to make a remark in the present day in company, the conversation would stop on a sudden. I am convinced of this."

His health does not seem to have prevented him from indulging somewhat in that dissipation which is the natural outlet for the young energies of ardent temperaments, unconscious how scanty a portion of vital strength had been allotted him; but a strictly regulated and abstinent life would have appeared to him pedantic and sentimental. He did not, however, to any serious extent, allow wine to usurp on his intellect, or games of chance to impair his means, for, in his letters to his brothers, he speaks of having drunk too much as a rare piece of joviality, and of having won £10 at cards as a great hit. His bodily vigour, too, must, at this time, have been considerable, as he signalised himself, at Hampstead, by giving a severe drubbing to a butcher, whom he saw beating a little boy, to the enthusiastic admiration of a crowd of bystanders. Plain, manly, practical life on the one hand, and a free exercise of his rich imagination on the other, were the ideal of his existence: his poetry never weakened his action, and his simple, everyday habits never coarsened the beauty of the world within him.

The following letters of this time are preserved:

My Dear Taylor,   23 *January*, 1818.

I have spoke to Haydon about the drawing. He would do it with all his Art and Heart too, if so I will it; however, he has written this to me; but I must tell you, first, he intends painting a finished Picture from the Poem. Thus he writes— "When I do anything for your Poem it must be effectual— an honour to both of us: to hurry up a sketch for the season won't do. I think an engraving from your head, from a chalk drawing of mine, done with all my might, to which I would put my name, would answer Taylor's idea better than the other. Indeed, I am sure of it."

. . . What think you of this? Let me hear. I shall have my second Book in readiness forthwith.

Yours most sincerely,

JOHN KEATS.

23 *January*, 1818.

My Dear Bailey,

Twelve days have pass'd since your last reached me.—What has gone through the myriads of human minds since the 12th? We talk of the immense number of books, the volumes ranged thousands by thousands—but perhaps more goes through the human intelligence in twelve days than ever was written.— *How has that unfortunate family lived through the twelve ?* One saying of yours I shall never forget: you may not recollect it, it being, perhaps, said when you were looking on the surface and seeming of Humanity alone, without a thought of the past or the future, or the deeps of good and evil. You were at that moment estranged from speculation, and I think you have arguments ready for the man who would utter it to you. This is a formidable preface for a simple thing—merely you said, "Why should woman suffer?" Aye, why should she? "By heavens, I'd coin my very soul, and drop my blood for drachmas!" These things are, and he, who feels how incompetent the most skyey knight-errantry is to heal this bruised fairness, is like a sensitive leaf on the hot hand of thought.

Your tearing, my dear friend, a spiritless and gloomy letter up, to re-write to me, is what I shall never forget—it was to me a real thing.

Things have happened lately of great perplexity; you must have heard of them; Reynolds and Haydon retorting and re-criminating, and parting for ever. The same thing has happened between Haydon and Hunt. It is unfortunate: men should bear with each other: there lives not the man who may not be cut up, aye, lashed to pieces, on his weakest side. The best of men have but a portion of good in them—a kind of spiritual yeast in their frames, which creates the ferment of existence—by which a man is propell'd to act, and strive, and buffet with circumstance. The sure way, Bailey, is first to know a man's faults, and then be passive. If, after that, he insensibly draws you towards him, then you have no power to break the link. Before I felt interested in either Reynolds or Haydon, I was well read in their faults; yet, knowing them, I have been cementing gradually with both. I have an affection for them both, for reasons almost opposite; and to both must I of necessity cling, supported always by the hope, that when a little time, a few years, shall have tried me more fully in their esteem, I may be able to bring them together. The time must come, because

they have both hearts; and they will recollect the best parts
of each other, when this gust is overblown.

I had a message from you through a letter to Jane—I
think, about Cripps. There can be no idea of binding until a
sufficient sum is sure for him; and even then the thing should
be maturely considered by all his helpers. I shall try my luck
upon as many fat purses as I can meet with. Cripps is improving very fast: I have the greater hopes of him because he is
so slow in development. A man of great executing powers at
twenty, with a look and a speech the most stupid, is sure to
do something.

I have just looked through the second side of your letter.
I feel a great content at it.

I was at Hunt's the other day, and he surprised me with a
real authenticated lock of *Milton's Hair*. I know you would
like what I wrote thereon, so here it is—as they say of a
Sheep in a Nursery Book:

ON SEEING A LOCK OF MILTON'S HAIR

Chief of organic numbers!
Old Scholar of the Spheres!
Thy spirit never slumbers,
But rolls about our ears
For ever and for ever!
O what a mad endeavour
    Worketh He,
Who to thy sacred and ennobled hearse
Would offer a burnt sacrifice of verse
    And melody.

How heaven-ward thou soundest!
Live Temple of sweet noise,
And Discord unconfoundest,
Giving Delight new joys,
And Pleasure nobler pinions:
O where are thy dominions?

    Lend thine ear
To a young Delian oath—aye, by thy soul,
By all that from thy mortal lips did roll,
And by the kernel of thy earthly love,
Beauty in things on earth and things above,
    I swear!

When every childish fashion
Has vanished from my rhyme,
Will I, grey gone in passion,
Leave to an after-time,
    Hymning and Harmony
Of thee and of thy works, and of thy life;
But vain is now the burning and the strife:

> Pangs are in vain, until I grow high-rife
>   With old Philosophy,
> And wed with glimpses of futurity.
>
> For many years my offerings must be hushed;
> When I do speak, I'll think upon this hour,
> Because I feel my forehead hot and flushed,
> Even at the simplest vassal of thy power,
>   A lock of thy bright hair,—
>   Sudden it came,
> And I was startled when I caught thy name
>   Coupled so unaware;
> Yet at the moment temperate was my blood—
> I thought I had beheld it from the flood!

This I did at Hunt's, at his request. Perhaps I should have done something better alone and at home.

I have sent my first book to the press, and this afternoon shall begin preparing the second. My visit to you will be a great spur to quicken the proceeding. I have not had your sermon returned. I long to make it the subject of a letter to you. What do they say at Oxford?

I trust you and Gleig pass much fine time together. Remember me to him and Whitehead. My brother Tom is getting stronger, but his spitting of blood continues.

I sat down to read *King Lear* yesterday, and felt the greatness of the thing up to the writing of a sonnet preparatory thereto: in my next you shall have it.

There were some miserable reports of Rice's health—I went, and lo! Master Jemmy had been to the play the night before, and was out at the time. He always comes on his legs like a cat.

I have seen a good deal of Wordsworth. Hazlitt is lecturing on Poetry at the Surrey Institution. I shall be there next Tuesday.

> Your most affectionate friend,
>
>   JOHN KEATS.

The assumption, in the above lines, of Beauty being "the kernel" of Milton's love, rather accords with the opinion of many of Keats's friends, that at this time he had not studied *Paradise Lost*, as he did afterwards. His taste would naturally have rather attracted him to those poems which Milton had drawn out of the heart of old mythology, *Lycidas* and *Comus*; and those "two exquisite jewels, hung, as it were, in the ears of antiquity," the

Penseroso and *Allegro*, had no doubt been well enjoyed; but his full appreciation of the great poem was reserved for the period which produced *Hyperion* as clearly under Miltonic influence, as *Endymion* is imbued with the spirit of Spenser, Fletcher, and Ben Jonson.

From a Letter to Mr. Reynolds.

HAMPSTEAD,
31 *January*, 1818.

Now I purposed to write to you a serious poetical letter, but I find that a maxim I met with the other day is a just one: "On cause mieux quand on ne dit pas *causons*." I was hindered, however, from my first intention by a mere muslin handkerchief, very neatly pinned—but "Hence, vain deluding," etc. Yet I cannot write in prose; it is a sunshiny day and I cannot, so here goes.

Hence Burgundy, Claret, and Port,
  Away with old Hock and Madeira,
Too earthly ye are for my sport;
  There's a beverage brighter and clearer.
Instead of a pitiful rummer,
My wine overbrims a whole summer;
  My bowl is the sky,
  And I drink at my eye,
  Till I feel in the brain
  A Delphian pain—
Then follow, my Caius! then follow:
  On the green of the hill
  We will drink our fill
  Of golden sunshine,
  Till our brains intertwine
With the glory and grace of Apollo!

God of the Meridian,
  And of the East and West,
To thee my soul is flown,
  And my body is earthward press'd.—·
It is an awful mission,
A terrible division;
And leaves a gulph austere
To be filled with worldly fear,
Aye, when the soul is fled
To high above our head,
Affrighted do we gaze
After its airy maze,
As doth a mother wild,
When her young infant child
Is in an eagle's claws—
And is not this the cause
Of madness?—God of Song,
Thou bearest me along

Through sights I scarce can bear:
O let me, let me share
With the hot lyre and thee,
The staid Philosophy.
Temper my lonely hours,
And let me see thy bow'rs
More unalarm'd!

My dear Reynolds, you must forgive all this ranting; but
the fact is, I cannot write sense this morning; however, you
shall have some. I will copy out my last sonnet.

When I have fears that I may cease to be.[1]

I must take a turn, and then write to Teignmouth. Remember me to all, not excepting yourself.

Your sincere friend,

JOHN KEATS.

HAMPSTEAD,
3 *February*, 1818.

MY DEAR REYNOLDS,

I thank you for your dish of filberts. Would I could get a
basket of them by way of dessert every day for the sum of
twopence (two sonnets on Robin Hood sent by the twopenny
post). Would we were a sort of ethereal pigs, and turned loose
to feed upon spiritual mast and acorns! which would be merely
being a squirrel and feeding upon filberts; for what is a squirrel
but an airy pig, or a filbert but a sort of archangelical acorn?
About the nuts being worth cracking, all I can say is, that
where there are a throng of delightful images ready drawn,
simplicity is the only thing. It may be said that we ought to
read our contemporaries, that Wordsworth, etc., should have
their due from us. But, for the sake of a few fine imaginative
or domestic passages, are we to be bullied into a certain
philosophy engendered in the whims of an egotist? Every man
has his speculations, but every man does not brood and peacock
over them till he makes a false coinage and deceives himself.
Many a man can travel to the very bourne of Heaven, and yet
want confidence to put down his half-seeing. Sancho will
invent a journey heavenward as well as anybody. We hate
poetry that has a palpable design upon us, and, if we do not
agree, seems to put its hand into its breeches pocket. Poetry
should be great and unobtrusive, a thing which enters into
one's soul, and does not startle it or amaze it with itself, but
with its subject. How beautiful are the retired flowers! How

[1] See the *Literary Remains*.

would they lose their beauty were they to throng into the
highway, crying out, "Admire me, I am a violet! Dote upon
me, I am a primrose!" Modern poets differ from the Eliza-
bethans in this: each of the moderns, like an Elector of Hanover,
governs his petty state, and knows how many straws are
swept daily from the causeways in all his dominions, and has
a continual itching that all the house-wives should have their
coppers well scoured. The ancients were Emperors of vast
provinces; they had only heard of the remote ones, and
scarcely cared to visit them. I will cut all this. I will have no
more of Wordsworth or Hunt in particular. Why should we
be of the tribe of Manasseh, when we can wander with Esau?
Why should we kick against the pricks when we can walk on
roses? Why should we be owls, when we can be eagles? Why
be teased with "nice-eyed wagtails," when we have in sight
"the cherub Contemplation"? Why with Wordsworth's
"Matthew with a bough of wilding in his hand," when we can
have Jacques "under an oak," etc.? The secret of the "bough
of wilding" will run through your head faster than I can
write it. Old Matthew spoke to him some years ago on some
nothing, and because he happens in an evening walk to imagine
the figure of the old man, he must stamp it down in black and
white, and it is henceforth sacred. I don't mean to deny
Wordsworth's grandeur and Hunt's merit, but I mean to say
we need not be teased with grandeur and merit when we can
have them uncontaminated and unobtrusive. Let us have the
old Poets and Robin Hood. Your letter and its sonnets gave
me more pleasure than will the Fourth Book of *Childe Harold*,
and the whole of anybody's life and opinions.

In return for your dish of filberts, I have gathered a few
catkins.[1] I hope they'll look pretty.

No, those days are gone away, etc.

I hope you will like them—they are at least written in the
spirit of outlawry. Here are the Mermaid lines:

Souls of Poets dead and gone, etc.

In the hope that these scribblings will be some amusement
for you this evening, I remain, copying on the hill,

Your sincere friend and co-scribbler,

JOHN KEATS.

[1] Mr. Reynolds had enclosed Keats some Sonnets on Robin Hood, to
which these fine lines are an answer.

Keats was perhaps unconsciously swayed in his estimate of Wordsworth at this moment by an incident which had occurred at Mr. Haydon's. The young Poet had been induced to repeat to the elder the fine "Hymn to Pan," out of *Endymion*, which Shelley, who did not much like the poem, used to speak of as affording the "surest promise of ultimate excellence." Wordsworth only remarked, "it was a pretty piece of Paganism." The mature and philosophic genius, penetrated with Christian associations, probably intended some slight rebuke to his youthful compeer, whom he saw absorbed in an order of ideas that to him appeared merely sensuous, and would have desired that the bright traits of Greek mythology should be sobered down by a graver faith, as in his own *Dion* and *Laodamia*; but, assuredly, the phrase could not have been meant contemptuously, as Keats took it, and was far more annoyed at it than at pages of *Quarterly* abuse, or *Blackwood's* ridicule.

[Postmark, HAMPSTEAD, 19 *February*, 1818.]

MY DEAR REYNOLDS,

I had an idea that a man might pass a very pleasant life in this manner—let him on a certain day read a certain page of full poesy or distilled prose, and let him wander with it, and muse upon it, and reflect from it, and bring home to it, and prophesy upon it, and dream upon it, until it becomes stale. But will it do so? Never. When man has arrived at a certain ripeness of intellect, any one grand and spiritual passage serves him as a starting-post towards all "the two-and-thirty palaces." How happy is such a voyage of conception, what delicious diligent indolence! A doze upon a sofa does not hinder it, and a nap upon clover engenders ethereal finger-pointings; the prattle of a child gives it wings, and the converse of middle-age a strength to beat them; a strain of music conducts to "an odd angle of the Isle," and when the leaves whisper, it puts a girdle round the earth. Nor will this sparing touch of noble books be any irreverence to their writers; for perhaps the honours paid by man to man are trifles in comparison to the benefit done by great works to the "spirit and pulse of good" by their mere passive existence. Memory should not be called knowledge. Many have original minds who do not think it: they are led away by custom. Now it appears to me that almost any man may, like the spider, spin from his own inwards, his own airy citadel. The points of leaves and twigs on which the spider begins her work are few, and she fills the air with a beautiful circuiting. Man should be content with as few points to tip with the fine web of his soul, and weave a tapestry empyrean—full of symbols for his spiritual eye, of softness for his spiritual touch, of space for his wanderings, of distinctness for his luxury. But the minds of mortals are so different, and bent on such diverse journeys, that it may at first appear impossible for any common taste and fellowship to exist between two or three under these suppositions. It is however quite the contrary. Minds would leave each other in contrary directions, traverse each other in numberless points, and at last greet each other at the journey's end. An old man and a child would talk together, and the old man be led on his path and the child left thinking. Man should not dispute or assert but whisper results to his neighbour, and thus by every germ of spirit sucking the sap from mould ethereal, every human [being] might become great, and humanity, instead of being a wide heath of furze and briars, with here and there a remote oak or pine, would become a grand democracy of forest trees! It has been an old comparison for our urging on—the bee-hive; however, it seems to me that we should rather be the flower than the bee. For it is a false notion that more is gained by receiving than giving—no, the receiver and the giver are equal in their benefits. The flower, I doubt not, receives a fair guerdon from the bee. Its leaves blush deeper in the next spring. And who shall say, between man and woman, which is the most delighted? Now it is more noble to sit like Jove than to fly like Mercury:—let us not therefore go hurrying about and collecting honey, bee-like buzzing here and there for a knowledge of what is to be arrived at; but let us open our leaves like a flower, and be passive and receptive, budding patiently under the eye of Apollo, and taking hints from every noble insect that favours us with a visit. Sap will be given us for meat, and dew for drink.

I was led into these thoughts, my dear Reynolds, by the beauty of the morning operating on a sense of idleness. I have not read any books—the morning said I was right—I had no idea but of the morning, and the thrush said I was right— seeming to say,

O thou! whose face hath felt the Winter's wind,
Whose eye hath seen the snow-clouds hung in mist,
And the black elm-tops among the freezing stars:
To thee the Spring will be a harvest-time.
O thou! whose only book hath been the light
Of supreme darkness which thou feddest on
Night after night, when Phœbus was away,
To thee the Spring will be a triple morn.
O fret not after knowledge!—I have none,
And yet my song comes native with the warmth.
O fret not after knowledge!—I have none,
And yet the Evening listens. He who saddens
At thought of idleness cannot be idle,
And he's awake who thinks himself asleep.

Now I am sensible all this is a mere sophistication (however it may neighbour to any truths) to excuse my own indulgence. So I will not deceive myself that man should be equal with Jove—but think himself very well off as a sort of scullion-mercury, or even a humble-bee. It is no matter whether I am right or wrong, either one way or another, if there is sufficient to lift a little time from your shoulders.

Your affectionate friend,

JOHN KEATS.

With his brothers at Teignmouth he kept up an affectionate correspondence, of which some specimens remain, and he visited them thrice in the early part of the year. The *Champion* herein mentioned was a periodical of considerable merit, in which Mr. Reynolds was engaged, and the article on Kean alluded to, as well as a later criticism of Keats on the same actor, are well worth preserving, both for their acute appreciation of a remarkable artist, and for their evidence that the genius and habit of poetry had produced its customary effect of making the poet a good writer of prose. Mr. Brown, whose name now frequently occurs, was a retired merchant, who had been the neighbour of the Keatses since the summer, and his congeniality of tastes and benevolence of disposition had made them intimates and friends. It will be often repeated in these pages—the oftener as they advance; and, in unison with that of the painter Severn, will close the series of honourable friendships associated with a poet's fame.

HAMPSTEAD,
22 *December*, 1817.

MY DEAR BROTHERS,

I must crave your pardon for not having written ere this.

. . . I saw Kean return to the public in *Richard III.*, and finely he did it, and, at the request of Reynolds, I went to criticise his Duke. The critique is in to-day's *Champion*, which I send you, with the *Examiner*, in which you will find very proper lamentation on the obsoletion of Christmas gambols and pastimes: but it was mixed up with so much egotism of that drivelling nature that all pleasure is entirely lost. Hone, the publisher's trial, you must find very amusing, and, as Englishmen, very encouraging: his *Not Guilty* is a thing, which not to have been, would have dulled still more Liberty's emblazoning. Lord Ellenborough has been paid in his own coin. Wooler and Hone have done us an essential service. I have had two very pleasant evenings with Dilke, yesterday and to-day, and am at this moment just come from him, and feel in the humour to go on with this, begun in the morning, and from which he came to fetch me. I spent Friday evening with Wells, and went next morning to see "Death on the Pale Horse." It is a wonderful picture, when West's age is considered; but there is nothing to be intense upon, no women one feels mad to kiss, no face swelling into reality. The excellence of every art is its intensity, capable of making all disagreeables evaporate from their being in close relationship with beauty and truth. Examine "King Lear," and you will find this exemplified throughout: but in this picture we have unpleasantness without any momentous depth of speculation excited, in which to bury its repulsiveness. The picture is larger than "Christ Rejected."

I dined with Haydon the Sunday after you left, and had a very pleasant day. I dined, too (for I have been out too much lately), with Horace Smith, and met his two brothers, with Hill and Kingston, and one Du Bois. They only served to convince me how superior humour is to wit, in respect to enjoyment. These men say things which make one start, without making one feel; they are all alike; their manners are alike; they all know fashionables; they have all a mannerism in their very eating and drinking, in their mere handling a decanter. They talked of Kean and his low company. "Would I were with that company instead of yours," said I to myself! I know such like acquaintance will never do for me, and yet I am going to Reynolds on Wednesday. Brown and Dilke walked with me and back from the Christmas pantomime. I had not a dispute, but a disquisition, with Dilke upon various subjects;

several things dove-tailed in my mind, and at once it struck me what quality went to form a man of achievement, especially in literature, and which Shakespeare possessed so enormously —I mean *negative capability*, that is, when a man is capable of being in uncertainties, mysteries, doubts, without any irritable reaching after fact and reason. Coleridge, for instance, would let go by a fine isolated verisimilitude caught from the penetralium of Mystery, from being incapable of remaining content with half-knowledge. This pursued through volumes would perhaps take us no farther than this, that with a great Poet the sense of Beauty overcomes every other consideration, or rather obliterates all consideration. Shelley's poem is out, and there are words about its being objected to as much as *Queen Mab* was. Poor Shelley, I think he has his quota of good qualities. . . . Write soon to your most sincere friend and affectionate brother,

JOHN.

23 *January*, 1818.

MY DEAR BROTHERS,

I was thinking what hindered me from writing so long, for I have so many things to say to you, and know not where to begin. It shall be upon a thing most interesting to you, my Poem. Well! I have given the first Book to Taylor; he seemed more than satisfied with it, and, to my surprise, proposed publishing it in quarto, if Haydon could make a drawing of some event therein, for a frontispiece. I called on Haydon. He said he would do anything I liked, but said he would rather paint a finished picture from it, which he seems eager to do. This, in a year or two, will be a glorious thing for us; and it will be, for Haydon is struck with the first Book. I left Haydon, and the next day received a letter from him, proposing to make, as he says, with all his might, a finished chalk sketch of my head, to be engraved in the first style, and put at the head of my Poem, saying, at the same time, he had never done the thing for any human being, and that it must have considerable effect, as he will put his name to it. I begin to-day to copy my second Book: "thus far into the bowels of the land." You shall hear whether it will be quarto or non-quarto, picture or non-picture. Leigh Hunt I showed my first Book to. He allows it not much merit as a whole; says it is unnatural, and made ten objections to it, in the mere skimming over. He

says the conversation is unnatural, and too high-flown for
Brother and Sister; says it should be simple—forgetting, do
ye mind, that they are both overshadowed by a supernatural
Power, and of force could not speak like Francesca, in the
Rimini. He must first prove that Caliban's poetry is unnatural. This, with me, completely overturns his objections.
The fact is, he and Shelley are hurt, and perhaps justly, at
my not having showed them the affair officiously; and, from
several hints I have had, they appear much disposed to dissect
and anatomise any trip or slip I may have made.—But who's
afraid? Ay! Tom! Demme if I am. I went last Tuesday, an
hour too late, to Hazlitt's Lecture on Poetry; got there just
as they were coming out, when all these pounced upon me:
Hazlitt, John Hunt and Son, Wells, Bewick, all the Landseers,
Bob Harris, aye and more.

I think a little change has taken place in my intellect lately;
I cannot bear to be uninterested or unemployed, I, who for
so long a time have been addicted to passiveness. Nothing
is finer for the purposes of great productions than a very
gradual ripening of the intellectual powers. As an instance
of this—observe—I sat down yesterday to read *King Lear*
once again: the thing appeared to demand the prologue of a
sonnet. I wrote it, and began to read. (I know you would
like to see it.)

ON SITTING DOWN TO READ "KING LEAR" ONCE AGAIN

O golden-tongued Romance with serene lute!
Fair plumed Syren! Queen! if far away!
Leave melodising on this wintry day,
Shut up thine olden volume, and be mute.
Adieu! for once again the fierce dispute,
Betwixt Hell torment and impassioned clay,
Must I burn through; once more assay
The bitter sweet of this Shakespearian fruit.
Chief Poet! and ye clouds of Albion,
Begetters of our deep eternal theme,
When I am through the old oak forest gone
Let me not wander in a barren dream,
But when I am consumed with the Fire,
Give me new Phœnix-wings to fly at my desire.

So you see I am getting at it with a sort of determination
and strength, though, verily, I do not feel it at this moment:
this is my fourth letter this morning, and I feel rather tired,
and my head rather swimming—so I will leave it open till
to-morrow's post.

I am in the habit of taking my papers to Dilke's and copying there; so I chat and proceed at the same time. I have been there at my work this evening, and the walk over the Heath takes off all sleep, so I will even proceed with you. . . . Constable, the bookseller, has offered Reynolds ten guineas a sheet to write for his Magazine. It is an Edinburgh one, which Blackwood's started up in opposition to. Hunt said he was nearly sure that the *Cockney School* was written by Scott [1]; so you are right, Tom! There are no more little bits of news I can remember at present.

I remain,

My dear brothers, your affectionate brother,

JOHN.

HAMPSTEAD,
16 February [1818].

MY DEAR BROTHERS,

When once a man delays a letter beyond the proper time, he delays it longer, for one or two reasons; first, because he must begin in a very common-place style, that is to say, with an excuse; and secondly, things and circumstances become so jumbled in his mind, that he knows not what, or what not, he has said in his last. I shall visit you as soon as I have copied my Poem all out. I am now much beforehand with the printers: they have done none yet, and I am half afraid they will let half the season by before the printing. I am determined they shall not trouble me when I have copied it all. Hazlitt's last lecture was on Thomson, Cowper, and Crabbe. He praised Thomson and Cowper, but he gave Crabbe an unmerciful licking. I saw Fazio the first night; it hung rather heavily on me. I am in the high way of being introduced to a squad of people, Peter Pindar, Mrs. Opie, Mrs. Scott. Mr. Robinson, a great friend of Coleridge's, called on me. Richards tells me that my Poems are known in the west country, and that he saw a very clever copy of verses headed with a motto from my sonnet to George. Honours rush so thickly upon me that I shall not be able to bear up against them. What think you— am I to be crowned in the Capitol ? Am I to be made a Mandarin ? No! I am to be invited, Mrs. Hunt tells me, to a party at Ollier's, to keep Shakespeare's birth-day. Shakespeare would stare to see me there. The Wednesday before last, Shelley,

---

[1] There seems to be no foundation for this assertion.

Hunt, and I, wrote each a sonnet on the river Nile: some day you shall read them all. I saw a sheet of *Endymion*, and have all reason to suppose they will soon get it done; there shall be nothing wanting on my part. I have been writing, at intervals, many songs and sonnets, and I long to be at Teignmouth to read them over to you; however, I think I had better wait till this book is off my mind; it will not be long first.

Reynolds has been writing two very capital articles, in the *Yellow Dwarf*, on Popular Preachers.

Your most affectionate brother,

JOHN.

These are the three sonnets on the Nile here alluded to, and very characteristic they are:

TO THE NILE

Son of the old moon-mountains African!
Stream of the Pyramid and Crocodile!
We call thee fruitful, and that very while
A desert fills our seeing's inward span:
Nurse of swart nations since the world began,
Art thou so fruitful? or dost thou beguile
Those men to honour thee, who, worn with toil,
Rest them a space 'twixt Cairo and Decan?
O may dark fancies err! They surely do;
'Tis ignorance that makes a barren waste
Of all beyond itself. Thou dost bedew
Green rushes like our rivers, and dost taste
The pleasant sun-rise. Green isles hast thou too,
And to the sea as happily dost haste.

J. K.

THE NILE

It flows through old hush'd Egypt and its sands,
Like some grave mighty thought threading a dream;
And times and things, as in that vision, seem
Keeping along it their eternal stands,—
Caves, pillars, pyramids, the shepherd bands
That roam'd through the young earth, the glory extreme
Of high Sesostris, and that southern beam,
The laughing queen that caught the world's great hands.

Then comes a mightier silence, stern and strong,
As of a world left empty of its throng,
And the void weighs on us; and then we wake,
And hear the fruitful stream lapsing along
'Twixt villages, and think how we shall take
Our own calm journey on for human sake.

L. H.

OZYMANDIAS

I saw a traveller from an antique land,
Who said:—Two vast and trunkless legs of stone
Stand in the desert. Near them, on the sand,
Half sunk, a shatter'd visage lies, whose frown,
And wrinkled lip, and sneer of cold command,
Tell that its sculptor well those passions read,
Which yet survive, stamp'd on these lifeless things,
The hand that mock'd them and the heart that fed;

And on the pedestal these words appear:—
"My name is Ozymandias, King of Kings:
Look on my works, ye Mighty, and despair!"
Nothing beside remains. Round the decay
Of that colossal wreck, boundless and bare,
The lone and level sands stretch far away.

P. B. S.

HAMPSTEAD,
21 *February* [1818].

MY DEAR BROTHERS,

I am extremely sorry to have given you so much uneasiness by not writing; however, you know good news is no news, or vice versa. I do not like to write a short letter to you, or you would have had one long before. The weather, although boisterous to-day, has been very much milder, and I think Devonshire is not the last place to receive a temperate change. I have been abominably idle since you left, but have just turned over a new leaf, and used as a marker a letter of excuse to an invitation from Horace Smith. I received a letter the other day from Haydon, in which he says his *Essays on the Elgin Marbles* are being translated into Italian, the which he superintends. I did not mention that I had seen the British Gallery; there are some nice things by Stark, and "Bathsheba" by Wilkie, which is condemned. I could not bear Alston's "Uriel."

The thrushes and blackbirds have been singing me into an idea that it was spring, and almost that leaves were on the trees. So that black clouds and boisterous winds seem to have mustered and collected in full divan, for the purpose of convincing me to the contrary. Taylor says my poem shall be out in a month. . . . The thrushes are singing now as if they would speak to the winds, because their big brother Jack—the Spring—was not far off. I am reading Voltaire and Gibbon, although I wrote to Reynolds the other day to prove reading of no use. I have not seen Hunt since. I am a good deal with

Dilke and Brown; they are kind to me. I don't think I could stop in Hampstead but for their neighbourhood. I hear Hazlitt's lectures regularly: his last was on Gray, Collins, Young, etc., and he gave a very fine piece of discriminating criticism on Swift, Voltaire, and Rabelais. I was very disappointed at his treatment of Chatterton. I generally meet with many I know there. Lord Byron's Fourth Canto is expected out, and I heard somewhere, that Walter Scott has a new Poem in readiness. . . . I have not yet read Shelley's Poem: I do not suppose you have it yet at the Teignmouth libraries. These double letters must come rather heavy; I hope you have a moderate portion of cash, but don't fret at all, if you have not.—Lord! I intend to play at cut and run as well as Falstaff, that is to say, before he got so lusty.

I remain, praying for your health, my dear brothers,

> Your affectionate brother,
>
> JOHN.

A lady, whose feminine acuteness of perception is only equalled by the vigour of her understanding, tells me she distinctly remembers Keats as he appeared at this time at Hazlitt's lectures. "His eyes were large and blue, his hair auburn; he wore it divided down the centre, and it fell in rich masses on each side his face; his mouth was full and less intellectual than his other features. His countenance lives in my mind as one of singular beauty and brightness—it had an expression as if he had been looking on some glorious sight. The shape of his face had not the squareness of a man's, but more like some women's faces I have seen—it was so wide over the forehead and so small at the chin. He seemed in perfect health, and with life offering all things that were precious to him."

Keats had lately vindicated those "who delight in sensation" against those who "hunger after Truth," and that, no doubt, was the tendency of his nature. But it is most interesting to observe how this dangerous inclination was in him continually balanced and modified by the purest appreciation of moral excellence, how far he was from taking the sphere he loved best to dwell in for the whole or even the best of creation. Never have words more effectively expressed the conviction of the superiority of

virtue above beauty than those in the following letter—
never has a poet more devoutly submitted the glory of
imagination to the power of conscience.

HAMPSTEAD,
21 April [1818].

MY DEAR BROTHERS,

I am certain, I think, of having a letter to-morrow morning;
for I expected one so much this morning, having been in town
two days, at the end of which my expectations began to get
up a little. I found two on the table, one from Bailey and one
from Haydon. I am quite perplexed in a world of doubts and
fancies; there is nothing stable in the world; uproar's your
only music. I don't mean to include Bailey in this, and so I
dismiss him from this, with all the opprobrium he deserves;
that is, in so many words, he is one of the noblest men alive
at the present day. In a note to Haydon, about a week ago
(which I wrote with a full sense of what he had done, and how
he had never manifested any little mean drawback in his
value of me), I said, if there were three things superior in
the modern world, they were "The Excursion," "Haydon's
Pictures" and Hazlitt's depth of Taste. So I believe—not thus
speaking with any poor vanity—that works of genius are the
first things in this world. No! for that sort of probity and disinterestedness which such men as Bailey possess does hold and
grasp the tip-top of any spiritual honours that can be paid to
anything in this world. And, moreover, having this feeling at
this present come over me in its full force, I sat down to write
to you with a grateful heart, in that I had not a brother who
did not feel and credit me for a deeper feeling and devotion for
his uprightness, than for any marks of genius however splendid.
I have just finished the revision of my first book, and shall
take it to Taylor's to-morrow.

Your most affectionate brother,

JOHN.

The correction and publication of *Endymion* were the
chief occupations of this half-year, and naturally furnish
much of the matter for Keats's correspondence. The
"Axioms" in the second letter to Mr. Taylor, his publisher, express with wonderful vigour and conciseness the
poet's notion of his own art, and are the more interesting

as they contain principles which superficial readers might have imagined he would have been the first to disregard and violate.

[Postmark, 30 January, 1818, HAMPSTEAD.]

MY DEAR TAYLOR,

These lines, as they now stand, about "happiness," have rung in my ears like "a chime a mending." See here:

> Behold
> Wherein lies happiness, Peona? fold, etc.

It appears to me the very contrary of "blessed." I hope this will appear to you more eligible:

> Wherein lies happiness? In that which becks
> Our ready minds to fellowship divine;
> A fellowship with essence, till we shine
> Full alchemised and free of space. Behold
> The clear religion of Heaven—Peona! fold, etc.

You must indulge me by putting this in; for, setting aside the badness of the other, such a preface is necessary to the subject. The whole thing must, I think, have appeared to you, who are a consecutive man, as a thing almost of mere words. But I assure you that, when I wrote it, it was a regular stepping of the imagination towards a truth. My having written that argument will perhaps be of the greatest service to me of anything I ever did. It set before me the gradations of happiness, even like a kind of pleasure-thermometer, and is my first step towards the chief attempt in the drama: the playing of different natures with joy and sorrow.

Do me this favour, and believe me,

Your sincere friend,
J. KEATS.

I hope your next work will be of a more general interest. I suppose you cogitate a little about it now and then.

HAMPSTEAD,
27 February [1818]

MY DEAR TAYLOR,

Your alteration strikes me as being a great improvement. And now I will attend to the punctuation you speak of. The comma should be at soberly, and in the other passage the comma should follow quiet. I am extremely indebted to you for this alteration, and also for your after admonitions. It is a sorry thing for me that any one should have to overcome prejudices in reading my verses. That affects me more than any hypercriticism on any particular passage. In *Endymion*, I have most likely but moved into the go-cart from the leading-strings. In poetry I have a few axioms, and you will see how far I am from their centre.

1st. I think poetry should surprise by a fine excess, and not by singularity; it should strike the reader as a wording of his own highest thoughts, and appear almost a remembrance.

2nd. Its touches of beauty should never be half-way, thereby making the reader breathless, instead of content. The rise, the progress, the setting of imagery, should, like the sun, come natural to him, shine over him, and set soberly, although in magnificence, leaving him in the luxury of twilight. But it is easier to think what poetry should be, than to write it. And this leads me to

Another axiom—That if poetry comes not as naturally as the leaves to a tree, it had better not come at all. However it may be with me, I cannot help looking into new countries with "Oh, for a muse of fire to ascend!" If *Endymion* serves me as a pioneer, perhaps I ought to be content, for, thank God, I can read, and perhaps understand, Shakespeare to his depths; and I have, I am sure, many friends, who, if I fail, will attribute any change in my life and temper to humbleness rather than pride—to a cowering under the wings of great poets, rather than to a bitterness that I am not appreciated. I am anxious to get *Endymion* printed that I may forget it, and proceed. I have copied the Third Book, and begun the Fourth. I will take care the printer shall not trip up my heels.

Remember me to Percy Street.

Your sincere and obliged friend,

JOHN KEATS.

P.S.—You shall have a short preface in good time.

TEIGNMOUTH,
14 *March* [1818].

DEAR REYNOLDS,

I escaped being blown over, and blown under, and trees and house being toppled on me. I have, since hearing of Brown's accident, had an aversion to a dose of parapet, and being also a lover of antiquities, I would sooner have a harmless piece of Herculaneum sent me quietly as a present than ever so modern a chimney-pot tumbled on to my head. Being agog to see some Devonshire, I would have taken a walk the first day, but the rain would not let me; and the second, but the rain would not let me; and the third, but the rain forbade it. Ditto fourth, ditto fifth, ditto—so I made up my mind to stop indoors, and catch a sight flying between the showers: and, behold, I saw a pretty valley, pretty cliffs, pretty brooks, pretty meadows, pretty trees, both standing as they were created, and blown down as they were uncreated. The green is beautiful, as they say, and pity it is that it is amphibious—*mais !* but alas! the flowers here wait as naturally for the rain twice a day as the mussels do for the tide; so we look upon a brook in these parts as you look upon a splash in your country. There must be something to support this—aye, fog, hail, snow, rain, mist blanketing up three parts of the year. This Devonshire is like Lydia Languish, very entertaining when it smiles, but cursedly subject to sympathetic moisture. You have the sensation of walking under one great Lamp-lighter: and you can't go on the other side of the ladder to keep your frock clean. Buy a girdle, put a pebble in your mouth, loosen your braces—for I am going among scenery whence I intend to tip you the Damosel Radcliffe. I'll cavern you, and grotto you, and water-fall you, and wood you, and water you, and immense-rock you, and tremendous-sound you, and solitude you. I'll make a lodgment on your glacis by a row of pines, and storm your covered way with bramble-bushes. I'll have at you with hip-and-haw small-shot, and cannonade you with shingles. I'll be witty upon salt fish, and impede your cavalry with clotted-cream. But ah, Coward! to talk at this rate to a sick man, or, I hope, to one that was sick—for I hope by this you stand on your right foot. If you are not—that's all—I intend to cut all sick people if they do not make up their minds to cut Sickness—a fellow to whom I have a complete aversion, and who, strange to say, is harboured and countenanced in several houses where I visit: he is sitting now, quite impudent, between me and Tom; he insults me at poor Jem Rice's; and you have seated him, before now, between us at the Theatre, when I thought he looked with a longing eye at poor Kean. I shall say, once for all, to my friends, generally and severally, cut that fellow, or I cut you.

I went to the Theatre here the other night, which I forgot to tell George, and got insulted, which I ought to remember to forget to tell anybody; for I did not fight, and as yet have had no redress.—"Lie thou there, sweet-heart!" I wrote to

Bailey yesterday, obliged to speak in a high way, and a damme who's afraid? for I had owed him [a letter] so long: however, he shall see I will be better in future. Is he in town yet? I have directed to Oxford as the better chance.

I have copied my fourth Book, and shall write the Preface soon. I wish it was all done; for I want to forget it, and make my mind free for something new. Atkins the coachman, Bartlet the surgeon, Simmons the barber, and the girls over at the bonnet-shop, say we shall now have a month of seasonable weather—warm, witty, and full of invention.

Write to me and tell me that you are well, or thereabouts; or, by the holy Beaucœur, which I suppose is the Virgin Mary, or the repented Magdalen (beautiful name, that Magdalen), I'll take to my wings and fly away to anywhere, but old or Nova Scotia.

I wish I had a little innocent bit of metaphysic in my head, to criss-cross the letter: but you know a favourite tune is hardest to be remembered when one wants it most; and you, I know, have, long ere this, taken it for granted that I never have any speculations without associating you in them, where they are of a pleasant nature: and you know enough of me to tell the places where I haunt most, so that if you think for five minutes after having read this, you will find it a long letter, and see written in the air before you,

Your affectionate friend,

JOHN KEATS.

TEIGNMOUTH,

MY DEAR REYNOLDS,   25 *March*, 1818.

In hopes of cheering you through a minute or two, I was determined, will he nill he, to send you some lines, so you will excuse the unconnected subjects and careless verse. You know, I am sure, Leland's *Enchanted Castle*, and I wish you may be pleased with my remembrance of it. The rain is come on again. I think with me Devonshire stands a very poor chance. I shall damn it up hill and down dale, if it keep up to the average of six fine days in three weeks. Let me hear better news of you.

Your affectionate friend,

JOHN KEATS.

Dear Reynolds! as last night I lay in bed,
There came before my eyes that wonted thread
Of shapes, and shadows, and remembrances,
That every other minute vex and please:

Things all disjointed come from north and south,—
Two Witch's eyes above a Cherub's mouth,
Voltaire with casque and shield and habergeon,
And Alexander with his night-cap on;
Old Socrates a tying his cravat,
And Hazlitt playing with Miss Edgeworth's Cat;
And Junius Brutus, pretty well, so so,
Making the best of 's way towards Soho.

Few are there who escape these visitings,—
Perhaps one or two whose lives have patent wings,
And thro' whose curtains peeps no hellish nose,
No wild-boar tushes, and no Mermaid's toes;
But flowers bursting out with lusty pride,
And young Æolian harps personified;
Some Titian colours touch'd into real life,—
The sacrifice goes on; the pontiff knife
Gleams in the Sun, the milk-white heifer lows,
The pipes go shrilly, the libation flows:
A white sail shows above the green-head cliff,
Moves round the point, and throws her anchor stiff;
The mariners join hymn with those on land.

You know the enchanted Castle,—it doth stand
Upon a rock, on the border of a Lake,
Nested in trees, which all do seem to shake
From some old magic-like Urganda's Sword.
O Phœbus! that I had thy sacred word
To show this Castle, in fair dreaming wise,
Unto my friend, while sick and ill he lies!

You know it well enough, where it doth seem
A mossy place, a Merlin's Hall, a dream;
You know the clear Lake, and the little Isles,
The mountains blue, and cold near neighbour rills,
All which elsewhere are but half animate;
There do they look alive to love and hate,
To smiles and frowns; they seem a lifted mound
Above some giant, pulsing underground.

Part of the Building was a chosen See,
Built by a banished Santon of Chaldee;
The other part, two thousand years from him,
Was built by Cuthbert de Saint Aldebrim;
Then there's a little wing, far from the Sun,
Built by a Lapland Witch turn'd maudlin Nun;
And many other juts of aged stone
Founded with many a mason-devil's groan.

The doors all look as if they oped themselves,
The windows as if latched by Fays and Elves,
And from them comes a silver flash of light,
As from the westward of a Summer's night;
Or like a beauteous woman's large blue eyes
Gone mad thro' olden songs and poesies.

See! what is coming from the distance dim!
A golden Galley all in silken trim!
Three rows of oars are lightening, moment whiles;
Into the verd'rous bosoms of those isles;
Towards the shade, under the Castle wall,
It comes in silence,—now 'tis hidden all.
The Clarion sounds, and from a Postern-gate
An echo of sweet music doth create
A fear in the poor Herdsman, who doth bring
His beasts to trouble the enchanted spring,—
He tells of the sweet music, and the spot,
To all his friends, and they believe him not.

O, that our dreamings all, of sleep or wake,
Would all their colours from the sunset take
From something of material sublime,
Rather than shadow our own soul's day-time
In the dark void of night. For in the world
We jostle—but my flag is not unfurl'd
On the Admiral-staff—and to philosophise
I dare not yet! Oh, never will the prize,
High reason, and the love of good and ill,
Be my award! Things cannot to the will
Be settled, but they tease us out of thought;
Or is it that imagination brought
Beyond its proper bound, yet still confin'd,
Lost in a sort of Purgatory blind,
Cannot refer to any standard law
Of either earth or heaven? It is a flaw
In happiness, to see beyond our bourn,—
It forces us in summer skies to mourn,
It spoils the singing of the Nightingale.

Dear Reynolds! I have a mysterious tale,
And cannot speak it: the first page I read
Upon a Limpit-rock of green sea-weed
Among the breakers; 'twas a quiet eve,
The rocks were silent, the wide sea did weave
An untumultuous fringe of silver foam
Along the flat brown sand; I was at home
And should have been most happy,—but I saw
Too far into the sea, where every maw
The greater on the less feeds evermore,—
But I saw too distinct into the core
Of an eternal fierce destruction,
And so from happiness I far was gone.
Still am I sick of it, and tho', to-day,
I've gather'd young spring-leaves, and flowers gay
Of periwinkle and wild strawberry,
Still do I that most fierce destruction see,—
The Shark at savage prey—the Hawk at pounce,—
The gentle Robin, like a Pard or Ounce,
Ravening a Worm—Away, ye horrid moods!
Moods of one's mind! You know I hate them well,
You know I'd sooner be a clapping Bell
To some Kamschatkan Missionary Church,
Than with these horrid moods be left i' the lurch.

MY DEAR RICE,

Being in the midst of your favourite Devon, I should not, by right, pen one word but it should contain a vast portion of wit, wisdom, and learning; for I have heard that Milton, ere he wrote his answer to Salmasius, came into these parts, and for one whole month, rolled himself for three whole hours a day, in a certain meadow hard by us, where the mark of his nose at equidistances is still shown. The exhibitor of the said meadow further saith, that, after these rollings, not a nettle sprang up in all the seven acres for seven years, and that from the said time a new sort of plant was made from the white-thorn, of a thornless nature, very much used by the bucks of the present day to rap their boots withal. This account made me very naturally suppose that the nettles and thorns ether-ealised by the scholar's rotatory motion, and garnered in his head, thence flew, after a process of fermentation, against the luckless Salmasius, and occasioned his well-known and unhappy end. What a happy thing it would be if we could settle our thoughts and make our minds up on any matter in five minutes, and remain content; that is, build a sort of mental cottage of feelings, quiet and pleasant—to have a sort of philosophical back-garden, and cheerful holiday-keeping front one. But, alas! this never can be; for, as the material cottager knows, there are such places as France and Italy, and the Andes, and burning mountains, so the spiritual cottager has know-ledge of the terra semi-incognita of things unearthly, and cannot, for his life, keep in the check-rein—or I should stop here, quiet and comfortable in my theory of—nettles. You will see, however, I am obliged to run wild, being attracted by the lode-stone, concatenation. No sooner had I settled the knotty point of Salmasius, than the devil put this whim into my head in the likeness of one of Pythagoras's question-ings—Did Milton do more good or harm in the world ? He wrote, let me inform you (for I have it from a friend who had it of ——), he wrote *Lycidas, Comus, Paradise Lost*, and other Poems, with much delectable prose; he was moreover an active friend to man all his life, and has been since his death. Very good. But, my dear fellow, I must let you know that, as there is ever the same quantity of matter constituting this habitable globe, as the ocean, notwithstanding the enormous

changes and revolutions taking place in some or other of
its demesnes, notwithstanding waterspouts, whirlpools, and
mighty rivers emptying themselves into it, it still is made up
of the same bulk, nor ever varies the number of its atoms;
and, as a certain bulk of water was instituted at the creation,
so, very likely, a certain portion of intellect was spun forth
into the thin air, for the brains of man to prey upon it. You will
see my drift, without any unnecessary parenthesis. That which
is contained in the Pacific could not be in the hollow of the
Caspian; that which was in Milton's head could not find room
in Charles the Second's. He, like a moon, attracted intellect
to its flow—it has not ebbed yet, but has left the shore-
pebbles all bare—I mean all bucks, authors of Hengist, and
Castlereaghs of the present day, who, without Milton's gor-
mandising, might have been all wise men. Now for as much
as I was very predisposed to a country I had heard you speak
so highly of, I took particular notice of everything during
my journey, and have bought some nice folio asses skins for
memorandums. I have seen everything but the wind—and
that they say, becomes visible by taking a dose of acorns, or
sleeping one night in a hog-trough, with your tail to the
sow-sow-west.

I went yesterday to Dawlish fair.

> Over the Hill and over the Dale,
> And over the Bourne to Dawlish,
> Where ginger-bread wives have a scanty sale,
> And ginger-bread nuts are smallish, etc.

Your sincere friend,

John Keats.

Mr. Reynolds seems to have objected to a Preface written
for *Endymion*, and Keats thus manfully and eloquently
remonstrates:

Teignmouth,
9 *April*, 1818.

My Dear Reynolds,

Since you all agree that the thing is bad, it must be so—
though I am not aware that there is anything like Hunt in it,
(and if there is, it is my natural way, and I have something
in common with Hunt). Look over it again, and examine into
the motives, the seeds, from which every one sentence sprang.

I have not the slightest feel of humility towards the public, or to anything in existence but the Eternal Being, the Principle of Beauty, and the Memory of great Men. When I am writing for myself, for the mere sake of the moment's enjoyment, perhaps nature has its course with me; but a Preface is written in to the public—a thing I cannot help looking upon as an enemy, and which I cannot address without feelings of hostility. If I write a Preface in a supple or subdued style, it will not be in character with me as a public speaker.

I would be subdued before my friends, and thank them for subduing me; but among multitudes of men I have no feel of stooping; I hate the idea of humility to them.

I never wrote one single line of poetry with the least shadow of public thought.

Forgive me for vexing you, and making a Trojan horse of such a trifle, both with respect to the matter in question, and myself; but it eases me to tell you: I could not live without the love of my friends; I would jump down Ætna for any great public good—but I hate a mawkish popularity. I cannot be subdued before them. My glory would be to daunt and dazzle the thousand jabberers about pictures and books. I see swarms of porcupines with their quills erect "like lime-twigs set to catch my wingèd book," and I would fright them away with a touch. You will say my Preface is not much of a touch. It would have been too insulting "to begin from Jove," and I could not [set] a golden head upon a thing of clay. If there is any fault in the Preface it is not affectation, but an undersong of disrespect to the public. If I write another Preface it must be done without a thought of those people. I will think about it. If it should not reach you in four or five days, tell Taylor to publish it without a Preface, and let the Dedication simply stand—"Inscribed to the Memory of Thomas Chatterton."

I had resolved last night to write to you this morning—I wish it had been about something else—something to greet you towards the close of your long illness. I have had one or two intimations of your going to Hampstead for a space; and I regret to see your confounded rheumatism keeps you in Little Britain, where I am sure the air is too confined.

Devonshire continues rainy. As the drops beat against my window, they give me the same sensation as a quart of cold water offered to revive a half-drowned devil—no feel of the clouds dropping fatness; but as if the roots of the earth were rotten, cold, and drenched. I have not been able to go to Kent's ca[ve?] at Babbicomb; however, on one very beautiful day I had a fine clamber over the rocks all along as far as that place.

I shall be in town in about ten days. We go by way of Bath on purpose to call on Bailey. I hope soon to be writing to you about the things of the north, purposing to wayfare all over those parts. I have settled my accoutrements in my own mind, and will go to gorge wonders. However, we'll have some days together before I set out.

I have many reasons for going wonder-ways; to make my winter chair free from spleen; to enlarge my vision; to escape disquisitions on poetry, and Kingston-criticism; to promote digestion and economise shoe-leather. I'll have leather buttons and belt; and, if Brown holds his mind, "over the hills we go." If my books will help me to it, then will I take all Europe in turn, and see the kingdoms of the earth and the glory of them. Tom is getting better: he hopes you may meet him at the top of the hill. My love to your nurse.

I am ever
Your affectionate friend,
JOHN KEATS.

TEIGNMOUTH,
10 *April*, 1818.

MY DEAR REYNOLDS,

I am anxious you should find this Preface tolerable. If there is an affectation in it 'tis natural to me. Do let the printer's devil cook it, and let me be as "the casing air."

You are too good in this matter; were I in your state, I am certain I should have no thought but of discontent and illness. I might, though, be taught patience. I had an idea of giving no Preface; however, don't you think this had better go? O! let it—one should not be too timid of committing faults.

The climate here weighs us [down] completely; Tom is quite low-spirited. It is impossible to live in a country which is continually under hatches. Who would live in a region of mists, game laws, indemnity bills, etc., when there is such a place as Italy? It is said this England from its clime produces a spleen, able to engender the finest sentiments, and covers the whole face of the isle with green. So it ought, I'm sure.

I should still like the Dedication simply, as I said in my last.

I wanted to send you a few songs, written in your favourite Devon. It cannot be! Rain, rain, rain! I am going this morning to take a facsimile of a letter of Nelson's, very much to his honour; you will be greatly pleased when you see it, in about a week.

What a spite it is one cannot get out! The little way I went yesterday, I found a lane banked on each side with a store of primroses, while the earlier bushes are beginning to leaf.

I shall hear a good account of you soon.

Your affectionate friend,

JOHN KEATS.

I cannot lay hands on the first Preface, but here is the second, which no one will regret to read again, both from its intrinsic truth and its representation, in the aptest terms, of the state of Keats's mind at this time, and of his honest judgment of himself.

Knowing within myself the manner in which this Poem has been produced, it is not without a feeling of regret that I make it public.

What manner I mean, will be quite clear to the reader, who must soon perceive great inexperience, immaturity, and every error denoting a feverish attempt, rather than a deed accomplished. The two first books, and indeed the two last, I feel sensible are not of such completion as to warrant their passing the press; nor should they if I thought a year's castigation would do them any good; it will not; the foundations are too sandy. It is just that this youngster should die away: a sad thought for me, if I had not some hope that while it is dwindling I may be plotting and fitting myself for verses fit to live.

This may be speaking too presumptuously and may deserve a punishment; but no feeling man will be forward to inflict it; he will leave me alone, with the conviction that there is not a fiercer hell than the failure in a great object. This is not written with the least atom of purpose to forestall criticisms, of course, but from the desire I have to conciliate men who are competent to look, and who do look with a zealous eye to the honour of English literature. The imagination of a boy is healthy, and the mature imagination of a man is healthy;

but there is a space of life between, in which the soul is in a ferment, the character undecided, the way of life uncertain, the ambition thick-sighted; thence proceeds mawkishness, and all the thousand bitters which those men I speak of must necessarily taste in going over the following pages. I hope I have not in too late a day touched the beautiful mythology of Greece and dulled its brightness; for I wish to try once more, before I bid it farewell.

Teignmouth,
27 April, 1818.

My Dear Reynolds,

It is an awful while since you have heard from me. I hope I may not be punished, when I see you well, and so anxious as you always are for me, with the remembrance of my so seldom writing when you were so horribly confined. The most unhappy hours in our lives are those in which we recollect times past to our own blushing. If we are immortal, that must be the Hell. If I must be immortal, I hope it will be after having taken a little of "that watery labyrinth," in order to forget some of my school-boy days, and others since those.

I have heard from George, at different times, how slowly you were recovering. It is a tedious thing; but all medical men will tell you how far a very gradual amendment is preferable. You will be strong after this, never fear.

We are here still enveloped in clouds. I lay awake last night listening to the rain, with a sense of being drowned and rotted like a grain of wheat. There is a continual courtesy between the heavens and the earth. The heavens rain down their unwelcomeness, and the earth sends it up again, to be returned to-morrow.

Tom has taken a fancy to a physician here, Dr. Turton, and, I think, is getting better; therefore I shall, perhaps, remain here some months. I have written to George for some books—shall learn Greek, and very likely Italian; and, in other ways, prepare myself to ask Hazlitt, in about a year's time, the best metaphysical road I can take. For, although I take Poetry to be chief, yet there is something else wanting to one who passes his life among books and thoughts on books. I long to feast upon old Homer as we have upon Shakespeare, and as I have lately upon Milton. If you understand Greek, and would read me passages now and then, explaining their meaning, 'twould be, from its mistiness, perhaps, a greater luxury than reading the thing one's self. I shall be happy when I can do the same for you.

I have written for my folio Shakespeare, in which there are the first few stanzas of my *Pot of Basil*. I have the rest here, finished, and will copy the whole out fair shortly, and George will bring it you. The compliment is paid by us to Boccace, whether we publish or no: so there is content in this world. Mine [my Poem] is short; you must be deliberate about yours: you must not think of it till many months after you are quite well:—then put your passion to it, and I shall be bound up with you in the shadows of mind, as we are in our matters of human life. Perhaps a stanza or two will not be too foreign to your sickness.

> Were they unhappy then? It cannot be:
> Too many tears, etc.

> But for the general award of love, etc.

> She wept alone for pleasures, etc.

The fifth line ran thus:

> What might have been, too plainly did she see.

Give my love to your mother and sisters. Remember me to the Butlers—not forgetting Sarah.

Your affectionate friend,

JOHN KEATS.

This adaptation of Boccaccio was intended to form part of a collection of Tales from the great Italian novelist, versified by Mr. Reynolds and himself. Two by Mr. Reynolds appeared in the *Garden of Florence*; *Isabella* was the only other one Keats completed.

TEIGNMOUTH,
27 April, 1818.

MY DEAR TAYLOR,

I think I did wrong to leave to you all the trouble of *Endymion*. But I could not help it then—another time I shall be more bent to all sorts of troubles and disagreeables. Young men, for some time, have an idea that such a thing as happiness is to be had, and therefore are extremely impatient under any unpleasant restraining. In time, however—of such stuff is the world about them—they know better, and instead of striving from uneasiness, greet it as an habitual sensation, a

panner which is to weigh upon them through life. And in proportion to my disgust at the task is my sense of your kindness
and anxiety. The book pleased me much. It is very free from
faults; and, although there are one or two words I should
wish replaced, I see in many places an improvement greatly
to the purpose.

I was proposing to travel over the North this summer.
There is but one thing to prevent me. I know nothing—I have
read nothing—and I mean to follow Solomon's directions,
"Get learning—get understanding." I find earlier days are
gone by—I find that I can have no enjoyment in the world
but continual drinking of knowledge. I find there is no worthy
pursuit but the idea of doing some good to the world. Some
do it with their society; some with their wit; some with their
benevolence; some with a sort of power of conferring pleasure
and good humour on all they meet—and in a thousand ways,
all dutiful to the command of great Nature. There is but one
way for me. The road lies through application, study, and
thought. I will pursue it; and, for that end, purpose retiring
for some years. I have been hovering for some time between
an exquisite sense of the luxurious, and a love for philosophy:
were I calculated for the former I should be glad. But as I am
not, I shall turn all my soul to the latter.

My brother Tom is getting better, and I hope I shall see
both him and Reynolds better before I retire from the world.
I shall see you soon, and have some talk about what books
I shall take with me.

Your very sincere friend,

JOHN KEATS.

It is difficult to add anything to the passages in these
letters, which show the spirit in which *Endymion* was
written and published. This first sustained work of a man
whose undoubted genius was idolised by a circle of affectionate friends, whose weaknesses were rather encouraged
than repressed by the intellectual atmosphere in which
he lived, who had rarely been enabled to measure his
spiritual stature with that of persons of other schools of
thought and habits of mind, appears to have been produced
with a humility that the severest criticism might not have
engendered. Keats, it is clear, did not require to be told
how far he was from the perfect poet. The very conscious-

ness of his capability to do something higher and better, which accompanies the lowly estimate of his work, kept the ideal ever before him, and urged him to complete it rather as a process of poetical education than as a triumph of contented power. Never was less presumption exhibited —never the sharp stroke of contemptuous censure less required. His own Preface was the more deprecatory, in that it did not deny that he was himself disappointed, and that he looked to future efforts to justify his claims to others, and himself to himself. This dissatisfaction with his book, and his brother's ill-health, cast over his mind the gloom which he hardly conceals in the letters of this period, though it is remarkable how free they are, at all times, from any merely querulous expressions, and from the vague sentimentality attributed to some of his literary associates.

TEIGNMOUTH,
3 *May* [1818].

My DEAR REYNOLDS,

What I complain of is, that I have been in so uneasy a state of mind as not to be fit to write to an invalid. I cannot write to any length under a disguised feeling. I should have loaded you with an addition of gloom, which I am sure you do not want. I am now, thank God, in a humour to give you a good groat's worth; for Tom, after a night without a wink of sleep, and over-burthened with fever, has got up, after a refreshing day-sleep, and is better than he has been for a long time. And you, I trust, have been again round the Common without any effect but refreshment. As to the matter, I hope I can say, with Sir Andrew, "I have matter enough in my head," in your favour. And now, in the second place, for I reckon that I have finished my Imprimis, I am glad you blow up the weather. All through your letter there is a leaning towards a climate-curse; and you know what a delicate satisfaction there is in having a vexation anathematised. One would think that there has been growing up, for these last four thousand years, a grand-child scion of the old forbidden tree, and that some modern Eve had just violated it; and that there was come, with double charge, "Notus and Afer (Auster?) black with thunderous clouds from Serraliona." Tom wants to be in town: we will have some such days upon the heath like that of last summer—and why not with the same book? or what do you say to a black-letter Chaucer, printed in 1596? Aye, I have got one, huzza! I shall have it bound in Gothique—a nice sombre binding; it will go a little way to unmodernise. And, also, I see no reason, because I have been away this last month, why I should not have a peep at your Spenserian—notwithstanding you speak of your office, in my thought, a little too early; for I do not see why a mind like yours is not capable of harbouring and digesting the whole mystery of Law as easily as Parson Hugh does pippins, which did not hinder him from his poetic canary. Were I to study Physic, or rather Medicine again, I feel it would not make the least difference in my poetry; when the mind is in its infancy a bias is in reality a bias, but when we have acquired more strength, a bias becomes no bias. Every department of knowledge we see excellent and calculated towards a great whole. I am so convinced of this that I am glad at not having given away my medical books, which I shall again look over, to keep alive the little I know thitherwards; and moreover intend, through you and Rice, to become a sort of pip-civilian. An extensive knowledge is needful to thinking people; it takes away the heat and fever, and helps, by widening speculation, to ease the burden of the Mystery, a thing which I begin to understand a little, and which weighed upon you in the most gloomy and true sentence in your letters. The difference of high sensations, with and without knowledge, appears to me this: in the latter case we are continually falling ten thousand fathoms deep, and being blown up again, without wings, and with all [the] horror of a bare-shouldered creature; in the former case, our shoulders are fledged, and we go through the same air and space without fear. This is running one's rigs on the score of abstracted benefit; when we come to human life and the affections, it is impossible to know how a parallel of breast and head can be drawn (you will forgive me for thus privately treading out [of] my depth, and take it for treading as school-boys tread the water); it is impossible to know how far knowledge will console us for the death of a friend, and the "ills that flesh is heir to." With respect to the affections and poetry, you must know by sympathy my thoughts that way, and I dare say these few lines will be but a ratification. I wrote them on May-day, and intend to finish the ode all in good time.

Mother of Hermes! and still youthful Maia!
    May I sing to thee
As thou wast hymned on the shores of Baiæ?
    Or may I woo thee
In earlier Sicilian? or thy smiles
Seek as they once were sought, in Grecian isles,
By bards who died content on pleasant sward,
Leaving great verse unto a little clan?
O, give me their old vigour, and unheard
Save of the quiet Primrose, and the span
    Of heaven and few ears,
Rounded by thee, my song should die away
    Content as theirs,
Rich in the simple worship of a day.

You may perhaps be anxious to know for fact to what sentence in your letter I allude. You say, "I fear there is little chance of anything else in this life." You seem by that to have been going through, with a more painful and acute zest, the same labyrinth that I have—I have come to the same conclusion thus far. My branchings-out therefrom have been numerous: one of them is the consideration of Wordsworth's genius, and as a help, in the manner of gold being the meridian line of worldly wealth, how he differs from Milton. And here I have nothing but surmises, from an uncertainty whether Milton's apparently less anxiety for humanity proceeds from his seeing farther or not than Wordsworth, and whether Wordsworth has, in truth, epic passion, and martyrs himself to the human heart, the main region of his song. In regard to his genius alone, we find what he says true, as far as we have experienced, and we can judge no farther but by larger experience; for axioms in philosophy are not axioms till they have been proved upon our pulses. We read fine things, but never feel them to the full until we have gone [over] the same steps as the author. I know this is not plain; you will know exactly my meaning when I say that now I shall relish *Hamlet* more than I ever have done—or better. You are sensible no man can set down venery as a bestial or joyless thing until he is sick of it, and therefore all philosophising on it would be mere wording. Until we are sick, we understand not; in fine, as Byron says, "Knowledge is sorrow"; and I go on to say that "Sorrow is wisdom"; and further, for aught we can know for certainty, "Wisdom is folly." So you see how I have run away from Wordsworth and Milton, and shall still run away from what was in my head to observe, that some kind of letters are good squares, others handsome ovals, others orbicular, others spheroid—and why should not there be another species with two rough edges, like a rat-trap? I hope you will find all my long letters of that species, and all will be well; for by merely touching the spring delicately and ethereally, the rough-edged will fly immediately into a proper compactness; and thus you may make a good wholesome loaf, with your own leaven in it, of my fragments. If you cannot find this said rat-trap sufficiently tractable, alas! for me, it being an impossibility in grain for my ink to stain otherwise. If I scribble long letters, I must play my vagaries. I must be too heavy, or too light, for whole pages; I must be quaint, and free of tropes and figures; I must play my draughts as I please, and for my advantage and your erudition, crown a white with a black, or a black with a white, and move into black or white, far and near as I please, I must go from Hazlitt to Patmore, and make Wordsworth and Coleman play at leap-frog, or keep one of them down a whole half-holiday at fly-the-garter; "from Gray to Gay, from Little to Shakespeare." I shall resume after dinner.

·   ·   ·   ·   ·   ·

This crossing a letter is not without its association—for chequer-work leads us naturally to a milkmaid, a milkmaid to Hogarth, Hogarth to Shakespeare; Shakespeare to Hazlitt, Hazlitt back to Shakespeare; and thus by merely pulling an apron-string we set a pretty peal of chimes at work. Let them chime on, while, with your patience, I will return to Words-worth—whether or no he has an extended vision or a circumscribed grandeur—whether he is an eagle in his nest or on the wing; and, to be more explicit, and to show you how tall I stand by the giant, I will put down a simile of human life as far as I now perceive it; that is, to the point to which I say we both have arrived at. Well, I compare human life to a large mansion of many apartments, two of which I can only describe, the doors of the rest being as yet shut upon me. The first we step into we call the Infant, or Thoughtless Chamber, in which we remain as long as we do not think. We remain there a long while, and notwithstanding the doors of the second chamber remain wide open, showing a bright appearance, we care not to hasten to it, but are at length imperceptibly impelled by the awakening of the thinking principle within us. We no sooner get into the second chamber, which

I shall call the Chamber of Maiden-thought, than we become intoxicated with the light and the atmosphere. We see nothing but pleasant wonders, and think of delaying there for ever in delight. However, among the effects this breathing is father of, is that tremendous one of sharpening one's vision into the heart and nature of man, of convincing one's nerves that the world is full of misery and heartbreak, pain, sickness, and oppression; whereby this Chamber of Maiden-thought becomes gradually darkened, and at the same time, on all sides of it, many doors are set open—but all dark—all leading to dark passages. We see not the balance of good and evil; we are in a mist, *we* are in that state, we feel the "Burden of the Mystery." To this point was Wordsworth come, as far as I can conceive, when he wrote *Tintern Abbey*, and it seems to me that his genius is explorative of those dark passages. Now if we live, and go on thinking, we too shall explore them. He is a genius and superior [to] us, in so far as he can, more than we, make discoveries and shed a light in them. Here I must think Wordsworth is deeper than Milton, though I think it has depended more upon the general and gregarious advance of intellect than individual greatness of mind. From the *Paradise Lost*, and the other works of Milton, I hope it is not too presuming, even between ourselves, to say, that his philosophy, human and divine, may be tolerably understood by one not much advanced in years. In his time, Englishmen were just emancipated from a great superstition, and men had got hold of certain points and resting-places in reasoning which were too newly born to be doubted, and too much oppressed by the rest of Europe, not to be thought ethereal and authentically divine. Who could gainsay his ideas on virtue, vice, and chastity, in *Comus*, just at the time of the dismissal of a hundred social disgraces? Who would not rest satisfied with his hintings at good and evil in the *Paradise Lost*, when just free from the Inquisition and burning in Smithfield? The Reformation produced such immediate and great benefits, that Protestantism was considered under the immediate eye of Heaven, and its own remaining dogmas and superstitions then, as it were, regenerated, constituted those resting-places and seeming sure points of reasoning. From that I have mentioned, Milton, whatever he may have thought in the sequel, appears to have been content with these by his writings. He did not think with the human heart as Wordsworth has done; yet Milton, as a philosopher, had surely as great powers as Wordsworth. What is then to be inferred ? O! many things: it proves there is really a grand march of intellect; it proves that a mighty Providence subdues the mightiest minds to the service of the time being, whether it be in human knowledge or religion.

I have often pitied a tutor who has to hear "Nom. Musa" so often dinn'd into his ears: I hope you may not have the same pain in this scribbling—I may have read these things before, but I never had even a thus dim perception of them; and, moreover, I like to say my lesson to one who will endure my tediousness, for my own sake.

After all there is something real in the world—Moore's present to Hazlitt is real. I like that Moore, and am glad I saw him at the Theatre just before I left town. Tom has spit a *leetle* blood this afternoon, and that is rather a damper—but I know—the truth is, there is something real in the world. Your third Chamber of Life shall be a lucky and a gentle one, stored with the wine of Love and the bread of Friendship.

When you see George, if he should not have received a letter from me, tell him he will find one at home most likely. Tell Bailey I hope soon to see him. Remember me to all. The leaves have been out here for many a day. I have written to George for the first stanzas of my *Isabel*. I shall have them soon, and will copy the whole out for you.

Your affectionate friend,

JOHN KEATS.

HAMPSTEAD,

25 *May*, 1818.

MY DEAR BAILEY,

I should have answered your letter on the moment, if I could have said Yes to your invitation. What hinders me is insuperable: I will tell it at a little length. You know my brother George has been out of employ for some time. It has weighed very much upon him, and driven him to scheme and turn over things in his mind. The result has been his resolution to emigrate to the back settlements of America, become farmer, and work with his own hands, after purchasing fourteen hundred acres of the American Government. This, for many reasons, has met with my entire consent—and the chief one is this; he is of too independent and liberal a mind to get on in trade in this country, in which a generous man with a scanty resource must be ruined. I would sooner he should till the ground than bow to a customer. There is no choice with him: he could not bring himself to the latter. I could not consent to his going alone—no; but that objection is done away with: he will marry, before he sets sail, a young lady he has known for several years, of a nature liberal and high-spirited enough to follow him to the banks of the Mississippi. He will set off in a month or six weeks, and you will see how I should wish to pass that time with him.—And then I must set out on a journey of my own. Brown and I are going on a pedestrian tour through the north of England, and Scotland, as far as John o' Grot's.

I have this morning such a lethargy that I cannot write. The reason of my delaying is oftentimes for this feeling—I wait for a proper temper. Now you ask for an immediate answer, I do not like to wait even till to-morrow. However, I am now so depressed that I have not an idea to put to paper; my hand feels like lead. And yet it is an unpleasant numbness; it does not take away the pain of existence. I don't know what to write.

[*Monday.*]—You see how I have delayed; and even now I have but a confused idea of what I should be about. My intellect must be in a degenerating state—it must be—for when I should be writing about—God knows what—I am troubling you with moods of my own mind, or rather body, for mind there is none. I am in that temper that if I were under water I would scarcely kick to come up to the top. I know very well 'tis all nonsense. In a short time I hope I shall be in a temper to feel sensibly your mention of my book. In vain have I waited till Monday to have any interest in that, or anything else. I feel no spur at my brother's going to America, and am almost stony-hearted about his wedding. All this will blow over. All I am sorry for is having to write to you in such a time—but I cannot force my letters in a hot-bed. I could not feel comfortable in making sentences for you. I am your debtor; I must ever remain so; nor do I wish to be clear of my rational debt: there is a comfort in throwing one-self on the charity of one's friends—'tis like the albatross sleeping on its wings. I will be to you wine in the cellar, and the more modestly, or rather, indolently, I retire into the backward bin, the more Falerne will I be at the drinking. There is one thing I must mention: my brother talks of sailing in a fortnight; if so, I will most probably be with you a week before I set out for Scotland. The middle of your first page should be sufficient to rouse me. What I said is true, and I have dreamt of your mention of it, and my not answering it has weighed on me since. If I come, I will bring your letter, and hear more fully your sentiments on one or two points. I will call about the Lectures at Taylor's, and at Little Britain, to-morrow. Yesterday I dined with Hazlitt, Barnes, and Wilkie, at Haydon's. The topic was the Duke of Wellington— very amusingly pro-and-con'd. Reynolds has been getting much better; and Rice may begin to crow, for he got a little so-so at a party of his, and was none the worse for it the next morning. I hope I shall soon see you, for we must have many new thoughts and feelings to analyse, and to discover whether a little more knowledge has not made us more ignorant.

Yours affectionately,

JOHN KEATS.

LONDON,
10 *June*, 1818.

MY DEAR BAILEY,

I have been very much gratified and very much hurt by your letters in the Oxford Paper; because, independent of that unlawful and mortal feeling of pleasure at praise, there is a glory in enthusiasm; and because the world is malignant enough to chuckle at the most honourable simplicity. Yes, on my soul, my dear Bailey, you are too simple for the world, and that idea makes me sick of it. How is it that, by extreme opposites, we have, as it were, got discontented nerves? You have all your life (I think so) believed everybody. I have suspected everybody. And, although you have been so deceived, you make a simple appeal. The world has something else to do, and I am glad of it. Were it in my choice, I would reject a Petrarchal coronation—on account of my dying day, and because women have cancers. I should not, by rights, speak in this tone to you, for it is an incendiary spirit that would do so. Yet I am not old enough or magnanimous enough to annihilate self—and it would, perhaps, be paying you an ill compliment. I was in hopes, some little time back, to be able to relieve your dulness by my spirits—to point out things in the world worth your enjoyment—and now I am never alone without rejoicing that there is such a thing as death—without placing my ultimate in the glory of dying for a great human purpose. Perhaps if my affairs were in a different state I should not have written the above—you shall judge: I have two brothers; one is driven, by the "burden of society," to America; the other, with an exquisite love of life, is in a lingering state. My love for my brothers, from the early loss of our parents, and even from earlier misfortunes, has grown into an affection, "passing the love of women." I have been ill-tempered with them, I have vexed them—but the thought of them has always stifled the impression that any woman might otherwise have made upon me. I have a sister too; and may not follow them either to America or to the grave. Life must be undergone; and I certainly derive some consolation from the thought of writing one or two more poems before it ceases.

I have heard some hints of your retiring to Scotland. I should like to know your feeling on it: it seems rather remote. Perhaps Gleig will have a duty near you. I am not certain whether I shall be able to go any journey, on account of my brother Tom and a little indisposition of my own. If I do not, you shall see me soon, if not on my return, or I'll quarter myself on you next winter. I had known my sister-in-law some time before she was my sister, and was very fond of her. I like her better and better. She is the most disinterested woman I ever knew—that is to say, she goes beyond degrees in it. To see an entirely disinterested girl quite happy is the most pleasant and extraordinary thing in the world. It depends upon a thousand circumstances. On my word it is extraordinary. Women must want imagination, and they may thank God for it; and so may we, that a delicate being can feel happy without any sense of crime. It puzzles me, and I have no sort of logic to comfort me: I shall think it over. I am not at home, and your letter being there I cannot look it over to answer any particular—only, I must say I feel that passage of Dante. If I take any book with me it shall be those minute volumes of Carey, for they will go into the aptest corner.

Reynolds is getting, I may say, robust. His illness has been of service to him. Like every one just recovered, he is high-spirited. I hear also good accounts of Rice. With respect to domestic literature, the *Edinburgh Magazine*, in another blow-up against Hunt, calls me "the amiable Mister Keats," and I have more than a laurel from the "Quarterly Reviewers," for they have smothered me in *Foliage*. I want to read you my *Pot of Basil*. If you go to Scotland, I should much like to read it there to you, among the snows of next winter. My brothers' remembrance to you.

Your affectionate friend,

JOHN KEATS.

Foliage was a volume of Poems chiefly classical, just published by Mr. Leigh Hunt. It contained the following sonnets to Keats. The *Edinburgh Magazine* was Blackwood's, and had begun the series of articles on the "Cockney School," to which further allusion will be made.

SONNET TO JOHN KEATS

'Tis well you think me truly one of those
Whose sense discerns the loveliness of things;
For surely as I feel the bird that sings
Behind the leaves, or dawn as it up grows,
Or the rich bee rejoicing as he goes,
Or the glad issue of emerging springs,
Or overhead the glide of a dove's wings,
Or turf, or tree, or, midst of all, repose:
And surely as I feel things lovelier still,
The human look, and the harmonious form
Containing woman, and the smile in ill,
And such a heart as Charles's,[1] wise and warm,—
As surely as all this, I see, ev'n now,
Young Keats, a flowering laurel on your brow.

ON RECEIVING A CROWN OF IVY FROM THE SAME

A crown of ivy! I submit my head
To the young hand that gives it—young, 'tis true,
But with a right, for 'tis a poet's too.
How pleasant the leaves feel! and how they spread
With their broad angles, like a nodding shed
Over both eyes! and how complete and new,
As on my hand I lean, to feel them strew
My sense with freshness—Fancy's rustling bed!
Tress-tossing girls, with smell of flowers and grapes,
Come dancing by, and downward piping cheeks,
And up-thrown cymbals, and Silenus old
Lumpishly borne, and many trampling shapes—
And lastly, with his bright eyes on her bent,
Bacchus—whose bride has of his hand fast hold.

---

[1] Charles Cowden Clarke.

ON THE SAME

It is a lofty feeling and a kind,
Thus to be topped with leaves;—to have a sense
Of honour-shaded thought—an influence
As from great Nature's fingers, and be twined
With her old, sacred, verdurous ivy-bind,
As though she hallowed with that sylvan fence
A head that bows to her benevolence,
'Midst pomp of fancied trumpets in the wind.
'Tis what's within us crowned. And kind and great
Are all the conquering wishes it inspires—
Love of things lasting, love of the tall woods,
Love of love's self, and ardour for a state
Of natural good befitting such desires,
Towns without gain, and haunted solitudes.

Whatever extravagance a stranger might find in these
verses, was probably justified to the poet by the author's
friendship, and in the Preface to *Foliage* there is, among
other ingenious criticisms, a passage on Shakespeare's
scholarship, which seems to me to have more than an
accidental bearing on the kind of classical knowledge which
Keats really possessed. "Though not a scholar," writes
Mr. Hunt, "he needed nothing more than the description
given by scholars, good or indifferent, in order to pierce
back at once into all the recesses of the original country.
They told him where they had been, and he was there in
an instant, though not in the track of their footing—
Battendo l'ali verso l'aurea fronde. The truth is, he felt the
Grecian mythology not as a set of schoolboy common-
places which it was thought wrong to give up, but as
something which it requires more than mere scholarship
to understand—as the elevation of the external world and
of accomplished humanity to the highest pitch of the
graceful, and as embodied essences of all the grand and
lovely qualities of nature. His description of Proserpine
and her flowers, in the *Winter's Tale*, of the characteristic
beauties of some of the Gods in *Hamlet*, and that single
couplet in the *Tempest*,

Ye nymphs called Naiads of the wandering brooks,
With your sedged crowns and *ever harmless looks*,

are in the deepest taste of antiquity, and show that all
great poets look at themselves and the fine world about
them in the same clear and ever-living fountains."

Every word of this might have applied to Keats, who, at this time, himself seems to have been studying Shakespeare with the greatest diligence. Captain Medwin, in his *Life of Shelley*, mentions that he has seen a folio edition of Shakespeare with Keats's annotations, and he gives as a specimen part of Agamemnon's speech in *Troilus and Cressida:*

> Sith every action that has gone before,
> Whereof we have record, trial did draw,
> Bias, and thwart, not answering the aim,
> And that unbodied figure of the thought
> That gave it surmised shape.

On which Keats remarks:

The genius of Shakespeare was an innate universality; wherefore he laid the achievements of human intellect prostrate beneath his indolent and kingly gaze: he could do easily men's utmost—his plan of tasks to come was not of this world. If what he proposed to do hereafter would not, in the idea, answer the aim, how tremendous must have been his conception of ultimates!

The agreeable diversion to his somewhat monotonous life by a walking-tour through the Lakes and Highlands with his friend Mr. Brown was now put into execution. They set off in the middle of June for Liverpool, where they parted with George Keats, who embarked with his wife for America. On the road he stopped to see a former fellow-student at Guy's, who was settled as a surgeon in a country town, and whom he informed that he had definitively abandoned that profession and intended to devote himself to poetry. Mr. Stephens remembers that he seemed much delighted with his new sister-in-law, who was a person of most agreeable appearance, and introduced her with evident satisfaction. From Lancaster they started on foot, and Mr. Brown has recorded the rapture of Keats when he became sensible, for the first time, of the full effect of mountain scenery. At a turn of the road above Bowness, where the Lake of Windermere first bursts on the view, he stopped as if stupefied with beauty. That evening he read aloud the poem of the *Pot of Basil*, which he had just completed. His disappointment at missing Wordsworth was very great, and he hardly concealed his vexation when he found that he owed the privation to the interest which the elder poet was taking in the General Election. This annoyance would perhaps have been diminished if the two poets had happened to be on the same side in politics; but, as it was, no views and objects could be more opposed.

A portion of a rambling journal of this tour remains in various letters.

KESWICK,
29 *June* [1818].

MY DEAR TOM,

I cannot make my journal as distinct and actual as I could wish, from having been engaged in writing to George, and therefore I must tell you, without circumstance, that we proceeded from Ambleside to Rydal, saw the waterfalls there, and called on Wordsworth, who was not at home, nor was anyone of his family. I wrote a note and left it on the mantelpiece. Thence, on we came to the foot of Helvellyn, where we slept, but could not ascend it for the mist. I must mention that from Rydal we passed Thirlswater, and a fine pass in the mountains. From Helvellyn we came to Keswick on Derwent Water. The approach to Derwent Water surpassed Windermere: it is richly wooded, and shut in with rich-toned mountains. From Helvellyn to Keswick was eight miles to breakfast, after which we took a complete circuit of the lake, going about ten miles, and seeing on our way the fall of Lodore. I had an easy climb among the streams, about the fragments of rocks, and should have got, I think, to the summit, but unfortunately I was damped by slipping one leg into a squashy hole. There is no great body of water, but the accompaniment is delightful; for it oozes out from a cleft in perpendicular rocks, all fledged with ash and other beautiful trees. It is a strange thing how they got there. At the south end of the lake, the mountains of Borrowdale are perhaps as fine as anything we have seen. On our return from this circuit, we ordered dinner, and set forth about a mile and a half on the Penrith road, to see the Druid temple. We had a fag up hill, rather too near dinnertime, which was rendered void by the gratification of seeing those aged stones on a gentle rise in the midst of the mountains, which at that time darkened all round, except at the fresh opening of the Vale of St. John. We went to bed rather fatigued, but not so much so as to hinder us getting up this morning to Mount Skiddaw. It promised all along to be fair, and we had fagged and tugged nearly to the top, when, at half-past six, there came a mist upon us, and shut out the view. We did not, however, lose anything by it: we were high enough without mist to see the coast of Scotland, the Irish Sea, the hills beyond Lancaster, and nearly all the large ones of Cumberland and Westmoreland, particularly Helvellyn and Scawfell. It grew colder and colder as we ascended, and we were glad, at about three parts of the way, to taste a little rum which the guide brought with him, mixed, mind ye, with mountain water. I took two glasses going and one returning. It is about six miles from where I am writing to the top; so we have walked ten miles before breakfast to-day. We went up with two others, very good sort of fellows. All felt, on arising into the cold air, that same elevation which a cold bath gives one. I felt as if I were going to a tournament.

Wordsworth's house is situated just on the rise of the foot of Mount Rydal; his parlour-window looks directly down Windermere; I do not think I told you how fine the Vale of Grassmere is, and how I discovered " the ancient woman seated on Helm Crag."

July 1st.—We are this morning at Carlisle. After Skiddaw, we walked to Ireby, the oldest market town in Cumberland, where we were greatly amused by a country dancing-school, holden at the "Tun." It was indeed "no new cotillion fresh from France." No, they kickit and jumpit with mettle extraordinary, and whiskit, and friskit, and toed it, and go'd it, and twirl'd it, and whirl'd it, and stamped it, and sweated it, tattooing the floor like mad. The difference between our country dances and these Scottish figures is about the same as leisurely stirring a cup of tea and beating up a batter-pudding. I was extremely gratified to think that, if I had pleasures they knew nothing of, they had also some into which I could not possibly enter. I hope I shall not return without having got the Highland fling. There was as fine a row of boys and girls as you ever saw; some beautiful faces, and one exquisite mouth. I never felt so near the glory of patriotism, the glory of making, by any means, a country happier. This is what I like better than scenery. I fear our continued moving from place to place will prevent our becoming learned in village affairs: we are mere creatures of rivers, lakes, and mountains. Our yesterday's journey was from Ireby to Wigton, and from Wigton to Carlisle. The cathedral does not appear very fine; the castle is very ancient, and of brick. The city is very various: old, white-washed narrow streets, broad, red-brick ones, more modern. I will tell you anon whether the inside of the cathedral is worth looking at. It is built of sandy red stone, or brick. We have now walked 114 miles, and are merely a little tired in the thighs and a little blistered. We shall ride 38 miles to Dumfries, when we shall linger awhile about Nithsdale and Galloway. I have written two letters to Liverpool. I found a letter from sister George; very delightful indeed: I shall preserve it in the bottom of my knapsack for you.

2 July.

ON VISITING THE TOMB OF BURNS

The town, the churchyard, and the setting sun,
The clouds, the trees, the rounded hills all seem,
Though beautiful, cold—strange—as in a dream,
I dreamed long ago, now new begun.
The short-lived, paly Summer is but won
From Winter's ague, for one hour's gleam;
Though sapphire-warm, their stars do never beam:
All is cold Beauty; pain is never done:
For who has mind to relish, Minos-wise,
The Real of Beauty, free from that dead hue
Sickly imagination and sick pride
Cast wan upon it! Burns! with honour due
I oft have honour'd thee. Great shadow, hide
Thy face; I sin against thy native skies.

You will see by this sonnet that I am at Dumfries. We have dined in Scotland. Burns's tomb is in the church-yard corner, not very much to my taste, though on a scale large enough to show they wanted to honour him. Mrs. Burns lives in this place; most likely we shall see her to-morrow. This sonnet I have written in a strange mood, half-asleep. I know not how it is, the clouds, the sky, the houses, all seem anti-Grecian and anti-Charlemagnish. I will endeavour to get rid of my prejudices and tell you fairly about the Scotch.

In Devonshire they say, "Well, where be ye going?" Here it is, "How is it wi' yoursel?" A man on the coach said the horses took a "hellish heap o' drivin"; the same fellow pointed out Burns's Tomb with a deal of life—"There! de ye see it, amang the trees—white, wi' a roond tap?" The first well-dressed Scotchman we had any conversation with, to our surprise, confessed himself a deist. The careful manner of delivering his opinions, not before he had received several encouraging hints from us, was very amusing. Yesterday was an immense horse-fair at Dumfries, so that we met numbers of men and women on the road, the women nearly all barefoot, with their shoes and clean stockings in hand, ready to put on and look smart in the towns. There are plenty of wretched cottages whose smoke has no outlet but by the door. We have now begun upon whisky, called here "whuskey," —very smart stuff it is. Mixed like our liquors, with sugar and water, 'tis called toddy; very pretty drink, and much praised by Burns.

Besides the above sonnet, Keats wrote another in the whisky-shop, into which the cottage where Burns was born was converted, which seems to me much the better of the two. The "local colour" is strong in it: it might have been written where "Willie brewed a peck o' maut," and its geniality would have delighted the object of its admiration. Nevertheless, the author wrote of it to Haydon thus disparagingly:

The "bonnie Doon" is the sweetest river I ever saw— overhung with fine trees as far as we could see. We stood sometime on the "brig" o'er which Tam o' Shanter fled— we took a pinch of snuff on the key stone—then we proceeded to the auld Kirk of Alloway. Then we went to the cottage in which Burns was born; there was a board to that effect by the door's side; it had the same effect as the same sort of memorial at Stratford-upon-Avon. We drank some toddy to Burns's memory with an old man who knew him. There was something good in his description of Burns's melancholy the last time he saw him. I was determined to write a sonnet in the cottage: I did, but it was so bad I cannot venture it here.

SONNET

This mortal body of a thousand days
    Now fills, O Burns, a space in thine own room,
Where thou didst dream alone on budded bays,
    Happy and thoughtless of thy day of doom!
My pulse is warm with thine old Barley-bree,
    My head is light with pledging a great soul,
My eyes are wandering, and I cannot see,
    Fancy is dead and drunken at its goal;

Yet can I stamp my foot upon thy floor,
  Yet can I ope thy window-sash to find
The meadow thou hast tramped o'er and o'er—
  Yet can I think of thee till thought is blind—
Yet can I gulp a bumper to thy name—
O smile among the shades, for this is fame!

The pedestrians passed by Solway Frith through that
delightful part of Kirkcudbrightshire, the scene of *Guy
Mannering*. Keats had never read the novel, but was much
struck with the character of Meg Merrilies as delineated
to him by Brown. He seemed at once to realise the creation
of the novelist, and, suddenly stopping in the pathway,
at a point where a profusion of honeysuckles, wild rose,
and foxglove mingled with the bramble and broom that
filled up the spaces between the shattered rocks, he cried
out, "Without a shadow of doubt, on that spot has old
Meg Merrilies often boiled her kettle."

AUCHTERCAIRN,
3 *July* [1818].

MY DEAR TOM,

We are now in Meg Merrilies' country, and have, this
morning, passed through some parts exactly suited to her.
Kirkcudbright County is very beautiful, very wild, with
craggy hills, somewhat in the Westmoreland fashion. We have
come down from Dumfries to the sea-coast part of it. The
following song you will have from Dilke, but perhaps you
would like it here:

Old Meg she was a gipsy,
  And lived upon the moors;
Her bed it was the brown heath turf,
  And her house was out of doors.
Her apples were swart blackberries,
  Her currants, pods o' broom;
Her wine was dew of the wild white rose,
  Her book a church-yard tomb.

Her brothers were the craggy hills,
  Her sisters larchen trees;
Alone with her great family
  She lived as she did please.
No breakfast had she many a morn,
  No dinner many a noon,
And, 'stead of supper, she would stare
  Full hard against the moon.

But every morn, of woodbine fresh
  She made her garlanding,
And, every night, the dark glen yew
  She wove, and she would sing.

And with her fingers, old and brown,
   She plaited mats of rushes,
And gave them to the cottagers
   She met among the bushes.

Old Meg was brave as Margaret Queen,
   And tall as Amazon;
An old red blanket cloak she wore,
   A ship-hat had she on:
God rest her aged bones somewhere!
   She died full long agone!

Yesterday was passed in Kirkcudbright; the country is
very rich, very fine, and with a little of Devon. I am now
writing at Newton Stewart, six miles from Wigtown. Our
landlady of yesterday said, "very few Southerners passed
hereaways." The children jabber away, as if in a foreign
language; the bare-footed girls look very much in keeping—
I mean with the scenery about them. Brown praises their
cleanliness and appearance of comfort, the neatness of their
cottages, etc. It may be. They are very squat among trees
and fern, and heath and broom, on levels, slopes, and heights;
but I wish they were as snug as those up the Devonshire
valleys. We are lodged and entertained in great varieties. We
dined, yesterday, on dirty bacon, dirtier eggs, and dirtiest
potatoes, with a slice of salmon; we breakfast, this morning,
in a nice carpeted room, with sofa, hair-bottomed chairs, and
green-baized mahogany. A spring by the road-side is always
welcome: we drink water for dinner, diluted with a gill of
whisky.

July 6th.—Yesterday morning we set out for Glenluce,
going some distance round to see some rivers: they were
scarcely worth the while. We went on to Stranraer, in a burning
sun, and had gone about six miles when the mail overtook us:
we got up, were at Port Patrick in a jiffey, and I am writing
now in little Ireland. The dialects on the neighbouring shores
of Scotland and Ireland are much the same, yet I can perceive
a great difference in the nations, from the chamber-maid at
this *nate Toone* kept by Mr. Kelly. She is fair, kind, and ready
to laugh, because she is out of the horrible dominion of the
Scotch Kirk. These Kirk-men have done Scotland good. They
have made men, women, old men, young men, old women,
young women, boys, girls, and all infants, careful; so that
they are formed into regular phalanges of savers and gainers.
Such a thrifty army cannot fail to enrich their country, and

give it a greater appearance of comfort than that of their poor rash neighbourhood. These Kirk-men have done Scotland harm — they have banished puns, love, and laughing. To remind you of the fate of Burns:—poor, unfortunate fellow! his disposition was Southern! How sad it is when a luxurious imagination is obliged, in self-defence, to deaden its delicacy in vulgarity and in things attainable, that it may not have leisure to go mad after things that are not! No man, in such matters, will be content with the experience of others. It is true that out of suffering there is no dignity, no greatness, that in the most abstracted pleasure there is no lasting happiness. Yet, who would not like to discover, over again, that Cleopatra was a gipsy, Helen a rogue, and Ruth a deep one? I have not sufficient reasoning faculty to settle the doctrine of thrift, as it is consistent with the dignity of human society —with the happiness of cottagers: all I can do is by plump contrasts: were the fingers made to squeeze a guinea or a white hand?—were the lips made to hold a pen or a kiss? And yet, in cities, man is shut out from his fellows if he is poor; the cottager must be very dirty, and very wretched, if she be not thrifty—the present state of society demands this, and this convinces me that the world is very young, and in a very ignorant state. We live in a barbarous age. I would sooner be a wild deer, than a girl under the dominion of the Kirk; and I would sooner be a wild hog, than be the occasion of a poor creature's penance before those execrable elders.

It is not so far to the Giant's Causeway as we supposed: we thought it seventy, and hear it is only forty-eight miles— so we shall leave one of our knapsacks here at Donaghadee, take our immediate wants, and be back in a week, when we shall proceed to the County of Ayr. In the Packet, yesterday, we heard some ballads from two old men. One was a Romance, which seemed very poor; then there was *The Battle of the Boyne*, then *Robin Huid*, as they call him—"Before the King you shall go, go, go; before the King you shall go."

July 9th.—We stopped very little in Ireland; and that you may not have leisure to marvel at our speedy return to Port Patrick, I will tell you that it is as dear living in Ireland as at the Hummums—thrice the expence of Scotland—it would have cost us £15 before our return; moreover we found those forty-eight miles to be Irish ones, which reach to seventy English; so having walked to Belfast one day, and back to

Donaghadee the next, we left Ireland with a fair breeze. We slept last night at Port Patrick when I was gratified by a letter from you. On our walk in Ireland, we had too much opportunity to see the worse than nakedness, the rags, the dirt, and misery of the poor common Irish. A Scotch cottage, though in that sometimes the smoke has no exit but at the door, is a palace to an Irish one. We had the pleasure of finding our way through a peat-bog, three miles long at least—dreary, flat, dank, black, and spongy—here and there were poor dirty creatures, and a few strong men cutting or carting peat. We heard, on passing into Belfast, through a most wretched suburb, that most disgusting of all noises, worse than the bag-pipes, the laugh of a monkey, the chatter of women, the scream of macaw—I mean the sound of the shuttle. What a tremendous difficulty is the improvement of such people. I cannot conceive how a mind "with child" of philanthropy could grasp at its possibility—with me it is absolute despair. At a miserable house of entertainment, half-way between Donaghadee and Belfast, were two men sitting at whisky—one a labourer, and the other I took to be a drunken weaver: the labourer took me to be a Frenchman, and the other hinted at bounty-money, saying he was ready to take it. On calling for the letters at Port Patrick, the man snapped out, "What regiment?" On our return from Belfast we met a sedan—the Duchess of Dunghill. It is no laughing matter though. Imagine the worst dog-kennel you ever saw, placed upon two poles from a mouldy fencing. In such a wretched thing sat a squalid old woman, squat like an ape half-starved from a scarcity of biscuit in its passage from Madagascar to the Cape, with a pipe in her mouth, and looking out with a round-eyed, skinny-lidded inanity, with a sort of horizontal idiotic movement of her head: squat and lean she sat, and puffed out the smoke, while two ragged, tattered girls carried her along. What a thing would be a history of her life and sensations; I shall endeavour, when I have thought a little more, to give you my idea of the difference between the Scotch and Irish. The two Irishmen I mentioned were speaking of their treatment in England, when the weaver said—"Ah! you were a civil man, but I was a drinker."

Till further notice, you must direct to Inverness.

Your most affectionate Brother,

JOHN.

Returning from Ireland, the travellers proceeded north⁻ wards by the coast, Ailsa Rock constantly in their view. That fine object first appeared to them, in the full sunlight, like a transparent tortoise asleep upon the calm water, then, as they advanced, displaying its lofty shoulders, and, as they still went on, losing its distinctness in the mountains of Arran and the extent of Cantire that rose behind. At the inn at Girvan Keats wrote this:

SONNET ON AILSA ROCK [1]

Hearken, thou craggy ocean-pyramid,
  Give answer by thy voice—the sea-fowls' screams!
  When were thy shoulders mantled in huge streams?
When from the sun was thy broad forehead hid?
How long is't since the mighty Power bid
  Thee heave to airy sleep from fathom dreams—
  Sleep in the lap of thunder or sunbeams—
Or when grey clouds are thy cold coverlid?
Thou answer'st not; for thou art dead asleep.
  Thy life is but two dead eternities,
The last in air, the former in the deep!
  First with the whales, last with the eagle-skies!
Drown'd wast thou till an earthquake made thee steep,
  Another cannot wake thy giant size!

MAYBOLE,
11 *July* [1818].

My DEAR REYNOLDS,

I'll not run over the ground we have passed; that would be nearly as bad as telling a dream—unless, perhaps, I do it in the manner of the Laputan printing press; that is, I put down mountains, rivers, lakes, dells, glens, rocks, with beautiful, enchanting, gothic, picturesque, fine, delightful, enchanting, grand, sublime—a few blisters, etc.—and now you have our journey thus far, where I begin a letter to you because I am approaching Burns's cottage very fast. We have made continual inquiries from the time we left his tomb at Dumfries. His name, of course, is known all about: his great reputation among the plodding people is, "that he wrote a good *mony* sensible things." One of the pleasantest ways of annulling self is approaching such a shrine as the Cottage of Burns: we need not think of his misery—that is all gone, bad luck to it! I shall look upon it hereafter with unmixed pleasure, as I do on my Stratford-on-Avon day with Bailey. I shall fill this sheet for you in the Bardie's country, going

[1] In the Collected Works.

no farther than this, till I get to the town of Ayr, which will be a nine miles walk to tea.

We were talking on different and indifferent things, when, on a sudden, we turned a corner upon the immediate country of Ayr. The sight was as rich as possible. I had no conception that the native place of Burns was so beautiful; the idea I had was more desolate: his "Rigs of Barley" seemed always to me but a few strips of green on a cold hill.—Oh, prejudice! —It was as rich as Devon. I endeavoured to drink in the prospect, that I might spin it out to you, as the silk-worm makes silk from mulberry leaves. I cannot recollect it. Besides all the beauty, there were the mountains of Annan Isle, black and huge over the sea. We came down upon everything suddenly; there were in our way the "bonny Doon," with the brig that Tam o' Shanter crossed, Kirk Alloway, Burns's Cottage, and then the Brigs of Ayr. First we stood upon the Bridge across the Doon, surrounded by every phantasy of green in tree, meadow, and hill: the stream of the Doon, as a farmer told us, is covered with trees "from head to foot." You know those beautiful heaths, so fresh against the weather of a summer's evening; there was one stretching along behind the trees.

I wish I knew always the humour my friends would be in at opening a letter of mine, to suit it to them as nearly as possible. I could always find an egg-shell for melancholy, and, as for merriment, a witty humour will turn anything to account. My head is sometimes in such a whirl in considering the million likings and antipathies of our moments, that I can get into no settled strain in my letters. My wig! Burns and sentimentality coming across you and Frank Floodgate in the office. Oh, Scenery, that thou shouldst be crushed between two puns! As for them, I venture the rascalliest in the Scotch region. I hope Brown does not put them in his journal: if he does, I must sit on the cutty-stool all next winter. We went to Kirk Alloway. "A prophet is no prophet in his own country." We went to the Cottage and took some whisky. I wrote a sonnet for the mere sake of writing some lines under the roof: they are so bad I cannot transcribe them. The man at the cottage was a great bore with his anecdotes. I hate the rascal. His life consists in fuzy, fuzzy, fuzziest. He drinks glasses, five for the quarter, and twelve for the hour; he is a mahogany-faced old jackass who knew Burns: he ought to have been kicked for having spoken to him. He calls himself "a curious old bitch," but he is a flat old dog. I should like to employ Caliph Vathek to kick him. Oh, the flummery of a birth-place! Cant! cant! cant! cant! It is enough to give a spirit the guts-ache. Many a true word, they say, is spoken in jest—this may be because his gab hindered my sublimity: the flat dog made me write a flat sonnet. My dear Reynolds, I cannot write about scenery and visitings. Fancy is indeed less than present palpable reality, but it is greater than remembrance. You would lift your eyes from Homer only to see close before you the real Isle of Tenedos. You would rather read Homer afterwards than remember yourself. One song of Burns's is of more worth to you than all I could think for a whole year in his native country. His misery is a dead weight upon the nimbleness of one's quill; I tried to forget it—to drink toddy without any care—to write a merry sonnet—it won't do—he talked, he drank with blackguards; he was miserable. We can see horribly clear, in the works of such a man, his whole life, as if we were God's spies. What were his addresses to Jean in the after part of his life? I should not speak so to you. —Yet, why not? You are not in the same case—you are in the right path, and you shall not be deceived. I have spoken to you against marriage, but it was general. The prospect in those matters has been to me so blank, that I have not been unwilling to die. I would not now, for I have inducements to life—I must see my little nephews in America, and I must see you marry your lovely wife. My sensations are sometimes deadened for weeks together—but, believe me, I have more than once yearned for the time of your happiness to come, as much as I could for myself after the lips of Juliet. From the tenor of my occasional rhodomontade in chit-chat, you might have been deceived concerning me in these points. Upon my soul, I have been getting more and more close to you every day, ever since I knew you, and now one of the first pleasures I look to is your happy marriage—the more, since I have felt the pleasure of loving a sister-in-law. I did not think it possible to become so much attached in so short a time. Things like these, and they are real, have made me resolve to have a care of my health—you must be as careful.

The rain has stopped us to-day at the end of a dozen miles, yet we hope to see Loch Lomond the day after to-morrow. I will piddle out my information, as Rice says, next winter, at any time when a substitute is wanted for Vingt-un. We bear the fatigue very well: twenty miles a day in general. A cloud came over us in getting up Skiddaw.—I hope to be more lucky in Ben Lomond—and more lucky still in Ben Nevis. What I think you would enjoy is, picking about ruins, sometimes Abbey, sometimes Castle.

Tell my friends I do all I can for them, that is, drink their health in Toddy. Perhaps I may have some lines, by and by, to send you fresh, on your own letter.

Your affectionate friend,

JOHN KEATS.

Part of the next letter illustrates, with singular felicity, the peculiar action of a high imagination on the ordinary relations of the sexes. The youthful companions of Keats, who saw how gentle and courteous was his manner to women, and who held the common belief that every poet was essentially sentimental, could not comprehend his frequent avoidance of female society, and the apparent absence of any engrossing passion; the pardonable conceit of conscious genius suggested itself to them as the probable cause of this defective sympathy, and, when he manifested an occasional interest in any one person, it was attributed rather to satisfied vanity than to awakened love. But the careful study of the poetical character at once disproves these superficial interpretations, and the simple statement of his own feelings by such a man as Keats is a valuable addition to our knowledge of the most delicate and wonderful of the works of Nature—a poet's heart. For the time was at hand when one intense affection was about to absorb his entire being, and to hasten, by its very violence, the calamitous extinction against which it struggled in vain.

INVERARY,

18 July [1818].

MY DEAR BAILEY,

The only day I have had a chance of seeing you when you were last in London I took every advantage of—some devil led you out of the way. Now I have written to Reynolds to tell me where you will be in Cumberland—so that I cannot miss you. And here, Bailey, I will say a few words, written in a sane and sober mind (a very scarce thing with me), for they may, hereafter, save you a great deal of trouble about me, which you do not deserve, and for which I ought to be bastinadoed. I carry all matters to an extreme; so that when I have any little vexation, it grows, in five minutes, into a theme for Sophocles. Then, and in that temper, if I write to any friend, I have so little self-possession, that I give him matter for grieving, at the very time, perhaps, when I am laughing at a pun. Your last letter made me blush for the pain I had given you. I know my own disposition so well that I am certain of writing many times hereafter in the same strain to you: now, you know how far to believe in them. You must allow for Imagination. I know I shall not be able to help it.

I am sorry you are grieved at my not continuing my visits to Little Britain. Yet I think I have, as far as a man can do who has books to read and subjects to think upon. For that reason I have been nowhere else except to Wentworth Place, so nigh at hand. Moreover, I have been too often in a state of health that made it prudent not to hazard the night air. Yet, further, I will confess to you that I cannot enjoy society, small or numerous. I am certain that our fair are glad I should come for the mere sake of my coming; but I am certain I bring with me a vexation they are better without. If I can possibly, at any time, feel my temper coming upon me, I refrain even from a promised visit. I am certain I have not a right feeling towards women—at this moment I am striving to be just to them, but I cannot. Is it because they fall so far beneath my boyish imagination? When I was a schoolboy I thought a fair woman a pure goddess; my mind was a soft nest in which some one of them slept, though she knew it not. I have no right to expect more than their reality. I thought them ethereal, above men. I find them perhaps equal—great by comparison is very small. Insult may be inflicted in more ways than by word or action. One who is tender of being insulted does not like to think an insult against another. I do not like to think insults in a lady's company. I commit a crime with her which absence would not have known. Is it not extraordinary?— when among men, I have no evil thoughts, no malice, no spleen; I feel free to speak or to be silent; I can listen, and from every one I can learn; my hands are in my pockets, I am free from all suspicion, and comfortable. When I am among women, I have evil thoughts, malice, spleen; I cannot speak, or be silent; I am full of suspicion, and therefore listen to nothing; I am in a hurry to be gone. You must be charitable, and put all this perversity to my being disappointed since my boyhood. Yet with such feelings I am happier alone, among crowds of men, by myself, or with a friend or two. With all this, trust me, I have not the least idea that men of different feelings and inclinations are more short-sighted than myself. I never rejoiced more than at my brother's marriage, and shall do so at that of any of my friends. I must absolutely get over this—but how? the only way is to find the root of the evil, and so cure it, "with backward mutters of dissevering power." That is a difficult thing; for an obstinate prejudice can seldom be produced but from a gordian complication of feelings, which must take time to unravel, and care to keep unravelled. I could say a good deal about this, but I will leave it, in hopes of better and more worthy dispositions— and, also, content that I am wronging no one, for, after all, I do think better of womankind than to suppose they care whether Mister John Keats, five feet high, likes them or not. You appeared to wish to know my moods on this subject: don't think it a bore, my dear fellow—it shall be my Amen.

I should not have consented to myself, these four months, tramping in the Highlands, but that I thought it would give me more experience, rub off more prejudice, use [me] to more hardship, identify finer scenes, load me with grander mountains, and strengthen more my reach in poetry, than would stopping at home among books, even though I should reach Homer. By this time I am comparatively a mountaineer; I have been among wilds and mountains too much to break out much about their grandeur. I have not fed upon oat-cake long enough to be very much attached to it. The first mountains I saw, though not so large as some I have since seen, weighed very solemnly upon me. The effect is wearing away, yet I like them mainly. We have come this evening with a guide—for without was impossible—into the middle of the Isle of Mull, pursuing our cheap journey to Iona, and perhaps Staffa. We would not follow the common and fashionable mode, for the great imposition of expense. We have come over heath, and rock, and river, and bog, to what, in England, would be called a horrid place. Yet it belongs to a shepherd pretty well off. The family speak not a word but Gaelic, and we have not yet seen their faces for the smoke, which, after visiting every cranny (not excepting my eyes, very much incommoded for writing), finds its way out at the door. I am more comfortable than I could have imagined in such a place, and so is Brown. The people are all very kind. We lost our way a little, yesterday; and inquiring at a cottage, a young woman, without a word, threw on her cloak, and walked a mile in a mizzling rain and splashy way, to put us right again.

I could not have had a greater pleasure in these parts than your mention of my sister. She is very much prisoned for me. I am afraid it will be some time before I can take her to many places I wish.

I trust we shall see you ere long in Cumberland—at least I hope I shall, before my visit to America, more than once. I intend to pass a whole year there, if I live to the completion of the three next. My sister's welfare, and the hopes of such a stay in America, will make me observe your advice. I shall be prudent, and more careful of my health than I have been.

I hope you will be about paying your first visit to town, after settling when we come into Cumberland. Cumberland, however, will be no distance to me after my present journey. I shall spin to you [in] a minute. I begin to get rather a contempt of distances. I hope you will have a nice convenient room for a library. Now you are so well in health, do keep it up by never missing your dinner, by not reading hard, and by taking proper exercise. You'll have a horse, I suppose, so you must make a point of sweating him. You say I must study Dante: well, the only books I have with me are those three little volumes. I read that fine passage you mention a few days ago. Your letter followed me from Hampstead to Port Patrick, and thence to Glasgow. You must think me, by this time, a very pretty fellow.

One of the pleasantest bouts we have had was our walk to Burns's Cottage, over the Doon, and past Kirk Alloway. I had determined to write a sonnet in the Cottage. I did; but it was so wretched I destroyed it: however, in a few days afterwards I wrote some lines cousin-german to the circumstance, which I will transcribe, or rather cross-scribe in the front of this.

Reynolds's illness has made him a new man; he will be stronger than ever: before I left London he was really getting a fat face.

Brown keeps on writing volumes of adventures to Dilke. When we get in of an evening, and I have perhaps taken my rest on a couple of chairs, he affronts my indolence and luxury, by pulling out of his knapsack, first, his paper; secondly, his pens; and lastly, his ink. Now I would not care if he would change a little. I say now, why not, Bailey, take out his pens first sometimes. But I might as well tell a hen to hold up her head before she drinks, instead of afterwards.

Your affectionate friend,

JOHN KEATS.

There is a charm in footing slow across a silent plain,
Where patriot battle has been fought, where glory had the gain;
There is a pleasure on the heath, where Druids old have been,
Where mantles grey have rustled by, and swept the nettled green;
There is a joy in every spot made known in times of old,
New to the feet altho' each tale a hundred times be told;
There is a deeper joy than all, more solemn in the heart,
More parching to the tongue than all, of more divine a smart,
When weary steps forget themselves upon a pleasant turf,
Upon hot sand, or flinty road, or sea-shore iron surf,
Toward the castle or the cot, where long ago was born
One who was great through mortal days, and died of fame unshorn.

Light heather-bells may tremble then—but they are far away;
Wood-lark may sing from sandy fern—the Sun may hear his lay;
Runnels may kiss the grass on shelves and shallows clear,—
But their low voices are not heard, tho' come on travels drear;
Blood-red the Sun may set behind black mountain peaks,
Blue tides may sluice and drench their time in caves and weedy creeks
Eagles may seem to sleep wing-wide upon the air,
Ring-doves may fly convulsed across to some high cedared lair,—
But the forgotten eye is still fast lidded to the ground,
As Palmer's that with weariness mid-desert shrine hath found.

At such a time the soul's a child, in childhood is the brain,
Forgotten is the worldly heart,—alone, it beats in vain!
Aye, if a madman could have leave to pass a healthful day,
To tell his forehead's swoon and faint, when first began decay,
He might make tremble many a one, whose spirit had gone forth
To find a Bard's low cradle-place about the silent north!

Scanty the hour, and few the steps, beyond the bourn of care,
Beyond the sweet and bitter world,—beyond it unaware!
Scanty the hour, and few the steps,—because a longer stay
Would bar return and make a man forget his mortal way!
O horrible! to lose the sight of well-remembered face,
Of Brother's eyes, of Sister's brow,—constant to every place,
Filling the air as on we move with portraiture intense,
More warm than those heroic tints that pain a painter's sense,
When shapes of old come striding by, and visages of old,
Locks shining black, hair scanty grey, and passions manifold!

No, no,—that horror cannot be! for at the cable's length
Man feels the gentle anchor pull, and gladdens in its strength:
One hour, half idiot, he stands by mossy waterfall,
But in the very next he reads his soul's memorial;
He reads it on the mountain's height, where chance he may sit down,
Upon rough marble diadem, that hill's eternal crown.

Yet be his anchor e'er so fast, room is there for a prayer,
That man may never lose his mind in mountains black and bare:
That he may stray, league after league, some great birthplace to find,
And keep his vision clear from speck, his inward sight unblind.

DUNANCULLEN,
23 *July* [1818].

MY DEAR TOM,

Just after my last had gone to the post, in came one of the men with whom we endeavoured to agree about going to Staffa: he said what a pity it was we should turn aside, and not see the curiosities. So we had a little tattle, and finally agreed that he should be our guide across the Isle of Mull. We set out, crossed two ferries, one to the Isle of Kerrera, of little distance; the other from Kerrera to Mull, nine miles across. We did it in forty minutes, with a fine breeze. The road through the island, or rather track, is the most dreary you can think of; between dreary mountains, over bog, and rock, and river, with our breeches tucked up, and our stockings in hand. About eight o'clock we arrived at a shepherd's hut, into which we could scarcely get for the smoke, through a door lower than my shoulders. We found our way into a little compartment, with the rafters and turf-thatch blackened with smoke, the earth-floor full of hills and dales. We had some white bread with us, made a good supper, and slept in our clothes in some blankets; our guide snored in another little bed about an arm's length off. This morning we came about *sax* miles to breakfast, by rather a better path, and we are now in, by comparison, a mansion. Our guide is, I think, a very obliging fellow. In the way, this morning, he sang us two Gaelic songs—one made by a Mrs. Brown, on her husband's being drowned—the other a Jacobin one on Charles Stuart. For some days Brown has been inquiring out his genealogy here; he thinks his grandfather came from Long Island. He got a parcel of people round him at a cottage door last evening, chatted with one who had been a Miss Brown, and who, I think, from a likeness, must have been a relation: he jawed with the old woman, flattered a young one, and kissed a child, who was afraid of his spectacles, and finally drank a pint of milk. They handle his spectacles as we do a sensitive leaf.

July 26th.—Well! we had a most wretched walk of thirty-seven miles, across the Island of Mull, and then we crossed to Iona, or Icolmkill; from Icolmkill we took a boat at a bargain to take us to Staffa, and land us at the head of Loch Nakeal, whence we should only have to walk half the distance to Oban again and by a better road. All this is well passed and done, with this singular piece of luck, that there was an interruption in the bad weather just as we saw Staffa, at which it is impossible to land but in a tolerably calm sea. But I will first mention Icolmkill. I know not whether you have heard much about this island; I never did before I came nigh it. It is rich in the most interesting antiquities. Who would expect to find the ruins of a fine cathedral church, of cloisters, colleges, monasteries, and nunneries, in so remote an island? The beginning of these things was in the sixth century, under the superstition of a would-be-bishop-saint, who landed from Ireland, and chose the spot for its beauty; for, at that time, the now treeless place was covered with magnificent woods. Columba in the Gaelic is Colm, signifying "dove"; "kill" signifies "church"; and I is as good as island: so I-colm-kill means the Island of St. Columba's Church. Now this St. Columba became the Dominic of the Barbarian Christians of the North, and was famed also far south, but more especially was reverenced by the Scots, the Picts, the Norwegians, and the Irish. In a course of years, perhaps the island was considered the most holy ground of the north; and the old kings of the afore-mentioned nations chose it for their burial-place. We were shown a spot in the church-yard where they say sixty-one kings are buried; forty-eight Scotch, from Fergus II. to Macbeth; eight Irish; four Norwegians; and one French. They lay in rows compact. Then we were shown other matters of later date, but still very ancient, many tombs of Highland chieftains—their effigies in complete armour, face upward, black and moss-covered; abbots and bishops of the island, always of the chief clans. There were plenty Macleans and Macdonalds; among these latter, the famous Macdonald, Lord of the Isles. There have been three hundred crosses in the island, but the Presbyterians destroyed all but two, one of which is a very fine one, and completely covered with a shaggy, coarse moss. The old school-master, an ignorant little man, but reckoned very clever, showed us these things. He is a Maclean, and as much above four feet as he is under four feet three inches. He stops at one glass of whisky, unless you press another, and at the second, unless you press a third.

l am puzzled how to give you an idea of Staffa. It can only

be represented by a first-rate drawing. One may compare the surface of the island to a roof: this roof is supported by grand pillars of basalt, standing together as thick as honeycomb. The finest thing is Fingal's Cave. It is entirely a hollowing out of basalt pillars. Suppose, now, the giants who rebelled against Jove had taken a whole mass of black columns and bound them together like bunches of matches, and then, with immense axes, had made a cavern in the body of these columns. Of course the roof and floor must be composed of the ends of these columns. Such is Fingal's Cave, except that the sea has done the work of excavation, and is continually dashing there. So that we walk along the sides of the cave, on the pillars which are left, as if for convenient stairs. The roof is arched somewhat Gothic-wise, and the length of some of the entire side-pillars is fifty feet. About the island you might seat an army of men, each on a pillar. The length of the cave is 120 feet, and from its extremity, the view into the sea, through the large arch at the entrance, is sublime. The colour of the columns is black, with a lurking gloom of purple therein. For solemnity and grandeur, it far surpasses the finest cathedrals. At the extremity of the cave there is a small perforation into another cave, at which, the waters meeting and buffeting each other, there is sometimes produced a report as if of a cannon, heard as far as Iona, which must be twelve miles. As we approached in the boat, there was such a fine swell of the sea that the pillars appeared immediately arising from the crystal. But it is impossible to describe it.

Not Aladdin magian
Ever such a work began;
Not the wizard of the Dee
Ever such a dream could see;
Not St. John, in Patmos' isle,
In the passion of his toil,
When he saw the churches seven,
Golden aisled, built up in heaven,
Gazed at such a rugged wonder!—
As I stood its roofing under,
Lo! I saw one sleeping there,
On the marble cold and bare;
While the surges washed his feet,
And his garments white did beat
Drenched about the sombre rocks;
On his neck his well-grown locks,
Lifted dry above the main,
Were upon the curl again.

"What is this? and what art thou?"
Whispered I, and touch'd his brow;
"What art thou? and what is this?"
Whispered I, and strove to kiss
The spirit's hand, to wake his eyes;
Up he started in a trice:
"I am Lycidas," said he,
"Fam'd in fun'ral minstrelsy!
This was architectur'd thus
By the great Oceanus!—
Here his mighty waters play
Hollow organs all the day;
Here, by turns, his dolphins all,
Finny palmers, great and small,
Come to pay devotion due,—
Each a mouth of pearls must strew!
Many a mortal of these days
Dares to pass our sacred ways;
Dares to touch, audaciously,
This cathedral of the sea!
I have been the pontiff-priest,
Where the waters never rest,
Where a fledgy sea-bird choir
Soars for ever! Holy fire
I have hid from mortal man;
Proteus is my Sacristan!
But the dulled eye of mortal
Hath passed beyond the rocky portal;
So for ever will I leave
Such a taint, and soon unweave
All the magic of the place."
So saying, with a Spirit's glance
He dived!

I am sorry I am so indolent as to write such stuff as this. It can't be helped.

The western coast of Scotland is a most strange place; it is composed of rocks, mountains, mountainous and rocky islands, intersected by lochs; you can go but a short distance anywhere from salt-water in the Highlands.

I assure you I often long for a seat and a cup o' tea at Well Walk, especially now that mountains, castles, and lakes are becoming common to me. Yet I would rather summer it out, for on the whole I am happier than when I have time to be glum: perhaps it may cure me. Immediately on my return I shall begin studying hard, with a peep at the theatre now and then. I have a slight sore throat, and think it better to stay a day or two at Oban; then we shall proceed to Fort William and Inverness. Brown, in his letters, puts down every little circumstance; I should like to do the same, but I confess myself too indolent, and besides, next winter they will come up in prime order as we speak of such and such things.

Remember me to all, including Mr. and Mrs. Bentley.

> Your most affectionate brother,
>
> JOHN.

From Fort William Keats mounted Ben Nevis. When on the summit a cloud enveloped him, and sitting on the stones, as it slowly wafted away, showing a tremendous precipice into the valley below, he wrote these lines:

> Read me a lesson, Muse, and speak it loud
> Upon the top of Nevis, blind in mist!
> I look into the chasms, and a shroud
> Vaporous doth hide them,—just so much I wist
> Mankind do know of hell; I look o'erhead,
> And there is sullen mist,—even so much
> Mankind can tell of heaven; mist is spread
> Before the earth, beneath me,—even such,
> Even so vague is man's sight of himself!
> Here are the craggy stones beneath my feet,—
> Thus much I know that, a poor witless elf,
> I tread on them,—that all my eye doth meet
> Is mist and crag, not only on this height,
> But in the world of thought and mental might!

To Mrs. Wylie, the mother of his sister-in-law

> INVERNESS,
> 6 *August* [1818].

MY DEAR MADAM,

It was a great regret to me that I should leave all my friends, just at the moment when I might have helped to soften away the time for them. I wanted not to leave my brother Tom, but more especially, believe me, I should like to have remained near you, were it but for an atom of consolation after parting with so dear a daughter. My brother George has ever been more than a brother to me; he has been my greatest friend, and I can never forget the sacrifice you have made for his happiness. As I walk along the mountains here I am full of these things, and lay in wait, as it were, for the pleasure of seeing you immediately on my return to town. I wish, above all things, to say a word of comfort to you, but I know not how. It is impossible to prove that black is white; it is impossible to make out that sorrow is joy, or joy is sorrow.

Tom tells me that you called on Mrs. Haslam, with a newspaper giving an account of a gentleman in a fur cap, falling over a precipice in Kirkcudbrightshire. If it was me, I did it in a dream, or in some magic interval between the first and second cup of tea; which is nothing extraordinary when we hear that Mahomet, in getting out of bed, upset a jug of water, and, whilst it was falling, took a fortnight's trip, as it seemed, to Heaven; yet was back in time to save one drop of water being spilt. As for fur caps, I do not remember one beside my own, except at Carlisle: this was a very good fur cap I met in High Street, and I dare say was the unfortunate one. I dare say that the Fates, seeing but two fur caps in the north, thought it too extraordinary, and so threw the dies which of them should be drowned. The lot fell upon Jones: I dare say his name was Jones. All I hope is that the gaunt ladies said not a word about hanging; if they did I shall repeat that I was not half-drowned in Kirkcudbright. Stop! let me see!—being half-drowned by falling from a precipice, is a very romantic affair: why should I not take it to myself? How glorious to be introduced in a drawing-room to a lady who reads novels, with "Mr. So-and-so—Miss So-and-so; Miss So-and-so, this is Mr. So-and-so, who fell off a precipice and was half-drowned." Now I refer to you, whether I should lose so fine an opportunity of making my fortune. No romance lady could resist me—none. Being run under a wagon; side-lamed in a playhouse; apoplectic through brandy; and a thousand other tolerably decent things for badness, would be nothing; but being tumbled over a precipice into the sea— oh! it would make my fortune—especially if you could continue to hint, from this bulletin's authority, that I was not upset on my own account, but that I dashed into the waves after Jessy of Dunblane, and pulled her out by the hair— but that, alas! she was dead, or she would have made me happy with her hand. However, in this you may use your own discretion. But I must leave joking, and seriously aver, that I have been very romantic indeed among these mountains and lakes. I have got wet through, day after day; eaten oat-cake, and drank whisky; walked up to my knees in bog; got a sore throat; gone to see Icolmkill and Staffa; met with unwholesome food, just here and there, as it happened; went up Ben Nevis—and—N.B., came down again: sometimes, when I am rather tired, I lean rather languishingly on a rock, and long for some famous beauty to get down from her palfrey

in passing, approach me, with—her saddle-bags, and give me
—a dozen or two capital roast-beef sandwiches.

When I come into a large town, you know there is no putting
one's knapsack into one's fob, so the people stare. We have
been taken for spectacle-vendors, razor-sellers, jewellers,
travelling linen-drapers, spies, excisemen, and many things
I have no idea of. When I asked for letters at Port Patrick,
the man asked—What regiment? I have had a peep also at
Little Ireland. Tell Henry I have not camped quite on the
bare earth yet, but nearly as bad, in walking through Mull;
for the shepherds' huts you can scarcely breathe in for the
smoke, which they seem to endeavour to preserve for smoking
on a large scale.

I assure you, my dear Madam, that one of the greatest
pleasures I shall have on my return, will be seeing you, and
that I shall ever be

Yours, with the greatest respect and sincerity,

JOHN KEATS.

It was Keats's intention to return by Edinburgh; but,
on arriving at Inverness, the inflammation in his throat,
brought on by the accidents and inconvenience of travel,
caused him, at his friend's solicitation, to return at once
to London. Some mutual friend had forwarded him an
invitation from Messrs. Blackwood, injudiciously adding
the suggestion that it would be very advisable for him
to visit the Modern Athens, and endeavour to conciliate
his literary enemies in that quarter. The sensibility and
moral dignity of Keats were outraged by this proposal:
it may be imagined what answer he returned, and also that
this circumstance may not have been unconnected with
the article on him which appeared in the August number
of the *Edinburgh Magazine*, as part of a series that had
commenced the previous year, and concerning which he
had already expressed himself freely.

Outside sheet of a letter to Mr. Bailey

There has been a flaming attack upon Hunt in the *Edinburgh
Magazine*. I never read anything so virulent—accusing him
of the greatest crimes, depreciating his wife, his poetry, his
habits, his company, his conversation. These philippics are

to come out in numbers—called *The Cockney School of Poetry*.
There has been but one number published—that on Hunt—
to which they have prefixed a motto from one Cornelius
Webb, "Poetaster"—who, unfortunately, was of our party
occasionally at Hampstead, and took it into his head to write
the following: something about, "We'll talk on Wordsworth,
Byron, a theme we never tire on"; and so forth till he comes
to Hunt and Keats. In the motto they have put Hunt and
Keats in large letters. I have no doubt that the second number
was intended for me but have hopes of its non-appearance,
from the following advertisement in last Sunday's *Examiner*:
"To Z.—The writer of the article signed Z, in Blackwood's
Edinburgh Magazine, for October, 1817, is invited to send his
address to the printer of the *Examiner*, in order that justice
may be executed on the proper person." I don't mind the
thing much—but if he should go to such lengths with me as
he has done with Hunt, I must infallibly call him to account,
if he be a human being, and appears in squares and theatres,
where we might "possibly meet."

Keats's first volume had been inscribed to Leigh Hunt,
and contained an ardent and affectionate Sonnet, written
"on the day when Mr. Leigh Hunt left prison." It was
therefore at once assumed by the critics that Keats was
not only a bad poet, but a bad citizen. At this time literary
criticism had assumed an unusually political complexion.
The triumph of the advocates of established rights and
enforced order, over all the hopes and dreams that the
French Revolution had generated, was complete, and it
was accompanied with the insolence of men whose cause
had little in it to move the higher impulses of our nature.
Proud of the overthrow of that fatal ambition, which had
turned into the gall of selfishness all the wholesome sympathy of a liberated nation for the wrongs of others, and
rejoicing in the pacification of Europe, they cared little
for the preservation of national liberties from arbitrary
power, or for the extirpation of those abuses and that
injustice which had first provoked the contest and would
surely lead to its renewal, if tolerated or sustained. It was,
perhaps, too much to expect a recognition of what the
French Revolution had done for the mind of man, from
those who had spent their blood and treasure in resisting

its immediate consequences, and some intolerance was to be forgiven in those who, when conjured in the name of Liberty, could point to the system of Napoleon, or in that of Humanity, to the "Reign of Terror." The pious Wordsworth and the politic Southey, who had hailed the day-star with songs of triumph, had fled affrighted from its bloody noon, and few persons of generous temper and honest purpose remained, whose imagination had not been tamed down before the terrible realities, or whose moral sense had not been shocked into despair.

Among these, however, were the men of letters, who were designated, in ridicule, "The Cockney School." The epithet had so much meaning as consisted in some of the leaders being Londoners, and engaged in the editorship of the public press of the metropolis. The strong and immediate contrasts between town and country seemed also to have the effect of rendering many of these writers insensible to that discrimination of the relative worth and importance of natural objects, which habit and taste requires, but which reason cannot strictly define. It is perfectly true that a blade of grass is, to the reverential observer, as great a miracle of divine workmanship as the solar system—that the valves of an unseemly shell may have, to the physiologist, all the importance of the circumfluent ocean—and that the poet may well find in a daisy "thoughts too deep for tears"—but there ever will be gradations of interest in the susceptibilities even of educated and accomplished men, and the admiration which would be recognised as just when applied to a rare or expansive object, will always appear unreal and coxcombical when lavished on what is trivial and common. Nor could these writers, as a School, be held altogether guiltless of the charge of literary conceit. The scantiness of general sympathy drove them into a coterie; and the evils inseparable from a limited intercourse with other minds grew up and flourished abundantly amongst them. They drew their inspiration from books and from themselves, and became, in many cases unconsciously, imitators of the peculiarities, as well as of the beauties, of the elder models of language and style. It was not so much that they were guilty of affected archaisms as that they delighted in giving that prominence to individual peculiarities, great and small, which impart to the works of some early poets an antiquarian as well as literary interest, but which had an almost comic effect when transferred to the habits and circumstances of a particular set of men in our own times. They fell into the error of demanding public and permanent attention for matters that could only claim a private and occasional interest, and thus have they not only damaged their contemporary reputation, but have barred up, in a great degree, their access to future fame.

Literary history affords us a singular parallel to the fate of this school, in that of the Italian-French poets of the seventeenth century, of whom Marino was the founder, and Boileau the destroyer. Allowing for the discrepancies of times and nations—the rich and indiscriminate diction, the copious and minute exercise of fancy, the constant disproportion between the matter and the form, which caused the author of the *Adonis* to be crowned at Naples, adored at Paris, and forgotten by posterity, were here revived, with, indeed, less momentary popularity, but, it is to be hoped, with a better chance of being remembered for what is really excellent and beautiful in their works. The spirit of Saint Amant, unequal in its conceptions, but admirable in its execution, might have lived again at Hampstead, with all its ostentatious contempt of superficial morality, but with its real profligacy converted into a jaunty freedom and sentimental good-nature. There too the spirit of Théophile de Viau might have audaciously confronted what appeared to him as the superstition of his time, and when vilified as "Roi des Libertins" by brutal and ignorant men, in comparison with whom his life was singularly pure, he might have been hunted thence as a felon over the face of Europe in the name of loyalty and religion. But while, in France, an ungenial and delusive criticism held up those remarkable authors to public ridicule and obloquy, at least the victims of Boileau recognised some power and faculty in the hand that struck them, whereas the reviewers of *Blackwood* and the *Quarterly* were persons evidently destitute of all poetic perception, directing an unrefined and unscrupulous satire against

political opponents, whose intellectual merits they had
no means of understanding. This, indeed, was no combat
of literary principles, no struggle of thoughts, no competition of modes of expression, it was simply the judgment
of the policeman and the beadle over mental efforts and
spiritual emanations.

The article which appeared in the *Quarterly* was dull
as well as ungenerous. It had no worth as criticism, for
the critic (as indeed the man) must be tested by what he
admires and loves, not only by what he dislikes and abuses;
and it was eminently stupid, for although the best burlesque
is often but the reverse of the most valuable work of art,
and the richest harvest of humour is among the high and
goodly growths of human intelligence, this book, as far
as the reviewer was capable of understanding it, might
just as well have been one of those merely extravagant and
ridiculous productions which it is sheer waste of time to
notice in any way. The only impression the review would
have left on the mind of a judicious reader would have
been that the writer knew nothing to enable him to discuss
the subject of poetry in any way, and his avowal that he
had not read, or could not read, the work he undertook to
criticise, was a vulgar impertinence which should have
prevented anyone from reading his criticism. The notice
in *Blackwood* was still more scurrilous, but more amusing,
and inserted quotations of some length, which no doubt
led the minds of many readers to very different conclusions
from those of the writer. The circumstance of Keats having
been brought up a surgeon, is the staple of the jokes of
the piece—he is told, "it is a better and a wiser thing to
be a starved apothecary, than a starved poet," and is
bidden "back to his gallipots"; just as an orthodox Jew
might have bidden Simon Peter back to his nets. At any
rate, this was hardly the way to teach refinement to low-
born poets, and to show the superior breeding of aristocratic
reviewers.

On looking back at the reception of Keats by his literary
contemporaries, the somewhat tardy appearance of the
justification of his genius by one who then held a wide
sway over the taste of his time appears as a most unfortunate incident. If the frank acknowledgment of the

respect with which Keats had inspired Mr. Jeffrey had been made in 1818 instead of 1820, the tide of public opinion would probably have been at once turned in his favour, and the imbecile abuse of his political, rather than literary, antagonists been completely exposed. In the very first sentence of his essay, indeed, Mr. Jeffrey lamented that these works had not come under his notice earlier, and, in the late edition of his collected articles, he expresses "the additional regret that he did not even then go more largely into the exposition of the merits of one, whom he ever regards as a poet of great power and promise, lost to us by a premature death." This notice in the *Edinburgh Review* referred principally to *Endymion*, of which, after a fair statement of objections to certain exaggerations and imperfections, it summed up the character and value as follows; and I think it nearly impossible to express, in fewer or better words, the impression usually left by this poem on those minds which, from their constitution, can claim to possess an opinion on the question:

It [*Endymion*] is, in truth, at least as full of genius as of absurdity, and he who does not find a great deal in it to admire and to give delight, cannot, in his heart, see much beauty in the two exquisite dramas to which we have already alluded [the *Faithful Shepherdess* of Fletcher, and the *Sad Shepherd* of Ben Jonson], or find any great pleasure in some of the finest creations of Milton and Shakespeare. There are very many such persons we readily believe, even among the reading and judicious part of the community—correct scholars we have no doubt many of them, and, it may be, very classical composers in prose and in verse, but utterly ignorant of the true genius of English poetry, and incapable of estimating its appropriate and most exquisite beauties. With that spirit we have no hesitation in saying Mr. Keats is deeply imbued, and of those beauties he has presented us with many sterling examples. We are very much inclined, indeed, to add that we do not know any book which we would sooner employ, as a test to ascertain whether any one had in him a native relish for poetry, and a genuine sensibility to its intrinsic charm.

This peculiar treatment of the Greek mythology, which was merely repulsive to the unscholarly views of pedants, and quite unintelligible to those who, knowing no more than Keats himself did of the Grecian language, were utterly incapable of comprehending the faculty by which the poet could communicate with Grecian nature, is estimated by Mr. Jeffrey with remarkable justice and force; but, perhaps, without a full conception of the process by which the will of Keats came into such entire harmony with the sensuous workings of the old Grecian spirit, that not only did his imagination delight in the same objects, but that it was, in truth, what theirs under certain circumstances might have been. He writes:

There is something very curious in the way in which Mr. Keats, and Mr. Barry Cornwall also, have dealt with the pagan mythology, of which they have made so much use in their poetry. Instead of presenting its imaginary persons under the trite and vulgar traits that belong to them in the ordinary systems, little more is borrowed from these than the general conception of their conditions and relations, and an original character and distinct individuality is bestowed upon them, which has all the merit of invention and all the grace and attraction of the fictions on which it is engrafted. The ancients, though they probably did not stand in any great awe of their deities, have yet abstained, very much, from any minute or dramatic representation of their feelings and affections. In Hesiod and Homer they are coarsely delineated, by some of their actions and adventures, and introduced to us merely as the agents in those particular transactions, while in the Hymns, from those ascribed to Orpheus and Homer down to those of Callimachus, we have little but pompous epithets and invocations, with a flattering commemoration of their most famous exploits, and are never allowed to enter into their bosoms, or follow out the train of their feelings with the presumption of our human sympathy. Except the love-song of the Cyclops to his sea-nymph in Theocritus—the Lamentation of Venus for Adonis in Moschus—and the more recent Legend of Apuleius, we scarcely recollect a passage in all the writings of antiquity in which the passions of an Immortal are fairly disclosed to the scrutiny and observation of men. The author before us, however, and some of his contemporaries, have dealt differently with the subject, and sheltering the violence of the fiction under the ancient traditionary fable, have created and imagined an entire new set of characters, and brought closely and minutely before us the loves and sorrows, and perplexities of beings, with whose names and supernatural attributes we had long been familiar, without any sense or feeling of their personal character.

It appears from the *Life of Lord Byron* that he was excited by this article into a rage of jealous injustice. The recognition by so high an authority of Keats as a poet, already great and becoming greater, was more than his patience could endure: for though he had been very well content to receive the hearty and honest admiration of Mr. Leigh Hunt and his friends, and to hold out a pretended liberal sympathy with their views and objects, yet when they came to see one another closer, as they did in the latter years of his life, the mutual repugnance could no longer be concealed, and flamed up almost into hatred. The noble poet wrote to the editor of the rival review, to send him—"no more Keats, I entreat: flay him alive—if some of you don't, I must skin him myself. There is no bearing the drivelling idiotism of the manikin." Again he writes: "Of the praises of that little . . . Keats—I shall observe, as Johnson did when Sheridan the actor got a pension—'What! has *he* got a pension?—Then it is time I should give up mine!' Nobody could be prouder of the praise of the *Edinburgh* than I was, or more alive to their censure, as I showed in *English Bards and Scotch Reviewers*. At present *all the men* they have ever praised are degraded by that insane article. Why don't they review and praise *Solomon's Guide to Health*? It is better sense, and as much poetry as Johnny Keats."

After this unmeasured language, one is surprised to find Lord Byron not only one of the sharpest reprovers of the critics upon Keats, but emphatic in the acknowledgment of his genius. In a long note (November 1831), he attributes his indignation to Keats's depreciation of Pope, which, he says, "hardly permitted me to do justice to his own genius which, *malgré* all the fantastic fopperies of his style, was undoubtedly of great promise. *His fragment of 'Hyperion' seems actually inspired by the Titans, and is as sublime as Æschylus.* He is a loss to our literature, and the more so, as he himself, before his death, is said to have been persuaded that he had not taken the right line, and was reforming his style upon the more classical models of the language." To Mr. Murray himself, a short time before, Byron had written, "You know very well that I did not approve of Keats's poetry, or principles of poetry, or of his abuse of Pope; but, as he is dead, omit *all* that is said *about him*, in any MSS. of mine or publication. His *Hyperion* is a fine monument, and will keep his name." This injunction, however, has been so little attended to by those who should have respected it, that the later editions of Lord Byron's works contain all the ribald abuse I have quoted, although the exclusion would, in literal terms, even extend to the well-known flippant and false, but not ill-natured, stanza of the eleventh canto of *Don Juan*:

> John Keats, who was kill'd off by one critique,
>   Just as he really promised something great,
> If not intelligible, without Greek
>   Contrived to talk about the Gods of late,
> Much as they might have been supposed to speak.
>   Poor fellow! His was an untoward fate;
> How strange the mind, that very fiery particle,
> Should let itself be snuff'd out by an article.

The excuse offered by Byron for all this inconsistency is by no means satisfactory, and this sort of repentant praise may be attributed to a mixed feeling of conscious injustice, and to a certain gratification at the notion that Keats had fallen victim to a kind of attack which his own superior vigour and stouter fibre had enabled him triumphantly to resist. In a letter to Murray (1821) Byron writes: "I knew, by experience, that a savage review is hemlock to a sucking author: and the one on me (which produced the *English Bards*, etc.) knocked me down—but I got up again. Instead of breaking a blood-vessel I drank three bottles of claret, and began an answer, finding that there was nothing in the article for which I could, lawfully, knock Jeffrey on the head, in an honourable way. However, I would not be the person who wrote that homicidal article, for all the honour and glory in the world; though I by no means approve of that school of scribbling which it treats upon." Keats, as has been shown, was very far from requiring three bottles of claret to give him the inclination to fight

the author of the slander, if he could have found him—
but the use *he* made of the attack was to purify his style,
correct his tendency to exaggeration, enlarge his poetical
studies, and produce, among other improved efforts, that
very *Hyperion* which called forth from Byron a eulogy as
violent and unqualified as the former onslaught.

"Review people," again wrote Lord Byron, "have no
more right to kill than any other footpads. However, he
who would die of an article in a review would have died of
something else equally trivial. The same nearly happened
to Kirke White, who died afterwards of a consumption."
Now, the cases of Keats and Kirke White are just so far
parallel, that Keats did die shortly after the criticisms upon
him, and also of consumption: his friends also, while he
still lived, spent a great deal of useless care upon these
critics and, out of an honest anger, gave encouragement
to the notion that their brutality had a most injurious
effect on the spirit and health of the poet; but a conscientious inquiry entirely dispels such a supposition. In
all this correspondence it must be seen how little importance Keats attaches to such opinions, how rarely he
alludes to them at all, and how easily, when he does so;
how lowly was his own estimate of the very works they
professed to judge, in comparison with what he felt himself
capable of producing, and how completely he, in his world
of art, rested above such paltry assailants. After his early
death the accusation was revived by the affectionate
indignation of Mr. Brown; and Shelley, being in Italy,
readily adopted the same tone. On the publication of the
volume containing *Lamia, Isabella, St. Agnes' Eve*, and
Hyperion, Shelley wrote a letter which, on second thoughts,
he left unfinished: it shows, however, how entirely he
believed Keats to be at the mercy of the critics, and how
he could bend for others that pride which ever remained
erect for himself.

To the Editor of the "Quarterly Review"

SIR,

Should you cast your eye on the signature of this letter
before you read the contents, you might imagine that they
related to a slanderous paper which appeared in your Review

some time since. I never notice anonymous attacks. The wretch who wrote it has doubtless the additional reward of a consciousness of his motives, besides the thirty guineas a sheet, or whatever it is that you pay him. Of course, you cannot be answerable for all the writings which you edit, and *I* certainly bear you no ill-will for having edited the abuse to which I allude—indeed, I was too much amused by being compared to Pharaoh, not readily to forgive editor, printer, publisher, stitcher, or any one, except the despicable writer, connected with something so exquisitely entertaining. Seriously speaking, I am not in the habit of permitting myself to be disturbed by what is said or written of me, though, I dare say, I may be condemned sometimes justly enough. But I feel, in respect to the writer in question, that "I am there sitting, where he durst not soar."

The case is different with the unfortunate subject of this letter, the author of *Endymion*, to whose feelings and situation I entreat you to allow me to call your attention. I write considerably in the dark; but if it is Mr. Gifford that I am addressing, I am persuaded that, in an appeal to his humanity and justice, he will acknowledge the *fas ab hoste doceri*. I am aware that the first duty of a Reviewer is towards the public, and I am willing to confess that the *Endymion* is a poem considerably defective, and that, perhaps, it deserved as much censure as the pages of your Review record against it; but, not to mention that there is a certain contemptuousness of phraseology from which it is difficult for a critic to abstain, in the review of *Endymion*, I do not think that the writer has given it its due praise. Surely the poem, with all its faults, is a very remarkable production for a man of Keats's age, and the promise of ultimate excellence is such as has rarely been afforded even by such as have afterwards attained high literary eminence. Look at book ii., line 833, etc., and book iii., lines 113 to 120; read down that page, and then again from line 193. I could cite many other passages, to convince you that it deserved milder usage. Why it should have been reviewed at all, excepting for the purpose of bringing its excellences into notice, I cannot conceive, for it was very little read, and there was no danger that it should become a model to the age of that false taste, with which I confess, that it is replenished.

Poor Keats was thrown into a dreadful state of mind by this review, which, I am persuaded, was not written with any intention of producing the effect, to which it has, at least, greatly contributed, of embittering his existence, and inducing a disease, from which there are now but faint hopes of his recovery. The first effects are described to me to have resembled insanity, and it was by assiduous watching that he was restrained from effecting purposes of suicide. The agony of his sufferings at length produced the rupture of a blood-vessel in the lungs, and the usual process of consumption appears to have begun. He is coming to pay me a visit in Italy; but I fear that, unless his mind can be kept tranquil, little is to be hoped from the mere influence of climate.

But let me not extort anything from your pity. I have just seen a second volume, published by him evidently in careless despair. I have desired my bookseller to send you a copy, and allow me to solicit your especial attention to the fragment of a poem entitled *Hyperion*, the composition of which was checked by the Review in question. The great proportion of this piece is surely in the very highest style of poetry. I speak impartially, for the canons of taste to which Keats has conformed in his other compositions, are the very reverse of my own. I leave you to judge for yourself; it would be an insult to you to suppose that, from motives however honourable, you would lend yourself to a deception of the public. . . .

This letter was never sent; but, in its place, when Keats was dead, Shelley used a very different tone, and hurled his contemptuous defiance at the anonymous slanderer, in these memorable lines:

> Our Adonais has drunk poison—oh!
> What deaf and viperous murderer could crown
> Life's early cup with such a draught of woe?
> The nameless worm would now itself disown:
> It felt, yet could escape the magic tone
> Whose prelude held all envy, hate and wrong,
> But what was howling in one breast alone,
> Silent with expectation of the song,
> Whose master's hand is cold, whose silver lyre unstrung.
>
> Live thou, whose infamy is not thy fame!
> Live! fear no heavier chastisement from me,
> Thou noteless blot on a remembered name!
> But be thyself, and know thyself to be!
> And ever in thy season be thou free
> To spill the venom when thy fangs o'erflow:
> Remorse and Self-contempt shall cling to thee;
> Hot Shame shall burn upon thy secret brow,
> And like a beaten hound tremble thou shalt—as now.
>
> *Adonais*—Stanzas 36, 37.

Now, from the enthusiastic friend, let us turn, joyfully, to the undeniable testimony of the poet himself, writing confidentially to his publisher. Mr. Hessey had sent him a letter that appeared in the *Morning Chronicle* of 3 October, earnestly remonstrating against these examples of tyrannous criticism, and asking whether they could have proceeded from the translator of Juvenal [Mr. Gifford], who had prefixed to his work "that manly and pathetic narrative of genius oppressed and struggling with innumerable difficulties, yet finally triumphing *under patronage and encouragement*; or from the biographer of Kirke White [Mr. Southey], who had expostulated with the monthly reviewer, who sat down to blast the hopes of a boy who had confessed to him all his hopes and all his difficulties." The letter was signed "J. S.," and its author remained unknown. The newspapers generally spoke favourably of *Endymion*, so that Keats could not even regard the offensive articles as the general expression of the popular voice: he may, indeed, have experienced a momentary annoyance, but, if no other evidence survived, the noble candour and simplicity of this answer is quite sufficient to place the question in its true light, and to silence for ever the exclamations either of honest wrath or contemptuous compassion. Still the malice was weak only because the genius was strong; the arrows were poisoned, though the armour they struck was proof and able to save the life within.

9 October, 1818.

My Dear Hessey,

You are very good in sending me the letters from the *Chronicle*, and I am very bad in not acknowledging such a kindness sooner: pray forgive me. It has so chanced that I have had that paper every day. I have seen to-day's. I cannot but feel indebted to those gentlemen who have taken my part. As for the rest, I begin to get a little acquainted with my own strength and weakness. Praise or blame has but a momentary effect on the man whose love of beauty in the abstract makes him a severe critic on his own works. My own domestic criticism has given me pain without comparison beyond what *Blackwood* or the *Quarterly* could inflict: and also when I feel I am right, no external praise can give me such a glow as my own solitary reperception and ratification of what is fine. J. S. is perfectly right in regard to the "slip-shod *Endymion*." That it is so is no fault of mine. No! though it may sound a little paradoxical, it is as good as I had power to make it by myself. Had I been nervous about it being a perfect piece, and with that view asked advice, and trembled over every page, it would not have been written; for it is not in my nature to fumble. I will write independently. I have written independently *without judgment*. I may write independently, and *with judgment*, hereafter. The Genius of Poetry must work out its own salvation in a man. It cannot be matured by law and precept, but by sensation and watchfulness in itself. That which is creative must create itself. In *Endymion* I leaped headlong into the sea, and thereby have become better acquainted with the soundings, the quick-sands, and the rocks, than if I had stayed upon the green shore, and piped a silly pipe, and took tea and comfortable advice. I was never afraid of failure; for I would sooner fail than not be among the greatest. But I am nigh getting into a rant; so, with remembrances to Taylor and Woodhouse, etc., I am,

Yours very sincerely,
John Keats.

On returning to the south, Keats found his brother alarmingly ill, and immediately joined him at Teignmouth. They returned together to Hampstead, where he gradually sunk under the disease, affectionately tended and fraternally mourned. He was of a most gentle and witty nature, and resembled John in character and appearance. In Keats's copy of Shakespeare, the words *Poor Tom* in *King Lear*, are pathetically underlined.

Teignmouth,
September, 1818.

My Dear Bailey,

When a poor devil is drowning, it is said he comes thrice to the surface before he makes his final sink; if, however, at the third rise, he can manage to catch hold of a piece of weed or rock, he stands a fair chance, as I hope I do now, of being saved. I have sunk twice in our correspondence, have risen twice, and have been too idle, or something worse, to extricate myself. I have sunk the third time, and just now risen again at this two of the clock p.m., and saved myself from utter perdition by beginning this, all drenched as I am, and fresh from the water. And I would rather endure the present inconvenience of a wet jacket than you should keep a laced one in store for me. Why did I not stop at Oxford in my way? How can you ask such a question? Why did I not promise to do so? Did I not, in a letter to you, make a promise to do so? Then how can you be so unreasonable as to ask me why I did not? This is the thing—(for I have been rubbing my invention; trying several sleights: I first polished a cold, felt it in my fingers, tried it on the table, but could not pocket it: I tried chilblains, rheumatism, gout, tight boots—nothing of that sort would do—so this is, as I was going to say, the thing)— I had a letter from Tom, saying how much better he had got, and thinking he had better stop. I went down to prevent his coming up. Will not this do? Turn it which way you like— it is selvaged all round. I have used it, these three last days, to keep out the abominable Devonshire weather. By the by, you may say what you will of Devonshire: the truth is, it is a splashy, rainy, misty, snowy, foggy, haily, floody, muddy, slipshod county. The hills are very beautiful, when you get a sight of 'em; the primroses are out—but then you are in; the cliffs are of a fine deep colour, but then the clouds are continually vieing with them. The women like your London people in a sort of negative way—because the native men are the poorest creatures in England. When I think of Wordsworth's Sonnet, *Vanguard of Liberty! ye men of Kent!* the degenerated race about me are *pulvis Ipecac. simplex*—a strong dose. Were I a corsair, I'd make a descent on the south coast of Devon, if I did not run the chance of having cowardice imputed to me. As for the men, they'd run away into the Methodist meeting-houses; and the women would be glad of it. Had England been a large Devonshire, we should not have won the Battle of Waterloo. There are knotted oaks, there are lusty rivulets, there are meadows such as are not elsewhere —but there are no thews and sinews. *Moore's Almanack* is here a curiosity: arms, neck, and shoulders may at least be seen there, and the ladies read it as some out-of-the-way romance. Such a quelling power have these thoughts over me that I fancy the very air of a deteriorating quality. I fancy the flowers, all precocious, have an Acrasian spell about them; I feel able to beat off the Devonshire waves like soap-froth. I think it well, for the honour of England, that Julius Cæsar did not first land in this county. A Devonshirer, standing on his native hills, is not a distinct object; he does not show against the light; a wolf or two would dispossess him. I like, I love England—I like its living men—give me a long brown plain for my money, so I may meet with some of Edmund Ironside's descendants; give me a barren mould, so I may meet with some shadowing of Alfred in the shape of a gipsy, a huntsman, or a shepherd. Scenery is fine, but human nature is finer; the sward is richer for the tread of a real nervous English foot; the eagle's nest is finer, for the mountaineer having looked into it. Are these facts or prejudices? Whatever they be, for them I shall never be able to relish entirely any Devonshire scenery. Homer is fine, Achilles is fine, Diomed is fine, Shakspeare is fine—Hamlet is fine, Lear is fine—but dwindled Englishmen are not fine. Where, too, the women are so passable, and have such English names, such as Ophelia, Cordelia, etc., that they should have such paramours, or rather imparamours! As for them, I cannot, in thought, help wishing, as did the cruel emperor, that they had but one head, and I might cut it off, to deliver them from any horrible courtesy they may do their undeserving countrymen. I wonder I meet with no born monsters. O! Devonshire, last night I thought the moon had dwindled in heaven.

I have never had your Sermon from Wordsworth, but Mr. Dilke lent it me. You know my ideas about Religion. I do not think myself more in the right than other people, and that nothing in this world is proveable. I wish I could enter into all your feelings on the subject, merely for one short ten minutes, and give you a page or two to your liking. I am sometimes so very sceptical as to think Poetry itself a mere Jack o' Lanthorn to amuse whoever may chance to be struck with its brilliance. As tradesmen say every thing is worth what it will fetch, so probably every mental pursuit takes its reality and worth from the ardour of the pursuer—being in itself a nothing. Ethereal things may at least be thus real, divided under three heads—things real, things semi-real, and nothings: things real, such as existences of sun, moon, and stars, and passages of Shakspeare; things semi-real, such as love, the clouds, etc., which require a greeting of the spirit to make them wholly exist; and nothings, which are made great and dignified by an ardent pursuit—which, by the by, stamp the Burgundy-mark on the bottles of our minds, insomuch as they are able to *"consecrate whate'er they look upon."* I have written a sonnet here of a somewhat collateral nature. So don't imagine it is "*apropos des bottes.*"

Four seasons fill the measure of the year, etc.[1]

Aye, this may be carried—but what am I talking of? It is an old maxim of mine, and of course must be well known, that every point of thought is the centre of an intellectual world. The two uppermost thoughts in a man's mind are the two poles of his world; he revolves on them, and every thing is southward and northward to him through their means. We take but three steps from feathers to iron. Now, my dear fellow, I must, once for all, tell you I have not one idea of the truth of any of my speculations: I shall never be a reasoner, because I care not to be in the right, when retired from bickering and in a proper philosophical temper. So you must not stare, if, in any future letter, I endeavour to prove that Apollo, as he had catgut strings to his lyre, used a cat's paw as a pecten— and, further, from [the] said pecten's reiterated and continual teasing, came the term *hen-pecked.*

My brother Tom desires to be remembered to you; he has just this moment had a spitting of blood, poor fellow! Remember me to Grey and Whitehead.

Your affectionate friend,
JOHN KEATS.

[Postmark, HAMPSTEAD, 27 *October*, 1818.]

MY DEAR WOODHOUSE,
  Your letter gave me great satisfaction, more on account of its friendliness than any relish of that matter in it which is accounted so acceptable in the "genus irritabile." The best answer I can give you is in a clerklike manner to make some observations on two principal points which seem to point like indices into the midst of the whole *pro* and *con* about genius, and views, and achievements, and ambition, *et cœtera.*
1st. As to the poetical character itself (I mean that sort, of which, if I am anything, I am a member; that sort distinguished from the Wordsworthian, or egotistical sublime; which is a thing *per se*, and stands alone), it is not itself—it has no self—it is every thing and nothing—it has no character —it enjoys light and shade—it lives in gusts, be it foul or fair,

[1] See the *Literary Remains.*

high or low, rich or poor, mean or elevated—it has as much delight in conceiving an Iago as an Imogen. What shocks the virtuous philosopher delights the cameleon poet. It does no harm from its relish of the dark side of things, any more than from its taste for the bright one, because they both end in speculation. A poet is the most unpoetical of anything in existence, because he has no identity; he is continually in for, and filling, some other body. The sun, the moon, the sea, and men and women, who are creatures of impulse, are poetical, and have about them an unchangeable attribute; the poet has none, no identity. He is certainly the most unpoetical of all God's creatures. If, then, he has no self, and if I am a poet, where is the wonder that I should say I would write no more? Might I not at that very instant have been cogitating on the characters of Saturn and Ops? It is a wretched thing to confess, but it is a very fact, that not one word I ever utter can be taken for granted as an opinion growing out of my identical nature. How can it, when I have no nature? When I am in a room with people, if I am free from speculating on creations of my own brain, then, not myself goes home to myself, but the identity of every one in the room begins to press upon me, [so] that I am in a very little time annihilated —not only among men; it would be the same in a nursery of children. I know not whether I make myself wholly understood: I hope enough to let you see that no dependence is to be placed on what I said that day.

In the second place, I will speak of my views, and of the life I purpose to myself. I am ambitious of doing the world some good: if I should be spared, that may be the work of future years—in the interval I will assay to reach to as high a summit in poetry as the nerve bestowed upon me will suffer. The faint conceptions I have of poems to come bring the blood frequently into my forehead. All I hope is, that I may not lose all interest in human affairs—that the solitary indifference I feel for applause, even from the finest spirits, will not blunt any acuteness of vision I may have. I do not think it will. I feel assured I should write from the mere yearning and fondness I have for the beautiful, even if my night's labours should be burnt every morning, and no eye ever shine upon them. But even now I am perhaps not speaking from myself, but from some character in whose soul I now live.

I am sure, however, that this next sentence is from myself.

—I feel your anxiety, good opinion, and friendship, in the highest degree, and am

Yours most sincerely,

JOHN KEATS.

29 *October*, 1818.

MY DEAR GEORGE,

There was a part in your letter which gave me great pain; that where you lament not receiving letters from England. I intended to have written immediately on my return from Scotland (which was two months earlier than I intended, on account of my own, as well as Tom's health), but then I was told by Mrs. W. that you had said you did not wish any one to write, till we had heard from you. This I thought odd, and now I see that it could not have been so. Yet, at the time, I suffered my unreflecting head to be satisfied, and went on in that sort of careless and restless life with which you are well acquainted. I am grieved to say that I am not sorry you had not letters at Philadelphia: you could have had no good news of Tom; and I have been withheld, on his account, from beginning these many days. I could not bring myself to say the truth, that he is no better, but much worse: however, it must be told, and you, my dear brother and sister, take example from me, and bear up against any calamity, for my sake, as I do for yours. Ours are ties, which, independent of their own sentiment, are sent us by Providence, to prevent the effects of one great solitary grief: I have Fanny,[1] and I have you— three people whose happiness, to me, is sacred, and it does annul that selfish sorrow which I should otherwise fall into, living, as I do, with poor Tom, who looks upon me as his only comfort. The tears will come into your eyes: let them; and embrace each other: thank Heaven for what happiness you have, and, after thinking a moment or two that you suffer in common with all mankind, hold it not a sin to regain your cheerfulness.

Your welfare is a delight to me which I cannot express. The moon is now shining full and brilliant; she is the same to me in matter that you are in spirit. If you were here, my dear sister, I could not pronounce the words which I can write to you from a distance. I have a tenderness for you, and an admiration which I feel to be as great and more chaste than I can have for any woman in the world. You will mention

[1] His sister.

Fanny—her character is not formed; her identity does not press upon me as yours does. I hope from the bottom of my heart that I may one day feel as much for her as I do for you. I know not how it is, my dear brother, I have never made any acquaintance of my own—nearly all through your medium; through you I know, not only a sister, but a glorious human being; and now I am talking of those to whom you have made me known, I cannot forbear mentioning Haslam, as a most kind, and obliging, and constant friend. His behaviour to Tom during my absence, and since my return, has endeared him to me for ever, besides his anxiety about you.

To-morrow I shall call on your mother and exchange information with her. I intend to write you such columns that it will be impossible for me to keep any order or method in what I write; that will come first which is uppermost in my mind; not that which is uppermost in my heart. Besides, I should wish to give you a picture of our lives here, whenever by a touch I can do it.

I came by ship from Inverness, and was nine days at sea without being sick. A little qualm now and then put me in mind of you; however, as soon as you touch the shore, all the horrors of sickness are soon forgotten, as was the case with a lady on board, who could not hold her head up all the way. We had not been into the Thames an hour before her tongue began to some tune—paying off, as it was fit she should, all old scores. I was the only Englishman on board. There was a downright Scotchman, who, hearing that there had been a bad crop of potatoes in England, had brought some triumphant specimens from Scotland. These he exhibited with natural pride to all the ignorant lightermen and watermen from the Nore to the Bridge. I fed upon beef all the way, not being able to eat the thick porridge which the ladies managed to manage, with large, awkward, horn-spoons into the bargain. Reynolds has returned from a six-weeks' enjoyment in Devonshire; he is well, and persuades me to publish my *Pot of Basil*, as an answer to the attack made on me in *Blackwood's Magazine* and the *Quarterly Review*. There have been two letters in my defence in the *Chronicle*, and one in the *Examiner*, copied from the Exeter paper, and written by Reynolds. I don't know who wrote those in the *Chronicle*. This is a mere matter of the moment: I think I shall be among the English Poets after my death. Even as a matter of present interest, the attempt to crush me in the *Quarterly* has only brought me more into notice, and it is a common expression among book-men, "I wonder the *Quarterly* should cut its own throat." It does me not the least harm in society to make me appear little and ridiculous: I know when a man is superior to me, and give him all due respect; he will be the last to laugh at me; and, as for the rest, I feel that I make an impression upon them which ensures me personal respect while I am in sight, whatever they may say when my back is turned.

The Misses —— are very kind to me, but they have lately displeased me much, and in this way:—now I am coming the Richardson!—On my return, the first day I called, they were in a sort of taking or bustle about a cousin of theirs, who, having fallen out with her grandpapa in a serious manner, was invited by Mrs. —— to take asylum in her house. She is an East-Indian, and ought to be her grandfather's heir. At the time I called, Mrs. —— was in conference with her up stairs, and the young ladies were warm in her praise down stairs, calling her genteel, interesting, and a thousand other pretty things, to which I gave no heed, not being partial to nine days' wonders. Now all is completely changed: they hate her, and, from what I hear, she is not without faults of a real kind; but she has others, which are more apt to make women of inferior claims hate her. She is not a Cleopatra, but is, at least, a Charmian: she has a rich Eastern look; she has fine eyes, and fine manners. When she comes into the room she makes the same impression as the beauty of a leopardess. She is too fine and too conscious of herself to repulse any man who may address her: from habit she thinks that *nothing particular*. I always find myself more at ease with such a woman: the picture before me always gives me a life and animation which I cannot possibly feel with anything inferior. I am, at such times, too much occupied in admiring to be awkward or in a tremble: I forget myself entirely, because I live in her. You will, by this time, think I am in love with her, so, before I go any farther, I will tell you I am not. She kept me awake one night, as a tune of Mozart's might do. I speak of the thing as a pastime and an amusement, than which I can feel none deeper than a conversation with an imperial woman, the very "yes" and "no" of whose life is to me a banquet. I don't cry to take the moon home with me in my pocket, nor do I fret to leave her behind me. I like her, and her like, because one has no *sensations*: what we both are is taken for granted. You will suppose I have, by this, had much talk with her—no such thing; there are the Misses —— on the look out. They think I don't admire her because I don't stare at her; they call her a flirt to me—what a want of knowledge! She walks across a room in such a manner that a man is drawn towards her with a magnetic power; this they call flirting! They do not know things; they do not know what a woman is. I believe, though, she has faults, the same as Charmian and Cleopatra might have had. Yet she is a fine thing, speaking in a worldly way; for there are two distinct tempers of mind in which we judge of things—the worldly, theatrical and pantomimical; and the unearthly, spiritual and ethereal. In the former, Bonaparte, Lord Byron, and this Charmian, hold the first place in our minds; in the latter, John Howard, Bishop Hooker rocking his child's cradle, and you, my dear sister, are the conquering feelings. As a man of the world, I love the rich talk of a Charmian; as an eternal being, I love the thought of you. I should like her to ruin me, and I should like you to save me.

> I am free from men of pleasure's cares,
> By dint of feelings far more deep than theirs.

This is "Lord Byron," and is one of the finest things he has said.

I have no town-talk for you: as for politics, they are, in my opinion, only sleepy, because they will soon be wide awake. Perhaps not; for the long-continued peace of England has given us notions of personal safety which are likely to prevent the re-establishment of our national honesty. There is, of a truth, nothing manly or sterling in any part of the Government. There are many madmen in the country, I have no doubt, who would like to be beheaded on Tower-hill, merely because of the sake of *éclat*; there are many men, who, like Hunt, from a principle of taste, would like to see things go on better; there are many, like Sir F. Burdett, who like to sit at the head of political dinners—but there are none prepared to suffer in obscurity for their country. The motives of our worst men are interest, and of our best vanity; we have no Milton, or Algernon Sidney. Governors, in these days, lose the title of man, in exchange for that of Diplomate or Minister. We breathe a sort of official atmosphere. All the departments of

Government have strayed far from simplicity, which is the greatest of strength. There is as much difference in this, between the present Government and Oliver Cromwell's, as there is between the Twelve Tables of Rome and the volumes of Civil Law which were digested by Justinian. A man now entitled Chancellor has the same honour paid him, whether he be a hog or a Lord Bacon. No sensation is created by greatness, but by the number of Orders a man has at his buttonhole. Notwithstanding the noise the Liberals make in favour of the cause of Napoleon, I cannot but think he has done more harm to the life of Liberty than any one else could have done. Not that the Divine Right gentlemen have done, or intend to do, any good—no, they have taken a lesson of him, and will do all the further harm he would have done, without any of the good. The worst thing he has taught them is, how to organise their monstrous armies. The Emperor Alexander, it is said, intends to divide his Empire, as did Dioclesian, creating two Czars besides himself, and continuing supreme monarch of the whole. Should he do so, and they, for a series of years, keep peaceable among themselves, Russia may spread her conquest even to China. I think it a very likely thing that China may fall of itself: Turkey certainly will. Meanwhile European North Russia will hold its horn against the rest of Europe, intriguing constantly with France. Dilke, whom you know to be a Godwin-perfectibility man, pleases himself with the idea that America will be the country to take up the human intellect where England leaves off. I differ there with him greatly: a country like the United States, whose greatest men are Franklins and Washingtons, will never do that: they are great men doubtless; but how are they to be compared to those, our countrymen, Milton and the two Sidneys? The one is a philosophical Quaker, full of mean and thrifty maxims; the other sold the very charger who had taken him through all his battles. Those Americans are great, but they are not sublime men; the humanity of the United States can never reach the sublime. Birkbeck's mind is too much in the American style; you must endeavour to enforce a little spirit of another sort into the settlement—always with great caution; for thereby you may do your descendants more good than you may imagine. If I had a prayer to make for any great good, next to Tom's recovery, it should be that one of your children should be the first American poet. I have a great mind to make a prophecy; and they say that prophecies work out their own fulfilment.

> 'Tis the witching hour of night,
> Orbed is the moon and bright,
> And the stars they glisten, glisten,
> Seeming with bright eyes to listen—
>   For what listen they?
> For a song and for a charm,
> See they glisten in alarm,
> And the moon is waxing warm
>   To hear what I shall say.

> Moon! keep wide thy golden ears—
> Hearken, stars! and hearken, spheres!—
> Hearken, thou eternal sky!
> I sing an infant's lullaby.
>   A pretty lullaby.
> Listen, listen, listen, listen,
> Glisten, glisten, glisten, glisten,
>   And hear my lullaby!
> Though the rushes that will make
> Its cradle still are in the lake—
> Though the linen that will be
> Its swathe, is on the cotton tree—
> Though the woollen that will keep
> It warm, is on the silly sheep—
> Listen, starlight, listen, listen,
> Glisten, glisten, glisten, glisten,
>   And hear my lullaby!
> Child, I see thee! Child, I've found thee
> Midst of the quiet all around thee!
> Child, I see thee! Child, I spy thee!
> And thy mother sweet is nigh thee!
> Child, I know thee! Child, no more,
> But a poet evermore!
> See, see, the lyre, the lyre,
> In a flame of fire,
> Upon the little cradle's top
> Flaring, flaring, flaring,
> Past the eyesight's bearing.
> Awake it from its sleep,
> And see if it can keep
> Its eyes upon the blaze—
>   Amaze, amaze!
> It stares, it stares, it stares,
> It dares what no one dares!
> It lifts its little hand into the flame
> Unharmed, and on the strings
> Paddles a little tune, and sings,
> With dumb endeavour sweetly—
> Bard art thou completely!
>   Little child
>   O' th' western wild,
> Bard art thou completely!
> Sweetly with dumb endeavour,

A poet now or never,
            Little child
            O' th' western wild,
A poet now or never!

Notwithstanding your happiness and your recommendations, I hope I shall never marry: though the most beautiful creature were waiting for me at the end of a journey or a walk; though the carpet were of silk, and the curtains of the morning clouds, the chairs and sofas stuffed with cygnet's down, the food manna, the wine beyond claret, the window opening on Winandermere, I should not feel, or rather my happiness should not be, so fine; my solitude is sublime—for, instead of what I have described, there is a sublimity to welcome me home; the roaring of the wind is my wife; and the stars through my window-panes are my children; the mighty abstract Idea of Beauty in all things, I have, stifles the more divided and minute domestic happiness. An amiable wife and sweet children I contemplate as part of that Beauty, but I must have a thousand of those beautiful particles to fill up my heart. I feel more and more every day, as my imagination strengthens, that I do not live in this world alone, but in a thousand worlds. No sooner am I alone, than shapes of epic greatness are stationed around me, and serve my spirit the office which is equivalent to a King's Bodyguard: "then Tragedy with scepter'd pall comes sweeping by": according to my state of mind, I am with Achilles shouting in the trenches, or with Theocritus in the vales of Sicily; or throw my whole being into Troilus, and, repeating those lines, "I wander like a lost soul upon the Stygian bank, staying for waftage," I melt into the air with a voluptuousness so delicate, that I am content to be alone. Those things, combined with the opinion I have formed of the generality of women, who appear to me as children to whom I would rather give a sugar-plum than my time, form a barrier against matrimony which I rejoice in. I have written this that you might see that I have my share of the highest pleasures of life, and that, though I may choose to pass my days alone, I shall be no solitary; you see there is nothing splenetic in all this. The only thing that can ever affect me personally for more than one short passing day is any doubt about my powers for poetry: I seldom have any; and I look with hope to the nighing time when I shall have none. I am as happy as a man can be—that is, in myself; I should be happier if Tom were well, and if I knew you were passing pleasant days. Then I should be most enviable—with the yearning passion I have for the Beautiful, connected and made one with the ambition of my intellect. Think of my pleasure in solitude in comparison with my commerce with the world: there I am a child, there they do not know me, not even my most intimate acquaintance; I give in to their feelings as though I were refraining from imitating a little child. Some think me middling, others silly, others foolish: every one thinks he sees my weak side against my will, when, in truth, it is with my will. I am content to be thought all this, because I have in my own breast so great a resource. This is one great reason why they like me so, because they can all show to advantage in a room, and eclipse (from a certain tact) one who is reckoned to be a good poet. I hope I am not here playing tricks "to make the angels weep." I think not; for I have not the least contempt for my species; and, though it may sound paradoxical, my greatest elevations of soul leave me every time more humbled. Enough of this, though, in your love for me, you will not think it enough.

Tom is rather more easy than he has been, but is still so nervous that I cannot speak to him of you—indeed it is the care I have had to keep his mind aloof from feelings too acute, that has made this letter so rambling. I did not like to write before him a letter he knew was to reach your hands; I cannot even now ask him for any message; his heart speaks to you.

Be as happy as you can, and believe me, dear Brother and Sister, your anxious and affectionate Brother,

JOHN.

This is my birth-day.

WELL WALK,
24 *November*, 1818.

MY DEAR RICE,

Your *amende honorable* I must call "*un surcroit d'amitié*," for I am not at all sensible of anything but that you were unfortunately engaged, and I was unfortunately in a hurry. I completely understand your feeling in this mistake, and find in it that balance of comfort which remains after regretting your uneasiness. I have long made up my mind to take for granted the genuine-heartedness of my friends, notwithstanding any temporary ambiguousness in their behaviour or their tongues—nothing of which, however, I had the least scent of this morning. I say, completely understand, for I am everlastingly getting my mind into such like painful trammels—and am even at this moment suffering under them in the case of a friend of ours. I will tell you two most unfortunate and parallel slips—it seems downright pre-intention: A friend says to me, "Keats, I shall go and see Severn this week."—"Ah! (says I) you want him to take your portrait." And again, "Keats," says a friend, "when will you come to town again?" "I will," says I, "let you have the MS. next week." In both these cases I appeared to attribute an interested motive to each of my friends' questions—the first made him flush, the second made him look angry:—and yet I am innocent in both cases; my mind leapt over every interval to what I saw was, *per se*, a pleasant subject with him. You see I have no allowances to make—you see how far I am from supposing you could show me any neglect. I very much regret the long time I have been obliged to exile from you, for I have one or two rather pleasant occasions to confer upon with you. What I have heard from George is favourable. I expect a letter from the settlement itself.

Your sincere friend,

JOHN KEATS.

I cannot give any good news of Tom.

WENTWORTH PLACE, HAMPSTEAD,
18 December, 1818.

MY DEAR WOODHOUSE,

I am greatly obliged to you. I must needs feel flattered by making an impression on a set of ladies. I should be content to do so by meretricious romance verse, if they alone, and not men, were to judge. I should like very much to know those ladies—though look here, Woodhouse—I have a new leaf to turn over: I must work; I must read; I must write. I am unable to afford time for new acquaintances. I am scarcely able to do my duty to those I have. Leave the matter to chance. But do not forget to give my remembrances to your cousin.

Yours most sincerely,

JOHN KEATS.

MY DEAR REYNOLDS,

Believe me, I have rather rejoiced at your happiness than fretted at your silence. Indeed I am grieved, on your account, that I am not at the same time happy. But I conjure you to think, at present, of nothing but pleasure; "Gather the rose," etc., gorge the honey of life. I pity you as much that it cannot last for ever, as I do myself now drinking bitters. Give yourself up to it—you cannot help it—and I have a consolation in thinking so. I never was in love, yet the voice and shape of a woman has haunted me these two days—at such a time when the relief, the feverish relief of poetry, seems a much less crime. This morning poetry has conquered—I have relapsed into those abstractions which are my only life—I feel escaped from a new, strange, and threatening sorrow, and I am thankful for it. There is an awful warmth about my heart, like a load of Immortality.

Poor Tom—that woman and poetry were ringing changes in my senses. Now I am, in comparison, happy. I am sensible this will distress you—you must forgive me. Had I known you would have set out so soon I would have sent you the *Pot of Basil*, for I had copied it out ready. Here is a free translation of a Sonnet of Ronsard, which I think will please you. I have the loan of his works—they have great beauties.

> Nature withheld Cassandra in the skies,
> For more adornment, a full thousand years;
> She took their cream of Beauty's fairest dies,
> And shaped and tinted her above all Peers:
> Meanwhile Love kept her dearly with his wings,
> And underneath their shadow filled her eyes
> With such a richness that the cloudy Kings
> Of high Olympus uttered slavish sighs.
> When from the Heavens I saw her first descend,
> My heart took fire, and only burning pains,
> They were my pleasures—they my Life's sad end;
> Love poured her beauty into my warm veins,
> [So that her image in my soul upgrew,
> The only thing adorable and true.—*Ed.*] [1]

---

[1] The second sonnet in the *Amours de Cassandre*: she was a damosel of Blois—"Ville de Blois—naissance de ma dame."

> "Nature ornant Cassandre, qui deuoit
> De sa douceur forcer les plus rebelles,
> La composa de cent beautez nouuelles
> Que dés mille ans en espargne elle auoit.—
> De tous les biens qu' Amour au Ciel couuoit
> Comme vu tresor cherement sous ces ailles,
> Elle enrichit les Graces immortelles
> De son bel oeil qui les Dieux esmouuoit.—
> Du Ciel à peine elle estoit descenduë
> Quand ie la vey, quand mon asme esperduë
> En deuint folle, et d'vn si poignant trait,
> Amour couler ses beautez en mes veines,
> Qu' autres plaisirs ie ne sens que mes peines,
> Ny autre bien qu' adorer son portrait."

I had not the original by me when I wrote it, and did not recollect the purport of the last lines.

I should have seen Rice ere this, but I am confined by Sawrey's mandate in the house now, and have, as yet, only gone out in fear of the damp night. I shall soon be quite recovered. Your offer I shall remember as though it had even now taken place in fact. I think it cannot be. Tom is not up yet—I cannot say he is better. I have not heard from George.

Your affectionate friend,

JOHN KEATS.

It may be as well at once to state that the lady alluded to in the above pages inspired Keats with the passion that only ceased with his existence. Where personal feelings of so profound a character are concerned, it does not become the biographer, in any case, to do more than to indicate their effect on the life of his hero, and where the memoir so nearly approaches the times of its subject that the persons in question, or, at any rate, their near relations, may be still alive, it will at once be felt how indecorous would be any conjectural analysis of such sentiments, or, indeed, any more intrusive record of them than is absolutely necessary for the comprehension of the real man. True, a poet's love is, above all other things, his life; true, a nature, such as that of Keats, in which the sensuous and the ideal were so interpenetrated that he might be said to think because he felt, cannot be understood without its affections; but no comment, least of all that of one personally a stranger, can add to the force of the glowing and solemn expressions that appear here and there in his correspondence. However sincerely the devotion of Keats may have been requited, it will be seen that his outward circumstances soon became such as to render a union very difficult, if not impossible. Thus these years were past in a conflict in which plain poverty and mortal sickness met a radiant imagination and a redundant heart. Hope was there, with Genius, his everlasting sustainer, and Fear never approached but as the companion of Necessity. The strong power conquered the physical man, and made the very intensity of his passion, in a certain sense, accessory to his death: he might have lived longer if he had lived less. But this should be no matter of self-

reproach to the object of his love, for the same may be
said of the very exercise of his poetic faculty, and of all
that made him what he was. It is enough that she has
preserved his memory with a sacred honour, and it is no
vain assumption, that to have inspired and sustained the
one passion of this noble being has been a source of grave
delight and earnest thankfulness, through the changes
and chances of her earthly pilgrimage.

When Keats was left alone by his brother's death, which
took place early in December, Mr. Brown pressed on him
to leave his lodgings and reside entirely in his house: this
he consented to, and the cheerful society of his friend
seemed to bring back his spirits, and at the same time to
excite him to fresh poetical exertions. It was then he began
Hyperion; that poem full of the "large utterance of the
early Gods," of which Shelley said, that the scenery and
drawing of Saturn dethroned by the fallen Titans surpassed those of Satan and his rebellious angels in *Paradise
Lost.* He afterwards published it as a fragment, and still
later re-cast it into the shape of a Vision, which remains
equally unfinished. Shorter poems were scrawled, as they
happened to suggest themselves, on the first scrap of paper
at hand, which was afterwards used as a mark for a book,
or thrown anywhere aside. It seemed as if, when his
imagination was once relieved, by writing down its effusions,
he cared so little about them that it required a friend at
hand to prevent them from being utterly lost. The admirable *Ode to a Nightingale* was suggested by the continual
song of the bird that, in the spring of 1819, had built her
nest close to the house, and which often threw Keats into
a sort of trance of tranquil pleasure. One morning he took
his chair from the breakfast-table, placed it on the grass-
plot under a plum-tree, and sat there for two or three
hours with some scraps of paper in his hands. Shortly afterwards Mr. Brown saw him thrusting them away, as waste-
paper, behind some books, and had considerable difficulty
in putting together and arranging the stanzas of the Ode.
Other poems as literally "fugitive" were rescued in much
the same way—for he permitted Mr. Brown to copy
whatever he could pick up, and sometimes assisted him.

The odes *To the Nightingale* and *To a Grecian Urn* were

first published in a periodical entitled the *Annals of Fine Arts*. Soon after he had composed them, he repeated, or rather chanted, them to Mr. Haydon, in the sort of recitative that so well suited his deep grave voice, as they strolled together through Kilburn meadows, leaving an indelible impression on the mind of his surviving friend.

The journal-letters to his brother and sister in America are the best records of his outer existence. I give them in their simplicity, being assured that thus they are best. They are full of a genial life which will be understood and valued by all to whom a book of this nature presents any interest whatever: and, when it is remembered how carelessly they are written, how little the writer ever dreamt of their being redeemed from the far West or exposed to any other eyes than those of the most familiar affection, they become a mirror in which the individual character is shown with indisputable truth, and from which the fairest judgment of his very self can be drawn.

[1818–19.]

My Dear Brother and Sister,

You will have been prepared, before this reaches you, for the worst news you could have; nay, if Haslam's letter arrived in proper time, I have a consolation in thinking the first shock will be passed before you receive this. The last days of poor Tom were of the most distressing nature; but his last moments were not so painful, and his very last was without a pang. I will not enter into any parsonic comments on death. Yet the commonest observations of the commonest people on death are true as their proverbs. I have a firm belief in immortality, and so had Tom.

During poor Tom's illness I was not able to write, and since his death the task of beginning has been a hindrance to me. Within this last week I have been everywhere, and I will tell you, as nearly as possible, how I go on. I am going to domesticate with Brown, that is, we shall keep house together. I shall have the front-parlour, and he the back one, by which I shall avoid the noise of Bentley's children, and be able to go on with my studies, which have been greatly interrupted lately, so that I have not the shadow of an idea of a book in my head, and my pen seems to have grown gouty for verse. How are you going on now? The going on of the world makes me dizzy.

There you are with Birkbeck, here I am with Brown; sometimes I imagine an immense separation, and sometimes, as at
present, a direct communication of spirit with you. That will
be one of the grandeurs of immortality. There will be no space,
and consequently the only commerce between spirits will be
by their intelligence of each other—when they will completely
understand each other, while we, in this world, merely comprehend each other in different degrees; the higher the degree
of good, so higher is our Love and Friendship. I have been so
little used to writing lately that I am afraid you will not smoke
my meaning, so I will give you an example. Suppose Brown, or
Haslam, or any one else, whom I understand in the next
degree to what I do you, were in America, they would be so
much the farther from me in proportion as their identity was
more impressed upon me. Now the reason why I do not feel,
at the present moment, so far from you, is that I remember
your ways, and manners, and actions; I know your manner
of thinking, your manner of feeling; I know what shape your
joy or your sorrow would take; I know the manner of your
walking, standing, sauntering, sitting down, laughing, punning,
and every action, so truly that you seem near to me. You will
remember me in the same manner, and the more when I tell
you that I shall read a page of Shakspeare every Sunday at
ten o'clock; you read one at the same time, and we shall be
as near each other as blind bodies can be in the same room.

Thursday.—This morning is very fine. What are you doing
this morning? Have you a clear hard frost, as we have? How
do you come on with the gun? Have you shot a Buffalo?
Have you met with any Pheasants? My thoughts are very
frequently in a foreign country. I live more out of England
than in it. The mountains of Tartary are a favorite lounge,
if I happen to miss the Alleghany ridge, or have no whim for
Savoy. There must be great pleasure in pursuing game—
pointing your gun—no, it won't do—now—no—rabbit it—
now, bang—smoke and feathers—where is it? Shall you be
able to get a good pointer or so? Now I am not addressing
myself to G. Minor—and yet I am, for you are one. Have you
some warm furs? By your next letter I shall expect to hear
exactly how you get on; smother nothing; let us have all—
fair and foul—all plain. Will the little bairn have made his
entrance before you have this? Kiss it for me, and when it
can first know a cheese from a caterpillar, show it my picture

twice a week. You will be glad to hear that Gifford's attack upon me has done me service—it has got my book among several *sets*, nor must I forget to mention, once more, what I suppose Haslam has told you, the present of a £25 note I had anonymously sent me. Another pleasing circumstance I may mention, on the authority of Mr. Neville, to whom I had sent a copy of *Endymion*. It was lying on his cousin's table, where it had been seen by one of the Misses Porter (of Romance celebrity), who expressed a wish to read it; after having dipped into it, in a day or two she returned it, accompanied by the following letter:

"DEAR SIR,

"As my brother is sending a messenger to Esher, I cannot but make the same the bearer of my regrets for not having had the pleasure of seeing you the morning you called at the gate. I had given orders to be denied, I was so very unwell with my still adhesive cold; but had I known it was you, I should have broken off the interdict for a few minutes, to say how very much I am delighted with *Endymion*. I had just finished the poem, and have now done as you permitted, lent it to Miss Fitzgerald.

"I regret you are not personally acquainted with the author, for I should have been happy to have acknowledged to him, through the advantage of your communication, the very rare delight my sister and myself have enjoyed from this first fruits of his genius. I hope the ill-natured review will not have damped such true Parnassian fire. It ought not, for when life is granted to the possessor, it always burns its brilliant way through every obstacle. Had Chatterton possessed sufficient manliness of mind to know the magnanimity of patience, and been aware that great talents have a commission from heaven, he would not have deserted his post, and his name might have paged with Milton.

"Ever much yours,
"JANE PORTER.

"DITTON COTTAGE, 4 *December*, 1818.
"To H. NEVILLE, ESQ., ESHER."

Now I feel more obliged than flattered by this—so obliged that I will not, at present, give you an extravaganza of a Lady Romance. I will be introduced to them first, if it be merely for the pleasure of writing you about them. Hunt has asked me to meet Tom Moore, so you shall hear of him also some day.

I am passing a quiet day, which I have not done for a long time, and if I do continue so, I feel I must again begin with my poetry, for if I am not in action, mind or body, I am in pain, and from that I suffer greatly by going into parties, when from the rules of society and a natural pride, I am obliged to smother my spirits and look like an idiot, because I feel my impulses, if given way to, would too much amaze them. I live under an everlasting restraint, never relieved except when I am composing, so I will write away.

Friday.—I think you knew before you left England, that my next subject would be the *Fall of Hyperion.* I went on a little with it last night, but it will take some time to get into the vein again. I will not give you any extracts, because I wish the whole to make an impression. I have, however, a few poems which you will like, and I will copy them out on the next sheet. I will write to Haslam this morning to know when the packet sails, and till it does I will write something every day. After that my journal shall go on like clockwork, and you must not complain of its dulness; for what I wish is to write a quantity to you, knowing well that dulness itself from me will be instructing to you. You may conceive how this not having been done has weighed upon me. I shall be better able to judge from your next what sort of information will be of most service or amusement to you. Perhaps, as you are fond of giving me sketches of characters, you may like a little pic-nic of scandal, even across the Atlantic. Shall I give you Miss —— ? She is about my height, with a fine style of coun- tenance of the lengthened sort; she wants sentiment in every feature; she manages to make her hair look well; her nostrils are very fine, though a little painful; her mouth is bad and good; her profile is better than her full face, which, indeed, is not full, but pale and thin, without showing any bone; her shape is very graceful, and so are her movements; her arms are good, her hands bad-ish, her feet tolerable. She is not seventeen, but she is ignorant; monstrous in her behaviour, flying out in all directions, calling people such names that I was forced lately to make use of the term—Minx: this is, I think, from no innate vice, but from a penchant she has for acting stylishly. I am, however, tired of such style, and shall decline any more of it. She had a friend to visit her lately;

you have known plenty such—she plays the music, but without one sensation but the feel of the ivory at her fingers; she is a downright Miss, without one set-off. We hated her, and smoked her, and baited her, and, I think, drove her away. Miss —— thinks her a paragon of fashion, and says she is the only woman in the world she would change persons with. What a stupe— she is as superior as a rose to a dandelion.

It is some days since I wrote the last page, but I never know; but I must write. I am looking into a book of Dubois'—he has written directions to the players. One of them is very good: "In singing, never mind the music—observe what time you please. It would be a pretty degradation, indeed, if you were obliged to confine your genius to the dull regularity of a fiddler—horse-hair and cat-guts. No, let him keep *your* time and play *your* time; *dodge him.*" I will now copy out the sonnet and letter I have spoken of. The outside cover was thus directed: "Messrs. Taylor and Hessey, Booksellers, 93, Fleet-street, London," and it contained this: "Messrs. Taylor and Hessey are requested to forward the enclosed letter by some *safe* mode of conveyance to the author of *Endymion*, who is not known at Teignmouth; or, if they have not his address, they will return the letter by post, directed as below, within a fortnight. Mr. P. Fenbank, P. O., Teignmouth, 9th November, 1818." In this sheet was enclosed the following, with a superscription, "Mr. John Keats, Teignmouth"; then came "Sonnet to John Keats," which I could not copy for any in the world but you, who know that I scout "mild light and loveliness," or any such nonsense, in myself.

> Star of high promise! Not to this dark age
> Do thy mild light and loveliness belong;
> For it is blind, intolerant, and wrong,
> Dead to empyreal soarings, and the rage
> Of scoffing spirits bitter war doth wage
> With all that bold integrity of song;
> Yet thy clear beam shall shine through ages strong,
> To ripest times a light and heritage.
> And those breathe now who dote upon thy fame,
> Whom thy wild numbers wrap beyond their being,
> Who love the freedom of thy lays, their aim
> Above the scope of a dull tribe unseeing,
> And there is one whose hand will never scant,
> From his poor store of fruits, all thou canst want.

> *(Turn over.)*

I turned over, and found a £25 note. Now this appears to me all very proper; if I had refused it, I should have behaved in a very braggadocio dunderheaded manner; and yet the present galls me a little, and I do not know that I shall not return it, if I ever meet with the donor, after whom to no purpose have I written.

I must not forget to tell you that a few days since I went with Dilke a-shooting on the heath, and shot a tomtit; there were as many guns abroad as birds.

Thursday.—On my word, I think so little, I have not one opinion upon anything except in matters of taste. I never can feel certain of any truth, but from a clear perception of its beauty, and I find myself very young-minded, even in that perceptive power, which I hope will increase. A year ago I could not understand, in the slightest degree, Raphael's Cartoons; now I begin to read them a little. And how did I learn to do so? By seeing something done in quite an opposite spirit; I mean a picture of Guido's, in which all the Saints, instead of that heroic simplicity and unaffected grandeur, which they inherit from Raphael, had, each of them, both in countenance and gesture, all the canting, solemn, melodramatic mawkishness of Mackenzie's Father Nicholas. When I was last at Haydon's, I looked over a book of prints, taken from the fresco of the church at Milan, the name of which I forget. In it were comprised specimens of the first and second age in Art in Italy. I do not think I ever had a greater treat, out of Shakspeare; full of romance and the most tender feeling; magnificence of drapery beyond everything I ever saw, not excepting Raphael's—but grotesque to a curious pitch; yet still making up a fine whole, even finer to me than more accomplished works, as there was left so much room for imagination. I have not heard one of this last course of Hazlitt's Lectures. They were upon Wit and Humour, the English Comic Writers, etc.

I do not think I have anything to say in the business-way. You will let me know what you would wish done with your property in England—what things you would wish sent out. But I am quite in the dark even as to your arrival in America. Your first letter will be the key by which I shall open your hearts and see what spaces want filling with any particular information. Whether the affairs of Europe are more or less interesting to you; whether you would like to hear of the Theatres, the Bear-Garden, the Boxers, the Painters, the Lecturers, the Dress, the progress of Dandyism, the progress of Courtship, or the fate of Mary M——, being a full, true, and *très* particular account of Miss Mary's ten suitors; how the first tried the effect of swearing, the second of stammering, the third of whispering, the fourth of sonnets, the fifth of Spanish-leather boots, the sixth of flattering her body, the seventh of flattering her mind, the eighth of flattering himself, the ninth of sticking to the mother, the tenth of kissing the chamber-maid and bidding her tell her mistress—but he was soon discharged.

And now, for the time, I bid you good-bye.

Your most affectionate Brother,

JOHN.

14 *February* [1819].

MY DEAR BROTHER AND SISTER,

How is it that we have not heard from you at the Settlement ? Surely the letters have miscarried. I am still at Wentworth Place; indeed, I have kept indoors lately, resolved, if possible, to rid myself of my sore throat; consequently I have not been to see your mother since my return from Chichester. Nothing worth speaking of happened at either place. I took down some of the thin paper, and wrote on it a little poem called *St. Agnes' Eve*, which you will have as it is, when I have finished the blank part of the rest for you. I went out twice, at Chichester, to old dowager card-parties. I see very little now, and very few persons—being almost tired of men and things. Brown and Dilke are very kind and considerate towards me. Another satire is expected from Lord Byron, called *Don Giovanni*. Yesterday I went to town for the first time these three weeks. I met people from all parts and of all sects. Mr. Woodhouse was looking up at a book-window in Newgate-street, and, being short-sighted, twisted his muscles into so queer a style, that I stood by, in doubt whether it was him or his brother, if he has one; and, turning round, saw Mr. Hazlitt, with his son. Woodhouse proved to be Woodhouse, and not his brother, on his features subsiding. I have had a little business with Mr. Abbey; from time to time he has behaved to me with a little *brusquerie*; this hurt me a little, especially when I knew him to be the only man in England who dared to say a thing to me I did not approve of, without its being resented, or, at least, noticed—so I wrote him about it, and have made an alteration in my favour. I expect from this to see more of Fanny, who has been quite shut up from me. I see Cobbett has been attacking the Settlement; but I cannot tell what to believe, and shall be all at elbows till I hear from you. Mrs. S. met me the other day. I heard she said a thing I am not at all contented with. Says she, "O, he is quite the little poet." Now this is abominable; you might as well say Bonaparte is "quite the little soldier." You see what it is to be under six feet, and not a Lord.

.   .   .   .   .   .

In my next packet I shall send you my *Pot of Basil*, *St. Agnes' Eve*, and, if I should have finished it, a little thing, called the *Eve of St. Mark*. You see what fine Mother Radcliffe names I have. It is not my fault; I did not search for them. I have not gone on with *Hyperion*, for, to tell the truth, I have not been in great cue for writing lately. I must wait for the spring to rouse me a little.

Friday, 18*th February*.—The day before yesterday I went to Romney-street; your mother was not at home. We lead very quiet lives here; Dilke is, at present, at Greek history and antiquities, and talks of nothing but the Elections of Westminster and the Retreat of the Ten Thousand. I never drink above three glasses of wine, and never any spirits and water; though, by the bye, the other day Woodhouse took me to his coffee-house, and ordered a bottle of claret. How I like claret! when I can get claret, I must drink it. 'Tis the only palate affair that I am at all sensual in. Would it not be a good spec. to send you some vine-roots? Could it be done? I'll inquire. If you could make some wine like claret, to drink on summer evenings in an arbour! It fills one's mouth with a gushing freshness, then goes down cool and feverless: then, you do not feel it quarrelling with one's liver. No; 'tis rather a peace-maker, and lies as quiet as it did in the grape. Then it is as fragrant as the Queen Bee, and the more ethereal part mounts into the brain, not assaulting the cerebral apart-ments, like a bully looking for his trull, and hurrying from door to door, bouncing against the wainscot, but rather walks like Aladdin about his enchanted palace, so gently that you do not feel his step. Other wines of a heavy and spirituous nature transform a man into a Silenus, this makes him a Hermes, and gives a woman the soul and immortality of an Ariadne, for whom Bacchus always kept a good cellar of claret, and even of that he never could persuade her to take above two cups. I said this same claret is the only palate-passion I have; I forgot game; I must plead guilty to the breast of a partridge, the back of a hare, the back-bone of a grouse, the wing and side of a pheasant, and a wood-cock *passim*. Talking of game (I wish I could make it), the lady whom I met at Hastings, and of whom I wrote you, I think, has lately sent me many presents of game, and enabled me to make as many. She made me take home a pheasant the other day, which I gave to Mrs. Dilke. The next I intend for your mother. I have not said in any letter a word about my own affairs. In a word, I am in no despair about them. My poem has not at all succeeded. In the course of a year or so I think I shall try the public again. In a selfish point of view I should suffer my pride and my contempt of public opinion to hold me silent; but for yours and Fanny's sake, I will pluck up spirit and try it again. I have no doubt of success in a course of years, if I persevere; but I must be patient; for the reviewers have enervated men's minds, and made them indolent; few think for themselves. These reviews are getting more and more powerful, especially the *Quarterly*. They are like a superstition, which, the more it prostrates the crowd, and the longer it continues, the more it becomes powerful, just in proportion to their increasing weakness. I was in hopes that, as people saw, as they must do now, all the trickery and iniquity of these plagues, they would scout them; but no; they are like the spectators at the Westminster cock-pit, they like the battle, and do not care who wins or who loses.

On Monday we had to dinner Severn and Cawthorn, the bookseller and print-virtuoso; in the evening Severn went home to paint, and we other three went to the play, to see Sheil's new tragedy ycleped *Evadne*. In the morning Severn and I took a turn round the Museum; there is a sphinx there of a giant size, and most voluptuous Egyptian expression; I had not seen it before. The play was bad, even in comparison with 1818, the "Augustan age of the drama." The whole was made up of a virtuous young woman, an indignant brother, a suspecting lover, a libertine prince, a gratuitous villain, a street in Naples, a cypress grove, lilies and roses, virtue and vice, a bloody sword, a spangled jacket, one "Lady Olivia," one Miss O'Neil, *alias* "Evadne," *alias* "Bellamira." The play is a fine amusement, as a friend of mine

once said to me: "Do what you will," says he, "a poor gentleman who wants a guinea cannot spend his two shillings better
than at the playhouse." The pantomime was excellent; I had
seen it before, and enjoyed it again.

Your mother and I had some talk about Miss ——. Says I,
"Will Henry have that Miss ——, a lath with a boddice, she
who has been fine-drawn—fit for nothing but to cut up into
cribbage-pins; one who is all muslin; all feathers and bone?
Once, in travelling, she was made use of as a linch-pin. I hope
he will not have her, though it is no uncommon thing to be
smitten with a staff—though she might be useful as his walking-
stick, his fishing-rod, his tooth-pick, his hat-stick (she runs so
much in his head). Let him turn farmer, she would cut into
hurdles; let him write poetry, she would be his turn-style.
Her gown is like a flag on a pole: she would do for him if he
turn freemason; I hope she will prove a flag of truce. When
she sits languishing, with her one foot on a stool, and one
elbow on the table, and her head inclined, she looks like
the sign of the Crooked Billet, or the frontispiece to
Cinderella, or a tea-paper wood-cut of Mother Shipton at
her studies."

The nothing of the day is a machine called the "Velocipede."
It is a wheel-carriage to ride cock-horse upon, sitting astride
and pushing it along with the toes, a rudder-wheel in hand.
They will go seven miles an hour. A handsome gelding will
come to eight guineas; however, they will soon be cheaper,
unless the army takes to them.

I look back upon the last month, and find nothing to write
about; indeed, I do not recollect one thing particular in it.
It's all alike; we keep on breathing; the only amusement is a
little scandal, of however fine a shape, a laugh at a pun—and
then, after all, we wonder how we could enjoy the scandal
or laugh at the pun.

I have been, at different times, turning it in my head,
whether I should go to Edinburgh, and study for a physician.
I am afraid I should not take kindly to it; I am sure I could
not take fees: and yet I should like to do so; it is not worse
than writing poems, and hanging them up to be fly-blown on
the Review shambles. Everybody is in his own mess: here is
the Parson at Hampstead quarrelling with all the world; he
is in the wrong by this same token; when the black cloth was
put up in the church, for the Queen's mourning, he asked the

workmen to hang it the wrong side outwards, that it might be better when taken down, it being his perquisite.

Friday, 19th March.—This morning I have been reading *The False One*. Shameful to say, I was in bed at ten—I mean, this morning. The "Blackwood's Reviewers" have committed themselves to a scandalous heresy; they have been putting up Hogg, the Ettrick Shepherd, against Burns: the senseless villains! The Scotch cannot manage themselves at all, they want imagination; and that is why they are so fond of Hogg, who has so little of it. This morning I am in a sort of temper, indolent and supremely careless; I long after a stanza or two of Thomson's *Castle of Indolence*; my passions are all asleep, from my having slumbered till nearly eleven, and weakened the animal fibre all over me, to a delightful sensation, about three degrees on this side of faintness. If I had teeth of pearl, and the breath of lilies, I should call it languor; but, as I am, I must call it laziness. In this state of effeminacy, the fibres of the brain are relaxed, in common with the rest of the body, and to such a happy degree, that pleasure has no show of enticement, and pain no unbearable frown; neither Poetry, nor Ambition, nor Love, have any alertness of countenance; as they pass by me, they seem rather like three figures on a Greek vase, two men and a woman, whom no one but myself could distinguish in their disguisement. This is the only happiness, and is a rare instance of advantage in the body overpowering the mind.

I have this moment received a note from Haslam, in which he writes that he expects the death of his father, who has been for some time in a state of insensibility; I shall go to town to-morrow to see him. This is the world; thus we cannot expect to give away many hours to pleasure; circumstances are like clouds, continually gathering and bursting; while we are laughing, the seed of trouble is put into the wide arable land of events; while we are laughing, it sprouts, it grows, and suddenly bears a poisonous fruit, which we must pluck. Even so we have leisure to reason on the misfortunes of our friends: our own touch us too nearly for words. Very few men have ever arrived at a complete disinterestedness of mind; very few have been interested by a pure desire of the benefit of others: in the greater part of the benefactors of humanity, some meretricious motive has sullied their greatness, some melodramatic scenery has fascinated them. From the manner in which I feel Haslam's misfortune I perceive how far I am from any humble standard of disinterestedness; yet this feeling ought to be carried to its highest pitch, as there is no fear of its ever injuring society. In wild nature, the Hawk would lose his breakfast of robins, and the Robin his of worms; the Lion must starve as well as the Swallow. The great part of men sway their way with the same instinctiveness, the same unwandering eye from their purposes, the same animal eagerness, as the Hawk: the Hawk wants a mate, so does the Man; look at them both; they set about it, and procure one in the same manner; they want both a nest, and they both set about one in the same manner. The noble animal, Man, for his amusement, smokes his pipe, the Hawk balances about the clouds: that is the only difference of their leisures. This is that which makes the amusement of life to a speculative mind; I go among the fields, and catch a glimpse of a stoat or a field-mouse, peeping out of the withered grass; the creature hath a purpose, and its eyes are bright with it; I go amongst the buildings of a city, and I see a man hurrying along—to what? —the creature hath a purpose, and its eyes are bright with it: —but then, as Wordsworth says, "We have all one human heart!" There is an electric fire in human nature, tending to purify; so that, among these human creatures, there is continually some birth of new heroism; the pity is, that we must wonder at it, as we should at finding a pearl in rubbish. I have no doubt that thousands of people, never heard of, have had hearts completely disinterested. I can remember but two, Socrates and Jesus. Their histories evince it. What I heard Taylor observe with respect to Socrates is true of Jesus: that, though he transmitted no writing of his own to posterity, we have his mind, and his sayings, and his greatness, handed down to us by others. Even here, though I am pursuing the same instinctive course as the veriest animal you can think of—I am, however, young, and writing at random, straining after particles of light in the midst of a great darkness, without knowing the bearing of any one assertion, of any one opinion —yet, in this may I not be free from sin? May there not be superior beings, amused with any graceful, though instinctive, attitude my mind may fall into, as I am entertained with the alertness of the stoat, or the anxiety of the deer? Though a quarrel in the street is a thing to be hated, the energies displayed in it are fine; the commonest man shows a grace in his quarrel. By a superior Being our reasonings may take the same tone; though erroneous, they may be fine. This is the very thing in which consists Poetry, and if so, it is not so fine a thing as Philosophy, for the same reason that an eagle is not so fine a thing as truth. Give me this credit, do you not think I strive to know myself? Give me this credit, and you will not think, that on my own account I repeat the lines of Milton:

> How charming is divine philosophy,
> Not harsh and crabbed, as dull fools suppose,
> But musical as is Apollo's lute.

No, not for myself, feeling grateful, as I do, to have got into a state of mind to relish them properly. Nothing ever becomes real till it is experienced; even a proverb is no proverb to you till life has illustrated it.

I am afraid that your anxiety for me leads you to fear for the violence of my temperament, continually smothered down: for that reason, I did not intend to have sent you the following Sonnet; but look over the two last pages, and ask yourself if I have not that in me which will bear the buffets of the world. It will be the best comment on my Sonnet; it will show you that it was written with no agony but that of ignorance, with no thirst but that of knowledge, when pushed to the point; though the first steps to it were through my human passions, they went away, and I wrote with my mind, and, perhaps, I must confess, a little bit of my heart.

> Why did I laugh to-night? No voice will tell, etc.[1]

I went to bed and enjoyed uninterrupted sleep: sane went to bed, and sane I arose.

15th April.—You see what a time it is since I wrote; all that time I have been, day after day, expecting letters from you. I write quite in the dark. In hopes of a letter to-day I deferred till night, that I might write in the light. It looks so much like rain, I shall not go to town to-day, but put it off till to-morrow. Brown, this morning, is writing some Spenserian stanzas against Miss B—— and me: so I shall amuse myself with him a little, in the manner of Spenser.

> He is to weet a melancholy carle:
> Thin in the waist, with bushy head of hair,
> As hath the seeded thistle, when a parle
> It holds with Zephyr, ere it sendeth fair
> Its light balloons into the summer air;

---

[1] See the *Literary Remains.*

Therto his beard had not begun to bloom,
No brush had touched his chin, or razor sheer;
No care had touched his cheek with mortal doom,
But new he was, and bright, as scarf from Persian loom.

Ne cared he for wine or half-and-half;
Ne cared he for fish, or flesh, or fowl;
And sauces held he worthless as the chaff;
He 'sdeigned the swine-head at the wassail-bowl;
Ne with lewd ribbalds sat he cheek by jowl;
Ne with sly lemans in the scorner's chair;
But after water-brooks this pilgrim's soul
Panted, and all his food was woodland air;
Though he would oft-times feast on gilliflowers rare.

The slang of cities in no wise he knew,
Tipping the wink to him was heathen Greek;
He sipped no "olden Tom," or "ruin blue,"
Or Nantz, or cherry-brandy, drank full meek
By many a damsel brave, and rouge of cheek;
Nor did he know each aged watchman's beat,
Nor in obscured purlieus would he seek
For curled Jewesses, with ankles neat,
Who, as they walk abroad, make tinkling with their feet.

This character would ensure him a situation in the establishment of the patient Griselda. Brown is gone to bed, and I am tired of writing; there is a north wind playing green-gooseberry with the trees, it blows so keen. I don't care, so it helps, even with a side-wind, a letter to me.

The fifth canto of Dante pleases me more and more; it is that one in which he meets with Paulo and Francesca. I had passed many days in rather a low state of mind, and in the midst of them I dreamt of being in that region of Hell. The dream was one of the most delightful enjoyments I ever had in my life; I floated about the wheeling atmosphere, as it is described, with a beautiful figure, to whose lips mine were joined, it seemed for an age; and in the midst of all this cold and darkness I was warm; ever-flowery tree-tops sprung up, and we rested on them, sometimes with the lightness of a cloud, till the wind blew us away again. I tried a Sonnet on it: there are fourteen lines in it, but nothing of what I felt. Oh! that I could dream it every night.

When lulled Argus, baffled, swooned and slept, etc.[1]

I want very much a little of your wit, my dear sister—a letter of yours just to bandy back a pun or two across the Atlantic, and send a quibble over the Floridas. Now, by this

[1] See the *Literary Remains*.

time you have crumpled up your large bonnet, what do you wear?—a cap! Do you put your hair in paper of nights? Do you pay the Misses Birkbeck a morning visit? Have you any tea, or do you milk-and-water with them? What place of worship do you go to—the Quakers, the Moravians, the Unitarians, or the Methodists? Are there any flowers in bloom you like? Any beautiful heaths? Any streets full of corset-makers? What sort of shoes have you to put those pretty feet of yours in? Do you desire compliments to one another? Do you ride on horseback? What do you have for breakfast, dinner, and supper, without mentioning lunch and bite, and wet and snack, and a bit to stay one's stomach? Do you get any spirits? Now you might easily distil some whisky, and, going into the woods, set up a whisky-shop for the monkeys! Do you and the other ladies get groggy on anything? A little so-so-ish, so as to be seen home with a lanthorn? You may perhaps have a game at Puss-in-the-corner: ladies are war-ranted to play at this game, though they have not whiskers. Have you a fiddle in the Settlement, or, at any rate, a Jew's-harp which will play in spite of one's teeth? When you have nothing else to do for a whole day, I'll tell you how you may employ it: first get up, and when you are dressed, as it would be pretty early, with a high wind in the woods, give George a cold pig, with my compliments, then you may saunter into the nearest coffee-house, and after taking a dram and a look at the *Chronicle*, go and frighten the wild bears on the strength of it. You may as well bring one home for breakfast, serving up the hoofs, garnished with bristles, and a grunt or two, to accompany the singing of the kettle. Then, if George is not up, give him a colder pig, always with my compliments. After you have eaten your breakfast, keep your eye upon dinner, it is the safest way; you should keep a hawk's eye over your dinner, and keep hovering over it till due time, then pounce upon it, taking care not to break any plates. While you are hovering with your dinner in prospect, you may do a thousand things—put a hedge-hog into George's hat, pour a little water into his rifle, soak his boots in a pail of water, cut his jacket round into shreds, like a Roman kilt, or the back of my grandmother's stays, tear off his buttons——

The following poem, the last I have written, is the first and only one with which I have taken even moderate pains; I have, for the most part, dashed off my lines in a hurry; this one I have done leisurely; I think it reads the more richly for it, and it will I hope encourage me to write other things in even a more peaceable and healthy spirit. You must recollect that Psyche was not embodied as a goddess before the time of Apuleius the Platonist, who lived after the Augustan age, and consequently the goddess was never worshipped or sacrificed to with any of the ancient fervour, and perhaps never thought of in the old religion: I am more orthodox than to let a heathen goddess be so neglected.

(Here follows the "Ode to Psyche" already published.)

I have been endeavouring to discover a better Sonnet stanza than we have. The legitimate does not suit the language well, from the pouncing rhymes; the other appears too elegiac, and the couplet at the end of it has seldom a pleasing effect. I do not pretend to have succeeded. It will explain itself:

If by dull rhymes our English must be chained, etc.[1]

This is the third of May, and everything is in delightful forwardness: the violets are not withered before the peeping of the first rose. You must let me know everything, now parcels go and come—what papers you have, and what newspapers you want, and other things. God bless you, my dear brother and sister.

Your ever affectionate brother,

JOHN KEATS.

The family of George Keats in America possess a Dante covered with his brother's marginal notes and observations, and these annotations on *Paradise Lost* appeared in an American periodical of much literary and philosophical merit, entitled *The Dial*; they were written in the fly-leaves of the book, and are in the tone of thought that generated *Hyperion*.

[1] See the *Literary Remains.*

NOTES ON MILTON

The genius of Milton, more particularly in respect to its span in immensity, calculated him by a sort of birthright for such an argument as the *Paradise Lost*. He had an exquisite passion for what is properly, in the sense of ease and pleasure, poetical luxury; and with that, it appears to me, he would fain have been content, if he could, so doing, preserve his self-respect and feeling of duty performed; but there was working in him, as it were, that same sort of thing which operates in the great world to the end of a prophecy's being accomplished. Therefore he devoted himself rather to the ardours than the pleasures of song, solacing himself, at intervals, with cups of old wine; and those are, with some exceptions, the finest parts of the poem. With some exceptions; for the spirit of mounting and adventure can never be unfruitful nor unrewarded. Had he not broken through the clouds which envelop so deliciously the Elysian fields of verse, and committed himself to the extreme, we should never have seen Satan as described.

> But his face
> Deep scars of thunder had entrenched, etc.

There is a greatness which the *Paradise Lost* possesses over every other Poem, the magnitude of contrast, and that is softened by the contrast being ungrotesque to a degree. Heaven moves on like music throughout.

Hell is also peopled with angels; it also moves on like music, not grating and harsh, but like a grand accompaniment in the bass to Heaven.

There is always a great charm in the openings of great Poems, particularly where the action begins, as that of Dante's Hell. Of Hamlet, the first step must be heroic and full of power; and nothing can be more impressive and shaded than the commencement here:

> Round he throws his baleful eyes
> That witnessed huge affliction and dismay,
> Mixed with obdurate pride and stedfast hate; etc.
> *Paradise Lost*, Book i., l. 56.

To slumber here, as in the vales of heaven.
> Book i., l. 321.

There is a cool pleasure in the very sound of *vale*.

The English word is of the happiest chance [choice]. Milton has put vales in Heaven and Hell with the very utter affection and yearning of a great Poet. It is a sort of Delphic abstraction, a beautiful thing made more beautiful by being reflected and put in a mist. The next mention of "vale" is one of the most pathetic in the whole range of poetry.

> Others more mild
> Retreated in a silent valley, sing,
> With notes angelical, to many a harp,
> Their own heroic deeds and hapless fall
> By doom of battle! and complain that fate
> Free virtue should inthrall to force or chance.
> Their song was partial; but the harmony
> (What could it less when spirits immortal sing?)
> Suspended hell, and took with ravishment
> The thronging audience.

> Book ii., l. 547.

How much of the charm is in the word *valley*!

The light and shade, the sort of black brightness, the ebon diamonding, the Ethiop immortality, the sorrow, the pain, the sad sweet melody, the phalanges of spirits so depressed as to be "uplifted beyond hope," the short mitigation of misery, the thousand melancholies and magnificencies of the following lines leave no room for anything to be said thereon, but "so it is."

> That proud honour claimed
> Azazel as his right, a cherub tall,
> Who forthwith from the glittering staff unfurled
> The imperial ensign, which, full high advanced,
> Shone like a meteor streaming to the wind,
> With gems and golden lustre rich emblazed,
> Seraphic arms and trophies; all the while
> Sonorous metal blowing martial sounds;
> At which the universal host up-sent
> A shout, that tore hell's concave, and beyond
> Frighted the reign of Chaos and old Night.
> All in a moment through the gloom were seen
> Ten thousand banners rise into the air
> With orient colours waving; with them rose
> A forest huge of spears; and thronging helms
> Appeared, and serried shields in thick array,
> Of depth immeasurable; anon they move
> In perfect phalanx to the Dorian mood
> Of flutes and soft recorders; such as raised
> To height of noblest temper heroes old
> Arming to battle; and instead of rage
> Deliberate valour breathed, firm and unmoved
> With dread of death to flight or foul retreat;
> Nor wanting power to mitigate and suage

With solemn touches troubled thoughts, and chase
Anguish, and doubt, and fear, and sorrow, and pain
From mortal or immortal minds. Thus they
Breathing united force, with fixed thought,
Moved on in silence to soft pipes, that charmed
Their painful steps o'er the burnt soil; and now
Advanced in view they stand, a horrid front
Of dreadful length and dazzling arms, in guise
Of warriors old with ordered spear and shield,
Awaiting what command their mighty chief
Had to impose.

Book i., ll. 533–67.

How noble and collected an indignation against kings, line 595, book i. His very wishing should have had power to pluck that feeble animal Charles from his bloody throne. The evil days had come to him; he hit the new system of things a mighty mental blow; the exertion must have had, or is yet to have, some sequences.

The management of this poem is Apollonian. Satan first "throws round his baleful eyes," then awakes his legions; he consults, he sets forward on his voyage, and just as he is getting to the end of it, see the Great God and our first Parent, and that same Satan, all brought in one vision; we have the invocation to light before we mount to heaven, we breathe more freely, we feel the great author's consolations coming thick upon him at a time when he complains most; we are getting ripe for diversity; the immediate topic of the poem opens with a grand perspective of all concerned.

Book iv. A friend of mine says this book has the finest opening of any; the point of time is gigantically critical, the wax is melted, the seal about to be applied, and Milton breaks out,

O for that warning voice, etc.

There is, moreover, an opportunity for a grandeur of tenderness. The opportunity is not lost. Nothing can be higher, nothing so more than Delphic.

There are two specimens of a very extraordinary beauty in the *Paradise Lost*; they are of a nature, so far as I have read, unexampled elsewhere; they are entirely distinct from the brief pathos of Dante, and they are not to be found even in Shakspeare. These are, according to the great prerogative of poetry, better described in themselves than by a volume. The one is in line 268, book iv.

> Not that fair field
> Of Enna, where Proserpine gathering flowers,
> Herself a fairer flower, by gloomy Dis
> Was gathered, which cost Ceres all that pain
> To seek her through the world.

The other is that ending "nor could the Muse defend her son."

> But drive far off the barbarous dissonance
> Of Bacchus and his revellers, the race
> Of that wild rout that tore the Thracian bard
> In Rhodope, where woods and rocks had ears
> To rapture, till the savage clamour drowned
> Both harp and voice; nor could the Muse defend
> Her son.

These appear exclusively Miltonic, without the shadow of another mind ancient or modern.

Book vi., line 58. *Reluctant*, with its original and modern meaning combined and woven together, with all its shades of signification, has a powerful effect.

Milton in many instances pursues his imagination to the utmost, he is "sagacious of his quarry," he sees beauty on the wing, pounces upon it, and gorges it to the producing his essential verse.

> So from the root springs lither the green stalk.

But in no instance is this sort of perseverance more exemplified, than in what may be called his *stationing* or *statuary*. He is not content with simple description, he must station; thus here we not only see how the birds *"with clang despised the ground,"* but we see them *"under a cloud in prospect."* So we see Adam *"fair indeed, and tall,"* *"under a plantain,"* and so we see Satan *"disfigured . . . on the Assyrian mount."*

The copy of "Spenser" which Keats had in daily use contains the following stanza, inserted at the close of canto ii. book v. His sympathies were very much on the side of the revolutionary "Gyant," who "undertook for to repair" the "realms and nations run awry," and to suppress "tyrants that make men subject to their law," "and lordings curbe that commons over-aw," while he grudged the legitimate victory, as he rejected the conservative philosophy, of the "righteous Artegall" and his comrade, the fierce defender of privilege and order. And he expressed, in this *ex post facto* prophecy, his conviction of the ultimate triumph of freedom and equality by the power of transmitted knowledge.

> In after-time, a sage of mickle lore
> Yclep'd Typographus, the Giant took,
> And did refit his limbs as heretofore,
> And made him read in many a learned book,
> And into many a lively legend look;
> Thereby in goodly themes so training him,
> That all his brutishness he quite forsook,
> When, meeting Artegall and Talus grim,
> The one he struck stone-blind, the other's eyes wox dim.

The *Literary Remains* will contain many sonnets and songs, written during these months, in the intervals of more complete compositions; but the following pieces are so fragmentary as more becomingly to take their place in the narrative of the author's life, than to show as substantive productions. Yet it is, perhaps, just in verses like these that the individual character pronounces itself most distinctly, and confers a general interest which more care of art at once elevates and diminishes. The occasional verses of a great poet are records, as it were, of his poetical table-talk, remembrances of his daily self and its intellectual companionship, more delightful from what they recall, than for what they are—more interesting for what they suggest, than for what they were ever meant to be.

FRAGMENT

> Where's the Poet? show him! show him!
> Muses nine! that I may know him!
> 'Tis the man who with a man
> Is an equal, be he King,
> Or poorest of the beggar-clan,
> Or any other wondrous thing
> A man may be 'twixt ape and Plato;
> 'Tis the man who with a bird,
> Wren, or Eagle, finds his way to
> All its instincts; he hath heard
> The Lion's roaring, and can tell
> What his horny throat expresseth;
> And to him the Tiger's yell
> Comes articulate and presseth
> On his ear like mother-tongue.

MODERN LOVE

And what is love? It is a doll dress'd up
For idleness to cosset, nurse, and dandle;
A thing of soft misnomers, so divine
That silly youth doth think to make itself
Divine by loving, and so goes on
Yawning and doting a whole summer long,
Till Miss's comb is made a pearl tiara,
And common Wellingtons turn Romeo boots;
Then Cleopatra lives at number seven,
And Anthony resides in Brunswick Square.
Fools! if some passions high have warm'd the world,
If Queens and Soldiers have play'd deep for hearts,
It is no reason why such agonies
Should be more common than the growth of weeds.
Fools! make me whole again that weighty pearl
The Queen of Egypt melted, and I'll say
That ye may love in spite of beaver hats.

FRAGMENT OF "THE CASTLE BUILDER"

.　　　.　　　.　　　.　　　.　　　.

To-night I'll have my friar,—let me think
About my room,—I'll have it in the pink;
It should be rich and sombre, and the moon,
Just in its mid-life in the midst of June,
Should look thro' four large windows and display
Clear, but for gold-fish vases in the way,
Their glassy diamonding on Turkish floor;
The tapers keep aside, an hour and more,
To see what else the moon alone can show;
While the night-breeze doth softly let us know
My terrace is well bower'd with oranges.
Upon the floor the dullest spirit sees
A guitar-riband and a lady's glove
Beside a crumple-leaved tale of love;
A tambour-frame, with Venus sleeping there,
All finished but some ringlets of her hair;
A viol, bow-strings torn, cross-wise upon
A glorious folio of Anacreon;
A skull upon a mat of roses lying,
Ink'd purple with a song concerning dying;
An hour-glass on the turn, amid the trails
Of passion-flower;—just in time there sails
A cloud across the moon,—the lights bring in!
And see what more my phantasy can win.
It is a gorgeous room, but somewhat sad;
The draperies are so, as tho' they had
Been made for Cleopatra's winding sheet;
And opposite the stedfast eye doth meet
A spacious looking-glass, upon whose face,
In letters raven-sombre, you may trace
Old "Mene, Mene, Tekel Upharsin."
Greek busts and statuary have ever been

Held, by the finest spirits, fitter far
Than vase grotesque and Siamesian jar;
Therefore 'tis sure a want of Attic taste
That I should rather love a Gothic waste
Of eyesight on cinque-coloured potter's clay,
Than on the marble fairness of old Greece.
My table-coverlets of Jason's fleece
And black Numidian sheep-wool should be wrought,
Gold, black, and heavy from the Lama brought.
My ebon sofas should delicious be
With down from Leda's cygnet progeny.
My pictures all Salvator's, save a few
Of Titian's portraiture, and one, though new,
Of Haydon's in its fresh magnificence.
My wine—O good! 'tis here at my desire,
And I must sit to supper with my friar.

·   ·   ·   ·   ·   ·

FRAGMENT

"Under the flag
Of each his faction, they to battle bring
Their embryo atoms."—MILTON.

Welcome joy, and welcome sorrow,
    Lethe's weed, and Hermes' feather;
Come to-day, and come to-morrow,
    I do love you both together!—
I love to mark sad faces in fair weather;
And hear a merry laugh amid the thunder;
    Fair and foul I love together:
Meadows sweet where flames are under,
And a giggle at a wonder;
Visage sage at pantomime;
Funeral, and steeple-chime;
Infant playing with a skull;
Morning fair, and shipwreck'd hull;
Nightshade with the woodbine kissing;
Serpents in red roses hissing;
Cleopatra regal-dress'd
With the aspic at her breast;
Dancing music, music sad,
Both together, sane and mad;
Muses bright, and Muses pale;
Sombre Saturn, Momus hale;—
Laugh and sigh, and laugh again;
Oh the sweetness of the pain!
Muses bright, and Muses pale,
Bare your faces of the veil;
Let me see: and let me write
Of the day, and of the night—
Both together:—let me slake
All my thirst for sweet heart-ache!
Let my bower be of yew,
Interwreath'd with myrtles new;
Pines and lime-trees full in bloom,
And my couch a low grass tomb.

A singular instance of Keats's delicate perception occurred in the composition of the *Ode on Melancholy*. In the original manuscript he had intended to represent the vulgar con nection of Melancholy with gloom and horror, in contrast with the emotion that incites to

> glut thy sorrow on a morning rose,
> Or on the rainbow of the salt sand-wave,
> Or on the wealth of globed peonies;

and which essentially

> lives in Beauty—Beauty that must die,
> And Joy, whose hand is ever at his lips
> Bidding adieu.

The first stanza, therefore, was the following, as grim a picture as Blake or Fuseli could have dreamed and painted:

> Though you should build a bark of dead men's bones,
>   And rear a phantom gibbet for a mast,
> Stitch shrouds together for a sail, with groans
>   To fill it out, blood-stained and aghast;
> Although your rudder be a dragon's tail
>   Long severed, yet still hard with agony,
>   Your cordage large uprootings from the skull
> Of bald Medusa, certes you would fail
>   To find the Melancholy—whether she
>   Dreameth in any isle of Lethe dull.

But no sooner was this written than the poet became conscious that the coarseness of the contrast would destroy the general effect of luxurious tenderness which it was the object of the poem to produce, and he confined the gross notion of Melancholy to less violent images, and let the ode at once begin:

> No, no! go not to Lethe, neither twist
>   Wolf's-bane, tight-rooted, for its poisonous wine;
> Nor suffer thy pale forehead to be kissed
>   By nightshade, ruby grape of Proserpine, etc.

The *Eve of St. Agnes* was begun on a visit in Hampshire, at the commencement of this year, and finished on his return to Hampstead. It is written still under Spenserian influences, but with a striking improvement in form, both of diction and versification; the story is easily conducted, and the details picturesque in the highest degree, without the intricate designing of the earlier poems. Lord Jeffrey remarks: "The glory and charm of the poem is the description of the fair maiden's antique chamber and of all that passes in that sweet and angel-guarded sanctuary, every part of which is touched with colours at once rich and delicate, and the whole chastened and harmonised in the midst of its gorgeous distinctness by a pervading grace and purity, that indicate not less clearly the exaltation, than the refinement of the author's fancy."

The greater part of this summer [1819] was passed at Shanklin, in the Isle of Wight, in company with Mr. Brown, who earnestly encouraged the full development of the genius of his friend. A combination of intellectual effort was here attempted which could hardly have been expected to be very successful. They were to write a play between them—Brown to supply the fable, characters, and dramatic conduct—Keats, the diction and the verse. The two com posers sat opposite at a table, and as Mr. Brown sketched out the incidents of each scene, Keats translated them into his rich and ready language. As a literary diversion, this process was probably both amusing and instructive, but it does not require any profound æsthetic pretensions to pronounce that a work of art thus created could hardly be worthy of the name. Joint compositions, except of a humorous character, are always dangerous attempts, and it is doubtful whether such a transference of faculties as they presuppose, is possible at all; at any rate, the unity of form and feeling must receive an injury hard to be compensated by any apparent improvement of the several parts. Nay, it is quite conceivable that two men, either of whom would have separately produced an effective work, should give an incomplete and hybrid character to a common production, sufficient to neutralise every excellence and annihilate every charm. A poem or a drama is not a picture, in which one artist may paint the landscape, and another the figures; and a certain imperfection and inferiority of parts is often more agreeable than an attempt at that entire completeness which it is only given to the very highest to attain. The incidents, as suggested by Mr. Brown, after some time struck Keats as too melodramatic, and he completed the fifth act alone. This tragedy, *Otho the Great*, was sent to Drury Lane, and accepted by Elliston, with a promise to bring it forward the same season. Kean seems to have been pleased with the principal character, and to have expressed a desire to act it. The manager, however, from some unknown cause, declared himself unable to perform his engagement, and Mr. Brown, who conducted the negotiation without mention of Keats's name, withdrew the manuscript and offered it to Covent Garden, where it met with no better fate, to the considerable annoyance of the author, who wrote to his friend Rice, "'Twould do one's heart good to see Macready in Ludolph." The unfitness of this tragedy for representation is too apparent to permit the managers of the two theatres to be accused of injustice or partiality. Had the name of Keats been as popular as it was obscure, and his previous writing as successful as it was misrepresented and misunderstood, there was not sufficient interest in either the plot or the characters to keep the play on the stage for a week. The story is confused and unreal, and the personages are mere embodied passions; the heroine and her brother walk through the whole piece like the demons of an old romance, and the historical character, who gives his name to the play, is almost excluded from its action and made a part of the pageantry. To the reader, however, the want of interest is fully redeemed by the beauty and power of passages continually recurring, and which are not cited here, only because it is pleasanter for everyone to find them out for himself. There is scarce a page without some touch of a great poet, and the contrast between the glory of the diction and the poverty of the invention is very striking. I own I doubt whether, if the contrivance of the double authorship had not been resorted to, Keats could of himself, at least at this time, have produced a much better play: the failure of Coleridge's *Remorse* is an example to the point, and it is probable that the philosophic generalities of the one poet did not stand more in the way of dramatic excellence than the superhuman imagery and creative fancy of the other; it is conceivable that Keats might have written a *Midsummer Night's Dream*, just as Coleridge might have written a *Hamlet*; but in both that great human element would have been wanting, which

Shakespeare so wonderfully combines with abstract reflection and with fairyland.

As soon as Keats had finished *Otho*, Mr. Brown suggested to him the character and reign of King Stephen, beginning with his defeat by the Empress Maud and ending with the death of his son Eustace, as a fine subject for an English historical tragedy. This Keats undertook, assuming, however, to himself the whole conduct of the drama, and wrote some hundred and thirty lines; this task, however, soon gave place to the impressive tale of *Lamia*, which had been in hand for some time, and which he wrote with great care, after much study of Dryden's versification. It is quite the perfection of narrative poetry. The story was taken from that treasure-house of legendary philosophy, Burton's *Anatomy of Melancholy*.

He contemplated a poem of some length on the subject of *Sabrina*, as suggested by Milton, and often spoke of it, but I do not find any fragments of the work.

A letter to Mr. Reynolds, dated Shanklin, 12 July, contains allusions to his literary progress and his pecuniary difficulties.

You will be glad to hear, under my own hand (though Rice says we are like Sauntering Jack and Idle Joe), how diligent I have been, and am being. I have finished the [first] act, and in the interval of beginning the second have proceeded pretty well with *Lamia*, finishing the first part, which consists of about four hundred lines. . . . I have great hopes of success, because I make use of my judgment more deliberately than I have yet done; but in case of failure with the world, I shall find my content. And here (as I know you have my good at heart as much as a brother) I can only repeat to you what I have said to George—that however I should like to enjoy what the competences of life procure, I am in no wise dashed at a different prospect. I have spent too many thoughtful days, and moralised through too many nights for that, and fruitless would they be indeed, if they did not, by degrees, make me look upon the affairs of the world with a healthy deliberation. I have of late been moulting: not for fresh feathers and wings—they are gone, and in their stead I hope to have a pair of patient sublunary legs. I have altered, not from a chrysalis into a butterfly, but the contrary; having two little loopholes, whence I may look out into the stage of the world; and that world, on our coming here, I almost forgot. The first time I sat down to write, I could scarcely believe in the necessity for so doing. It struck me as a great oddity. Yet the very corn which is now so beautiful, as if it had only took to ripening yesterday, is for the market; so, why should I be delicate?

·   ·   ·   ·   ·   ·   ·

SHANKLIN,
2 *August*, 1819.

MY DEAR DILKE,

I will not make my diligence an excuse for not writing to you sooner, because I consider idleness a much better plea. A man in the hurry of business of any sort is expected, and ought to be expected, to look to everything; his mind is in a whirl, and what matters it, what whirl? But to require a letter of a man lost in idleness is the utmost cruelty; you cut the thread of his existence; you beat, you pummel him; you sell his goods and chattels; you put him in prison; you impale him; you crucify him. If I had not put pen to paper since I saw you, this would be to me a *vi et armis* taking up before the judge; but having got over my darling lounging habits a little, it is with scarcely any pain I come to this dating from Shanklin. The Isle of Wight is but so-so, etc. Rice and I passed rather a dull time of it. I hope he will not repent coming with me. He was unwell, and I was not in very good health; and I am afraid we made each other worse by acting upon each other's spirits. We would grow as melancholy as need be. I confess I cannot bear a sick person in a house, especially alone. It weighs upon me day and night, and more so when perhaps the cause is irretrievable. Indeed, I think Rice is in a dangerous state. I have had a letter from him which speaks favourably of his health at present. Brown and I are pretty well harnessed again to our dog-cart. I mean the tragedy, which goes on sinkingly. We are thinking of introducing an elephant, but have not historical reference within reach to determine us as to Otho's menagerie. When Brown first mentioned this I took it for a joke; however, he brings such plausible reasons, and discourses so eloquently on the dramatic effect, that I am giving it a serious consideration. The Art of Poetry is not sufficient for us, and if we get on in that as well as we do in painting, we shall, by next winter, crush the Reviews and the Royal Academy. Indeed, if Brown would take a little of my advice, he could not fail to be first pallette of his day. But, odd as it may appear, he says plainly that he cannot see any force in my plea of putting skies in the background, and leaving Indian-ink out of an ash-tree. The other day he was sketching Shanklin Church, and as I saw how the business was going on, I challenged him to a trial of skill: he lent me pencil and paper. We keep the sketches to contend for the prize at the Gallery. I will not say whose I think best, but really I do not think Brown's done to the top of the Art.

A word or two on the Isle of Wight. I have been no farther than Steephill. If I may guess, I should [say] that there is no finer part in the island than from this place to Steephill. I do not hesitate to say it is fine. Bonchurch is the best. But I have been so many finer walks, with a back-ground of lake and mountain, instead of the sea, that I am not much touched with it, though I credit it for all the surprise I should have felt if it had taken my cockney maidenhead. But I may call myself an old stager in the picturesque, and unless it be something very large and overpowering, I cannot receive any extraordinary relish.

I am sorry to hear that Charles is so much oppressed at Westminster, though I am sure it will be the finest touchstone for his metal in the world. His troubles will grow, day by day, less, as his age and strength increase. The very first battle he wins will lift him from the tribe of Manasseh. I do not know how I should feel were I a father, but I hope I should strive with all my power not to let the present trouble me. When your boy shall be twenty, ask him about his childish troubles, and he will have no more memory of them than you have of yours.

So Reynolds's piece succeeded: that is all well. Papers have, with thanks, been duly received. We leave this place on the 13th, and will let you know where we may be a few days after. Brown says he will write when the fit comes on him. If you will stand law expenses I'll beat him into one before his time.

Your sincere friend,

JOHN KEATS.

In August, the friends removed to Winchester, where Mr. Brown, however, soon left him alone. This was always a favourite residence of Keats: the noble cathedral and its quiet close—the greensward and elm-tree walks were especially agreeable to him. He wrote thence the following letters and extracts:

To Mr. Haydon

I came here in the hopes of getting a library, but there is none: the High Street is as quiet as a lamb. At Mr. Cross's is a very interesting picture of Albert Durer, who, being alive in such warlike times, was perhaps forced to paint in his gauntlets, so we must make all allowances.

.   .   .   .   .   .

I have done nothing, except for the amusement of a few people who refine upon their feelings till anything in the *un*-understandable way will go down with them. I have no cause to complain, because I am certain anything really fine will in these days be felt. I have no doubt that if I had written *Othello* I should have been cheered. I shall go on with patience.

To Mr. Bailey

We removed to Winchester for the convenience of a library, and find it an exceedingly pleasant town, enriched with a beautiful cathedral, and surrounded by a fresh-looking country. We are in tolerably good and cheap lodgings. Within these two months I have written fifteen hundred lines, most of which, besides many more of prior composition, you will probably see by next winter. I have written two tales, one from Boccaccio, called the *Pot of Basil*, and another called *St. Agnes' Eve*, on a popular superstition, and a third called *Lamia* (half-finished). I have also written parts of my *Hyperion*, and completed four acts of a tragedy. It was the opinion of most of my friends that I should never be able to write a scene: I will endeavour to wipe away the prejudice. I sincerely hope you will be pleased when my labours, since we last saw each other, shall reach you. One of my ambitions is to make as great a revolution in modern dramatic writing as Kean has done in acting. Another, to upset the drawling of the blue-stocking literary world. If, in the course of a few years, I do these two things, I ought to die content, and my friends should drink a dozen of claret on my tomb. I am convinced more and more every day that (excepting the human-friend philosopher) a fine writer is the most genuine being in the world. Shakspeare and the *Paradise Lost* every day become greater wonders to me. I look upon fine phrases like a lover.

I was glad to see, by a passage of one of Brown's letters, some time ago, from the North, that you were in such good spirits. Since that, you have been married, and in congratulating you, I wish you every continuance of them. Present my respects to Mrs. Bailey. This sounds oddly to me, and I dare say I do it awkwardly enough; but I suppose by this time it is nothing new to you.

Brown's remembrances to you. As far as I know, we shall remain at Winchester for a goodish while.

Ever your sincere friend,

JOHN KEATS.

WINCHESTER,
23 *August*, 1819.

MY DEAR TAYLOR,

.   .   .   .

I feel every confidence that, if I choose, I may be a popular writer. That I will never be; but for all that I will get a livelihood. I equally dislike the favour of the public with the love of a woman. They are both a cloying treacle to the wings of independence. I shall now consider them (the people) as debtors to me for verses, not myself to them for admiration, which I can do without. I have of late been indulging my spleen by composing a preface AT them; after all resolving never to write a preface at all. "*There* are so many verses," would I have said to them; "give so much means for me to buy pleasure with, as a relief to my hours of labour." You will observe at the end of this, if you put down the letter, "How a solitary life engenders pride and egotism!" True—I know it does: but this pride and egotism will enable me to write finer things than anything else could, so I will indulge it. Just so much as I am humbled by the genius above my grasp, am I exalted and look with hate and contempt upon the literary world. A drummer-boy who holds out his hand familiarly to a field-marshal—that drummer-boy with me is the good word and favour of the public. Who could wish to be among the commonplace crowd of the little-famous, who are each individually lost in a throng made up of themselves? Is this worth louting or playing the hypocrite for? To beg suffrages for a seat on the benches of a myriad-aristocracy in letters? This is not wise—I am not a wise man. 'Tis pride. I will give you a definition of a proud man. He is a man who has neither vanity nor wisdom—one filled with hatred cannot be vain, neither can he be wise. Pardon me for hammering instead of writing. Remember me to Woodhouse, Hessey, and all in Percy Street.

Ever yours sincerely,

JOHN KEATS.

WINCHESTER,
25 *August* [1819].

MY DEAR REYNOLDS,

By this post I write to Rice, who will tell you why we have left Shanklin, and how we like this place. I have indeed scarcely anything else to say, leading so monotonous a life, unless I was to give you a history of sensations and day nightmares. You would not find me at all unhappy in it, as all my thoughts and feelings, which are of the selfish nature, home speculations, every day continue to make me more iron. I am convinced more and more, every day, that fine writing is, next to fine doing, the top thing in the world; the *Paradise Lost* becomes a greater wonder. The more I know what my diligence may in time probably effect, the more does my heart distend with pride and obstinacy. I feel it in my power to become a popular writer. I feel it in my power to refuse the poisonous suffrage of a public. My own being, which I know to be, becomes of more consequence to me than the crowds of shadows in the shape of men and women that inhabit a kingdom. The soul is a world of itself, and has enough to do in its own home. Those whom I know already, and who have grown as it were a part of myself, I could not do without; but for the rest of mankind, they are as much a dream to me as Milton's *Hierarchies*. I think if I had a free and healthy and lasting organisation of heart, and lungs as strong as an ox, so as to be able [to bear] unhurt the shock of extreme thought and sensation without weariness, I could pass my life very nearly alone, though it should last eighty years. But I feel my body too weak to support me to this height; I am obliged continually to check myself, and be nothing.

It would be vain for me to endeavour after a more reasonable manner of writing to you. I have nothing to speak of but myself, and what can I say but what I feel? If you should have any reason to regret this state of excitement in me, I will turn the tide of your feelings in the right channel, by mentioning that it is the only state for the best sort of poetry—that is all I care for, all I live for. Forgive me for not filling up the whole sheet; letters become so irksome to me, that the next time I leave London I shall petition them all to be spared to me. To give me credit for constancy, and at the same time waive letter-writing, will be the highest indulgence I can think of.

Ever your affectionate friend,
JOHN KEATS.

WINCHESTER,
Wednesday evening.

MY DEAR DILKE,

Whatever I take to, for the time, I cannot leave off in a hurry; letter-writing is the go now; I have consumed a quire at least. You must give me credit, now, for a free letter, when it is in reality an interested one on two points, the one requestive, the other verging to the pros and cons. As I expect they will lead me to seeing and conferring with you for a short time, I shall not enter at all upon a letter I have lately received from George, of not the most comfortable intelligence, but proceed to these two points, which, if you can Hume out into sections and subsections, for my edification, you will oblige me. The first I shall begin upon; the other will follow like a tail to a comet. I have written to Brown on the subject, and can but go over the same ground with you in a very short time, it not being more in length than the ordinary paces between the wickets. It concerns a resolution I have taken to endeavour to acquire something by temporary writing in periodical works. You must agree with me how unwise it is to keep feeding upon hopes, which depending so much on the state of temper and imagination, appear gloomy or bright, near or afar off, just as it happens. Now an act has three parts—to act, to do, and to perform.—I mean I should *do* something for my immediate welfare. Even if I am swept away like a spider from a drawing-room, I am determined to spin—homespun, anything for sale. Yea, I will traffic, anything but mortgage my brain to Blackwood. I am determined not to lie like a dead lump. You may say I want tact. That is easily acquired. You may be up to the slang of a cock-pit in three battles. It is fortunate I have not, before this, been tempted to venture on the common. I should, a year or two ago, have spoken my mind on every subject with the utmost simplicity. I hope I have learned a little better, and am confident I shall be able to cheat as well as any literary Jew of the market, and shine up an article on anything, without much knowledge of the subject, aye, like an orange. I would willingly have recourse to other means. I cannot; I am fit for nothing but literature. Wait for the issue of this tragedy? No: there cannot be greater uncertainties, east, west, north, and south, than concerning dramatic composition. How many months must I wait! Had I not better begin to look about me now? If better events supersede this necessity, what harm will be done? I have no trust whatever in poetry. I don't wonder at it: the marvel is to me how people read so much of it. I think you will see the reasonableness of my plan. To forward it, I purpose living in cheap lodgings in town, that I may be in the reach of books and information, of which there is here a plentiful lack. If I can [find] any place tolerably comfortable, I will settle myself and fag till I can afford to buy pleasure, which, if [I] never can afford, I must go without. Talking of pleasure, this moment I was writing with one hand, and with the other holding to my mouth a nectarine. Good God, how fine! It went down soft, pulpy, slushy, oozy—all its delicious *embonpoint* melted down my throat like a large beatified strawberry. Now I come to my request. Should you like me for a neighbour again? Come, plump it out, I won't blush. I should also be in the neighbourhood of Mrs. Wylie, which I should be glad of, though that, of course, does not influence me. Therefore will you look about Rodney Street for a couple of rooms for me—rooms like the gallant's legs in Massinger's time, "as good as the times allow, Sir!" I have written to-day to Reynolds, and to Woodhouse. Do you know him? He is a friend of Taylor's, at whom Brown has taken one of his funny odd dislikes. I'm sure he's wrong, because Woodhouse likes my poetry—conclusive. I ask your opinion, and yet I must say to you, as to him (Brown), that if you have anything to say against it I shall be as obstinate and heady as a Radical. By the *Examiners* coming in your handwriting you must be in town. They have put me into spirits. Notwithstanding my aristocratic temper, I cannot help being very much pleased with the present public proceedings. I hope sincerely I shall be able to put a mite of help to the liberal side of the question before I die. If you should have left town again (for your holidays cannot be up yet), let me know when this is forwarded to you. A most extraordinary mischance has befallen two letters I wrote Brown—one from London, whither I was obliged to go on business for George; the other from this place since my return. I can't make it out. I am excessively sorry for it. I shall hear from Brown and from you almost together, for I have sent him a letter to-day.

Ever your sincere friend,

JOHN KEATS.

WINCHESTER,
5 *September* [1819].

MY DEAR TAYLOR,

This morning I received yours of the 2nd, and with it a letter from Hessey, enclosing a bank post bill of £30, an ample sum I assure you—more I had no thought of. You should not have delayed so long in Fleet Street; leading an inactive life as you did was breathing poison: you will find the country air do more for you than you expect. But it must be proper country air. You must choose a spot. What sort of a place is Retford? You should have a dry, gravelly, barren, elevated country, open to the currents of air, and such a place is generally furnished with the finest springs. The neighbourhood of a rich, enclosed, fulsome, manured, arable land, especially in a valley, and almost as bad on a flat, would be almost as bad as the smoke of Fleet Street. Such a place as this was Shanklin, only open to the south-east, and surrounded by hills in every other direction. From this south-east came the damps from the sea, which, having no egress, the air would for days together take on an unhealthy idiosyncrasy altogether enervating and weakening as a city smoke. I felt it very much. Since I have been here in Winchester I have been improving in health: it is not so confined, and there is, on one side of the city, a dry chalky down, where the air is worth sixpence a pint. So if you do not get better at Retford, do not impute it to your own weakness until you have well considered the nature of the air and soil—especially as Autumn is encroaching—for the Autumn fog over a rich land is like the steam from cabbage water. What makes the great difference between valesmen, flatlandmen, and mountaineers? The cultivation of the earth in a great measure. Our health, temperament, and disposition, are taken more (notwithstanding the contradiction of the history of Cain and Abel) from the air we breathe than is generally imagined. See the difference between a peasant and a butcher. I am convinced a great cause of it is the difference of the air they breathe: the one takes his mingled with the fume of slaughter, the other from the dank exhalement from the glebe; the teeming damp that comes up from the plough-furrow is of more effect in taming the fierceness of a strong man than his labour. Let him be mowing furze upon a mountain, and at the day's end his thoughts will run upon a pick-axe if he ever had handled one—let him leave the plough, and he will think quietly of his supper. Agriculture is the tamer of men—the steam from the earth is like drinking their mother's milk—it enervates their nature. This appears a great cause of the imbecility of the Chinese: and if this sort of atmosphere is a mitigation to the energies of a strong man, how much more must it injure a weak one, unoccupied, unexercised. For what is the cause of so many men maintaining a good state in cities, but occupation? An idle man, a man who is not sensitively alive to self-interest, in a city, cannot continue long in good health. This is easily explained. If you were to walk leisurely through an unwholesome path in the fens, with a little horror of them, you would be sure to have your ague. But let Macbeth cross the same path, with the dagger in the air leading him on, and he would never have an ague or anything like it. You should give these things a serious consideration. Notts, I believe, is a flat country. You should be on the slope of one of the dry barren hills in Somersetshire. I am convinced there is as harmful air to be breathed in the country as in town.

I am greatly obliged to you for your letter. Perhaps, if you had had strength and spirits enough, you would have felt offended by my offering a note of hand, or, rather, expressed it. However, I am sure you will give me credit for not in anywise mistrusting you; or imagining that you would take advantage of any power I might give you over me. No, it proceeded from my serious resolve not to be a gratuitous borrower, from a great desire to be correct in money-matters, to have in my desk the chronicles of them to refer to, and know my worldly non-estate: besides, in case of my death, such documents would be but just, if merely as memorials of the friendly turns I had done to me.

Had I known of your illness I should not have written in such fiery phrase in my first letter. I hope that shortly you will be able to bear six times as much.

Brown likes the tragedy very much, but he is not a fit judge of it, as I have only acted as midwife to his plot, and, of course, he will be fond of his child. I do not think I can make you any extracts without spoiling the effect of the whole when you come to read it. I hope you will then not think my labour misspent. Since I finished it I have finished *Lamia*, and am now occupied in revising *St. Agnes' Eve*, and studying Italian. Ariosto I find as diffuse, in parts, as Spenser. I understand completely the difference between them. I will cross the letter with some lines from *Lamia*.

Brown's kindest remembrances to you, and I am ever your most sincere friend,

JOHN KEATS.

I shall be alone here for three weeks, expecting [an] account of your health.

WINCHESTER,
22 *September*, 1819.

MY DEAR REYNOLDS,

I was very glad to hear from Woodhouse that you would meet in the country. I hope you will pass some pleasant time together, which I wish to make pleasanter by a brace of letters, very highly to be estimated, as really I have had very bad luck with this sort of game this season. I "kepen in solitarinesse," for Brown has gone a-visiting. I am surprised myself at the pleasure I live alone in. I can give you no news of the place here, or any other idea of it but what I have to this effect written to George. Yesterday, I say to him, was a grand day for Winchester. They elected a mayor. It was indeed high time the place should receive some sort of excitement. There was nothing going on—all asleep—not an old maid's sedan returning from a card-party; and if any old women got tipsy at christenings they did not expose it in the streets.

The side streets here are excessively maiden-lady like;

the door-steps always fresh from the flannel. The knockers have a staid, serious, nay, almost awful quietness about them. I never saw so quiet a collection of lions' and rams' heads. The doors [are] most part black, with a little brass handle just above the keyhole, so that in Winchester a man may very quietly shut himself out of his own house.

How beautiful the season is now. How fine the air—a temperate sharpness about it. Really, without joking, chaste weather—Dian skies. I never liked stubble-fields so much as now—aye, better than the chilly green of the Spring. Somehow, a stubble field looks warm, in the same way that some pictures look warm. This struck me so much in my Sunday's walk that I composed upon it.[1]

Season of mists and mellow fruitfulness, etc.

I hope you are better employed than in gaping after weather. I have been, at different times, so happy as not to know what weather it was. No, I will not copy a parcel of verses. I always somehow associate Chatterton with Autumn. He is the purest writer in the English language. He has no French idiom or particles, like Chaucer; 'tis genuine English idiom in English words. I have given up *Hyperion*—there were too many Miltonic inversions in it—Miltonic verse cannot be written but in an artful, or, rather, artist's humour. I wish to give myself up to other sensations. English ought to be kept up. It may be interesting to you to pick out some lines from *Hyperion*, and put a mark, +, to the false beauty, proceeding from art, and 1, 2, to the true voice of feeling. Upon my soul, 'twas imagination; I cannot make the distinction—every now and then there is a Miltonic intonation—but I cannot make the division properly. The fact is, I must take a walk; for I am writing a long letter to George, and have been employed at it all the morning. You will ask, have I heard from George? I am sorry to say, not the best news—I hope for better. This is the reason, among others, that if I write to you it must be in such a scrap-like way. I have no meridian to date interests from, or measure circumstances. To-night I am all in a mist: I scarcely know what's what. But you, knowing my unsteady and vagarish disposition, will guess that all this turmoil will be settled by to-morrow morning. It strikes me to-night that I have led a very odd sort of life for the two or three last

[1] See the fine lines, *To Autumn*, in the Collected Works.

years—here and there, no anchor—I am glad of it. If you can get a peep at Babbicomb before you leave the country, do. I think it the finest place I have seen, or is to be seen, in the south. There is a cottage there I took warm water at, that made up for the tea. I have lately shirk'd some friends of ours, and I advise you to do the same. I mean the blue-devils—I am never at home to them. You need not fear them while you remain in Devonshire. There will be some of the family waiting for you at the coach-office—but go by another coach.

I shall beg leave to have a third opinion in the first discussion you have with Woodhouse—just half-way between both. You know I will not give up any argument. In my walk to-day, I stoop'd under a railing that lay across my path, and asked myself "Why I did not get over"; "Because," answered I, "no one wanted to force you under." I would give a guinea to be a reasonable man—good, sound sense—a says-what-he-thinks-and-does-what-he-says-man—and did not take snuff. They say men near death, however mad they may have been, come to their senses: I hope I shall here in this letter; there is a decent space to be very sensible in—many a good proverb has been in less—nay, I have heard of the statutes at large being changed into the statutes at small, and printed for a watch-paper.

Your sisters, by this time, must have got the Devonshire "ees"—short ees—you know 'em; they are the prettiest ees in the language. O, how I admire the middle-sized delicate Devonshire girls of about fifteen. There was one at an inn door holding a quartern of brandy; the very thought of her kept me warm a whole stage—and a sixteen-miler too. "You'll pardon me for being jocular."

Ever your affectionate friend,
JOHN KEATS.

23 *September*, 1819.
To Mr. Brown

Now I am going to enter on the subject of self. It is quite time I should set myself doing something, and live no longer upon hopes. I have never yet exerted myself. I am getting into an idle-minded, vicious way of life, almost content to live upon others. In no period of my life have I acted with any self-will but in throwing up the apothecary profession. That I do not repent of. Look at ——; if he was not in the law, he would be acquiring, by his abilities, something towards his support. My occupation is entirely literary: I will do so, too. I will write, on the liberal side of the question, for whoever will pay me. I have not known yet what it is to be diligent. I purpose living in towns in a cheap lodging, and endeavouring, for a beginning, to get the theatricals of some paper. When I can afford to compose deliberate poems, I will. I shall be in expectation of an answer to this. Look on my side of the question. I am convinced I am right. Suppose the tragedy should succeed—there will be no harm done. And here I will take an opportunity of making a remark or two on our friendship, and on all your good offices to me. I have a natural timidity of mind in these matters; liking better to take the feeling between us for granted, than to speak of it. But, good God! what a short while you have known me! I feel it a sort of duty thus to recapitulate, however unpleasant it may be to you. You have been living for others more than any man I know. This is a vexation to me, because it has been depriving you, in the very prime of your life, of pleasures which it was your duty to procure. As I am speaking in general terms, this may appear nonsense; you, perhaps, will not understand it; but if you can go over, day by day, any month of the last year, you will know what I mean. On the whole, however, this is a subject that I cannot express myself upon. I speculate upon it frequently, and, believe me, the end of my speculations is always an anxiety for your happiness. This anxiety will not be one of the least incitements to the plan I purpose pursuing. I had got into a habit of mind of looking towards you as a help in all difficulties. This very habit would be the parent of idleness and difficulties. You will see it is a duty I owe myself to break the neck of it. I do nothing for my subsistence—make no exertion. At the end of another year you shall applaud me, not for verses, but for conduct. While I have some immediate cash, I had better settle myself quietly, and fag on as others do. I shall apply to Hazlitt, who knows the market as well as anyone, for something to bring me in a few pounds as soon as possible. I shall not suffer my pride to hinder me. The whisper may go round; I shall not hear it. If I can get an article in the *Edinburgh*, I will. One must not be delicate. Nor let this disturb you longer than a moment. I look forward, with a good hope that we shall one day be passing free, untrammelled, unanxious time together. That can never be if I continue a dead lump. I shall be expecting anxiously an answer from you. If it does not arrive in a few days this will have miscarried, and I shall come straight to —— before I go to town, which you, I am sure, will agree had better be done while I still have some ready cash. By the middle of October I shall expect you in London. We will then set at the theatres. If you have anything to gainsay, I shall be even as the deaf adder which stoppeth her ears.

On the same day he wrote another letter, having received one from Mr. Brown in the interval. He again spoke of his purpose.

Do not suffer me to disturb you unpleasantly: I do not mean that you should not suffer me to occupy your thoughts, but to occupy them pleasantly; for, I assure you, I am as far from being unhappy as possible. Imaginary grievances have always been more my torment than real ones. You know this well. Real ones will never have any other effect upon me than to stimulate me to get out of or avoid them. This is easily accounted for. Our imaginary woes are conjured up by our passions, and are fostered by passionate feeling: our real ones come of themselves, and are opposed by an abstract exertion of mind. Real grievances are displacers of passion. The imaginary nail a man down for a sufferer, as on a cross; the real spur him up into an agent. I wish, at one view, you would see my heart towards you. 'Tis only from a high tone of feeling that I can put that word upon paper—out of poetry. I ought to have waited for your answer to my last before I wrote this. I felt, however, compelled to make a rejoinder to yours. I had written to —— on the subject of my last, I scarcely know whether I shall send my letter now. I think he would approve of my plan; it is so evident. Nay, I am convinced, out and out, that by prosing for a while in periodical works, I may maintain myself decently.

The gloomy tone of this correspondence soon brought Mr. Brown to Winchester. Up to that period Keats had always expressed himself most averse to writing for any periodical publication. The short contributions to the *Champion* were rather acts of friendship than literary labours. But now Mr. Brown, knowing what his pecuniary circumstances were, and painfully conscious that the time spent in the creation of those works which were destined to be the delight and solace of thousands of his fellow-creatures, must be unprofitable to him in procuring the necessities of life, and, above all, estimating at its due value that spirit of independence which shrinks from materialising the obligations of friendship into daily bread, gave every encouragement to these designs, and only remonstrated against the project of the following note, both on account of the pain he would himself suffer from the privation of Keats's society, and from the belief that the scheme of life would not be successful.

WINCHESTER,
1 *October* [1819].

MY DEAR DILKE,

For sundry reasons which I will explain to you when I come to town, I have to request you will do me a great favour, as I must call it, knowing how great a bore it is. That your imagination may not have time to take too great an alarm, I state immediately that I want you to hire me a couple of rooms (a sitting-room and bed-room for myself alone) in Westminster. Quietness and cheapness are the essentials; but as I shall, with Brown, be returned by next Friday, you cannot, in that space, have sufficient time to make any choice selection, and need not be very particular, as I can, when on the spot, suit myself at leisure. Brown bids me remind you not to send the *Examiners* after the third. Tell Mrs. D. I am obliged to her for the late ones, which I see are directed in her hand. Excuse this mere business-letter, for I assure you I have not a syllable at hand on any subject in the world.

Your sincere friend,

JOHN KEATS.

The friends returned to town together, and Keats took possession of his new abode. But he had miscalculated his own powers of endurance: the enforced absence from his friends was too much for him, and a still stronger impulse drew him back again to Hampstead. She, whose name

Was ever on his lips
But never on his tongue,

exercised too mighty a control over his being for him to remain at a distance, which was neither absence nor

presence, and he soon returned to where at least he could
rest his eyes on her habitation, and enjoy each chance
opportunity of her society. I find a fragment written about
this date, and under this inspiration, but it is still an
interesting study of the human heart, to see how few
traces remain in his outward literary life of that passion
which was his real existence.

TO ——

What can I do to drive away
Remembrance from my eyes? for they have seen,
Aye, an hour ago, my brilliant Queen!
Touch has a memory. O say, love, say,
What can I do to kill it and be free
In my old liberty?
When every fair one that I saw was fair,
Enough to catch me in but half a snare,
Not keep me there:
When, howe'er poor or particolour'd things,
My muse had wings,
And ever ready was to take her course
Whither I bent her force,
Unintellectual, yet divine to me;—
Divine, I say!—What sea-bird o'er the sea
Is a philosopher the while he goes
Winging along where the great water throes?

How shall I do
To get anew
Those moulted feathers, and so mount once more
Above, above
The reach of fluttering Love,
And make him cower lowly while I soar?
Shall I gulp wine? No, that is vulgarism,
A heresy and schism,
Foisted into the canon law of love;—
No,—wine is only sweet to happy men;
More dismal cares
Seize on me unawares,—
Where shall I learn to get my peace again?
To banish thoughts of that most hateful land,
Dungeoner of my friends, that wicked strand
Where they were wreck'd and live a wrecked life;
That monstrous region, whose dull rivers pour,
Ever from their sordid urns unto the shore,
Unown'd of any weedy-haired gods;
Whose winds, all zephyrless, hold scourging rods,
Iced in the great lakes, to afflict mankind;
Whose rank-grown forests, frosted, black, and blind,
Would fright a Dryad; whose harsh herbaged meads
Make lean and lank the starv'd ox while he feeds;
There bad flowers have no scent, birds no sweet song
And great unerring Nature once seems wrong.

O, for some sunny spell
To dissipate the shadows of this hell!
Say they are gone,—with the new dawning light
Steps forth my lady bright!
O, let me once more rest
My soul upon that dazzling breast!
Let once again these aching arms be placed,
The tender gaolers of thy waist!
And let me feel that warm breath here and there
To spread a rapture in my very hair,—
O, the sweetness of the pain!
Give me those lips again!
Enough! Enough! It is enough for me
To dream of thee!

WENTWORTH PLACE, HAMPSTEAD,
17 *November* [1819].

MY DEAR TAYLOR,

I have come to a determination not to publish anything I have now ready written; but, for all that, to publish a poem before long, and that I hope to make a fine one. As the marvellous is the most enticing, and the surest guarantee of harmonious numbers, I have been endeavouring to persuade myself to untether Fancy, and to let her manage for herself. I and myself cannot agree about this at all. Wonders are no wonders to me. I am more at home amongst men and women. I would rather read Chaucer than Ariosto. The little dramatic skill I may as yet have, however badly it might show in a drama, would, I think, be sufficient for a poem. I wish to diffuse the colouring of *St. Agnes' Eve* throughout a poem in which character and sentiment would be the figures to such drapery. Two or three such poems, if God should spare me, written in the course of the next six years, would be a famous *Gradus ad Parnassum altissimum*. I mean they would nerve me up to the writing of a few fine plays—my greatest ambition, when I do feel ambitious. I am sorry to say that is very seldom. The subject we have once or twice talked of appears a promising one—the Earl of Leicester's history. I am this morning reading Holingshed's *Elizabeth*. You had some books awhile ago, you promised to send me, illustrative of my subject. If you can lay hold of them, or any other which may be serviceable to me, I know you will encourage my low-spirited muse by sending them, or rather by letting me know where our errand-cart man shall call with my little box. I will endeavour to set myself selfishly at work on this poem that is to be.

Your sincere friend,

JOHN KEATS.

About this time he wrote this to his brother George:

From the time you left us our friends say I have altered so completely I am not the same person. I dare say you have altered also. Mine is not the same hand I clenched at Hammond's.[1] We are like the relic garments of a saint, the same and not the same; for the careful monks patch it and patch it till there is not a thread of the original in it, and still they show it for St. Anthony's shirt. This is the reason why men who have been bosom-friends for a number of years afterwards meet coldly; neither of them know why. Some think I have lost that poetic fire and ardour they say I once had. The fact is, I perhaps have, but instead of that I hope I shall substitute a more thoughtful and quiet power. I am more contented to read and think, but seldom haunted with ambitious thoughts. I am scarcely content to write the best verse from the fever they leave behind. I want to compose without this fever; I hope I shall one day.

You cannot imagine how well I can live alone. I told the servant to-day I was not at home to anyone that called. I am not sure how I should endure loneliness and bad weather at the same time. It is beautiful weather now. I walk for an hour every day before dinner. My dear sister, I have all the *Examiners* ready for you. I will pack them up when the business with Mr. Abbey comes to a conclusion. I have dealt out your best wishes like a pack of cards, but, being always given to cheat, I have turned up ace. You see I am making game of you. I see you are not happy in America. As for pun-making, I wish it were as profitable as pin-making. There is but little business of that sort going on now. We struck for wages like the Manchester weavers, but to no purpose, for we are all out of employ. I am more lucky than some, you see, as I have an opportunity of exporting a pun—getting into a little foreign trade, which is a comfortable thing. You have heard of Hook the farce-writer. Horace Smith was asked if he knew him. "Oh, yes," says he, "Hook and I are very intimate." Brown has been taking French lessons at the cheap rate of two-and-sixpence a page, and Reynolds observed, "Gad, the man sells his lessons so cheap, he must have stolen them." I wish you could get change for a pun in silver currency, and get with three-and-a-half every night into Drury pit.

[1] The surgeon to whom he was apprenticed.

In the beginning of the winter George Keats suddenly appeared in England, but remained only for a short period. On his arrival in America, with his wife, he found that their limited means required an immediate retirement into, what were then, the solitudes of the Far West, but which the labour of enterprising men has now peopled with life and planted with civilisation. From Philadelphia these two children of the Old World, and nearly children in life (she was just sixteen), proceeded to Pittsburg and descended the Ohio to Cincinnati. Down that beautiful river, then undisturbed by the panting of the steamboat or the tumult of inhabited shores, their lonely boat found its way to Cincinnati, where they resided for some time. George Keats paid a visit shortly after to Kentucky, where he lived in the same house with Audubon the naturalist, who, seeing him one day occupied in chopping a log, after watching him with a curious interest, exclaimed, "You will do well in this country; I could chop that log in ten minutes; you have taken near an hour; but your persistence is worth more than my expertness." A boat in which he invested his money completely failed as a speculation, and his voyage to England seems to have been undertaken in the hope of raising capital for some more successful venture. I am unable to determine whether he took back with him any portion of what remained of John's fortune, but he did receive his share of his brother Tom's property, and he may possibly have repaid himself for what he had spent for John out of John's share. John's professional education had been so expensive that it only required a certain amount of that carelessness in money-matters incidental to men of higher natures to account for the continual embarrassment in which he found himself, without having indulged in any profligate habits. Tom's long sickness was also a great expense to the family, so that the assistance of the more prudent and fortunate brother was frequently required to make up deficiencies. This was, no doubt, the reason why, out of the £1100 left by Tom, George received £440, and John little more than £200. When George returned the second time to America he certainly left his brother's finances in a deplorable state; it is probable he was not aware how very small a sum re-

mained for John's subsistence, or it would have been hardly
justifiable for him to have repaid himself any portion of
what he had advanced, except he was convinced that
whatever he did take would be so reproductive that it was
indisputably the best thing to be done with the money at
the time, whatever was to be its ultimate destination.
The subject was so painful a one, and the increasing
melancholy, both physical and moral, of Keats so manifest,
that there can be no ground for discrediting his brother's
positive assertion that, when he left London, he had not
the courage to lay before him the real state of their affairs,
but that he kept to the pleasing side of things, and encouraged him in the belief that the American speculation would
produce enough to restore both of them to comfortable
circumstances. At the same time it might well be permitted
to John's friends, who did not know the details of the
affair, to be indignant at the state of almost destitution
to which so noble a man was reduced, while they believed
that his brother in America had the means of assisting
him. But, on the other hand, after Keats's death, when
George was ready to give the fullest explanation of the
circumstances, when the legal administration of John's
effects showed that no debts were owing to the estate,
and when, without the least obligation, he offered to do
his utmost to liquidate his brother's engagements, it was
only just to acknowledge that they had been deceived
by appearances, and that they fully acquitted him of
unfraternal and ungenerous conduct. Their accusations
rankled long and bitterly in his mind, and were the subject
of a frequent correspondence with his friends in England.
I have extracted the following portion of a letter, dated
"Louisville, 20 April, 1825," as an earnest expression of
his feelings, and also as giving an interesting delineation
of the poet's character, by one who knew him so well:
and I am glad to find such a confirmation of what has
been so often stated in these pages, that the faults of
Keats's disposition were precisely the contrary of those
attributed to him by common opinion.

LOUISVILLE,
20 April, 1825.

. . . Your letter has in some measure relieved my mind

of a load that has sorely pressed for years. I felt innocent of the unfeeling, mean, conduct imputed to me by some of my brother's friends, and knew that the knowledge of the facts would soon set that to rights; but I could not rest while under the impression that he really suffered through my not forwarding him money at the time when I promised, but had not the power. Your saying "that he knew nothing of want, either of friends or money," and giving proofs of the truth of it, made me breathe freely—enabled me to cherish his memory, without the feeling of having caused him misery, however unavoidably, while a living Friend and Brother. I do not doubt but that he complained of me; although he was the noblest fellow, whose soul was ever open to my inspection, his nervous, morbid temperament at times led him to misconstrue the motives of his best friends. I have been instrumental times innumerable in correcting erroneous impressions so formed of those very persons who have been most ready to believe the stories lately circulated against me, and I almost believe that if I had remained his companion, and had had the means, as I had the wish, to have devoted my life to his fame and happiness, he might have been living at this hour. His temper did not unfold itself to you, his friend, until the vigour of his mind was somewhat impaired, and he no longer possessed the power to resist the pettishness he formerly considered he had no right to trouble his friends with. From the time we were boys at school, where we loved, jangled, and fought alternately, until we separated in 1818, I in a great measure relieved him by continual sympathy, explanation, and inexhaustible spirits and good humour, from many a bitter fit of hypochondriasm. He avoided teasing anyone with his miseries but Tom and myself, and often asked our forgiveness; venting and discussing them gave him relief. I do not mean to say that he did not receive the most indulgent attention from his many devoted friends; on the contrary, I shall ever look with admiration on the exertions made for his comfort and happiness by his numerous friends. No one in England understood his character perfectly but poor Tom, and he had not the power to divert his frequent melancholy, and eventually increased his disease most fearfully by the horrors of his own lingering death. If I did not feel fully persuaded that my motive was to acquire an independence to support us all in case of necessity, I never should forgive myself for leaving him. Some extraordinary exertion was necessary to retrieve our affairs from the gradual decline they were suffering. That exertion I made, whether wisely or not, future events had to decide. After all, *Blackwood* and the *Quarterly*, associated with our family disease, consumption, were ministers of death sufficiently venomous, cruel, and deadly, to have consigned one of less sensibility to a premature grave. I have consumed many hours in devising means to punish those literary gladiators, but am always brought to the vexing conclusion that they are invulnerable to one of my prowess. Has much been said in John's defence against those libellers both of his character and writings ? His writings were fair game, and liable to be assailed by a sneaking poacher, but his character as represented by *Blackwood* was not. A good cudgelling should have been his reward if he had been within my reach. John was the very soul of courage and manliness, and as much like the *Holy Ghost* as *Johnny Keats*. I am much indebted for the interest you have taken in my vindication, and will observe further for your satisfaction, that Mr. Abbey, who had the management of our money concerns, in a letter lately received, expressed himself "satisfied that my statement of the account between John and me was correct." He is the only person who is in possession of data to refute or confirm my story. My not having written to you seems to have been advanced as a proof of my worthlessness. If it prove anything, it proves my humility, for I can assure you, if I had known you felt one-half the interest in my fate unconnected with my brother it appears you did, the explanation would have been made when I first became acquainted there was a necessity for it.—I should never have given up a communication with the only spirits in existence who are congenial to me, and at the same time know me. Understand me, when I failed to write, it was not from a diminished respect or friendliness towards you, but under the impression that I had moved out of your circle, leaving but faint traces that I had ever existed within it.

Soon after George's departure, Keats wrote to his sister-in-law, and there is certainly nothing in the letter betokening any diminution of his liveliness or sense of enjoyment. He seems, on the contrary, to regard his brother's voyage in no serious light—probably anticipating a speedy reunion, and with pleasant plans for a future that never was to come. But these loving brothers had now met and parted for the last time, and this gay letter remains the last record of a cheerful and hopeful nature that was about to be plunged into the darkness of pain and death, and of an affection which space could not diminish, and which time preserved, till after many years of honest, useful and laborious life, he who remained also passed away, transmitting to other generations a name that genius has illustrated above the blazon of ordinary nobilities.

My Dear Sister,

By the time you receive this your troubles will be over, and George have returned to you. On Henry's marriage there was a piece of bride's-cake sent me, but as it missed its way, I suppose the bearer was a conjuror, and wanted it for his own private use. Last Sunday George and I dined at ——. Your mother, with Charles, were there, and fool L——, who sent the sly disinterested shawl to Miss M——, with his own heathen name engraved in the middle of it. The evening before last we had a pianoforte dance at Mrs. Dilke's; there was little amusement in the room, but a Scotchman to hate: some persons you must have observed have a most unpleasant effect on you, when seen speaking in profile: this Scot is the most accomplished fellow in this way I ever met with: the effect was complete; it went down like a dose of bitters, and I hope will improve my digestion. At Taylor's, too, there was a Scotchman, but he was not so bad, for he was as clean as he could get himself. George has introduced an American to us: I like him in a moderate way. I told him I hated Englishmen, as they were the only men I knew. He does not understand this. Who would be Braggadocio to Johnny Bull? Johnny's house is his castle, and a precious dull castle it is: how many dull castles there are in so-and-so crescent! I never wish myself a general visitor and newsmonger, but when I write to you—I should then, for a day or two, like to have the knowledge of that L——, for instance; of all the people of a wide acquaintance to tell you about, only let me have his knowledge of family affairs, and I would set them in a proper light, but, bless me, I never go anywhere.

My pen is no more garrulous than my tongue. Any third person would think I was addressing myself to a lover of scandal, but I know you do not like scandal, but you love fun; and if scandal happen to be fun, that is no fault of ours. The best thing I have heard is your shooting, for it seems you follow the gun. I like your brothers the more I know of them, but I dislike mankind in general. Whatever people on the other side of the question may say, they cannot deny that they are always surprised at a good action, and never at a bad one. I am glad you have doves in America. *Gertrude of Wyoming*, and Birkbeck's book, should be bound together as a couple of decoy-ducks; one is almost as practical as the other. I have been sitting in the sun while I wrote this, until it has become quite oppressive: the Vulcan heat is the natural heat for January. Our Irish servant has very much piqued me this morning, by saying her father is very much like my Shakspeare, only he has more colour than the engraving. If you were in England, I dare say you would be able to pick out more amusement from society than I am able to do. To me it is all as dull here as Louisville is to you. I am tired of theatres; almost all parties I chance to fall into, I know by heart; I know the different styles of talk in different places; what subjects will be started; and how it will proceed; like an acted play, from the first to the last act. I know three witty people, all distinct in their excellence—Rice, Reynolds, and Richards—Rice is the wisest—Reynolds the playfullest— Richards the out-of-the-wayest. The first makes you laugh and think; the second makes you laugh and not think; the third puzzles your head; I admire the first, I enjoy the second, and I stare at the third; the first is claret, the second ginger-beer, the third is *crême de Byrapymdrag*; the first is inspired by Minerva, the second by Mercury, and the third by Harlequin Epigram, Esq.; the first is neat in his dress, the second careless, the third uncomfortable; the first speaks adagio, the second allegretto, and the third both together; the first is Swiftean, the second Tom Crib-ean, the third Shandean. I know three people of no wit at all, each distinct in his excellence, A., B. and C. A. is the foolishest, B. is the sulkiest, and C. is the negative; A. makes you yawn, B. makes you hate, and as for C. you never see him at all, though he were six feet high; I bear the first, I forbear the second, I am not certain that the third is; the first is gruel, the second ditch-water, and the third is spilt and ought to be wiped up; A. is inspired by Jack of the Clock, B. has been drilled by a Russian sergeant,

C. they say is not his mother's true child, but she bought [him] of the man who cries "young lambs to sell." . . . I will send you a close written sheet on the first of next month; but, for fear of missing the mail, I must finish here. God bless you, my dear sister.

Your affectionate brother,

JOHN KEATS.

The study of Italian, to which Keats had been latterly much addicted, had included Ariosto, and the humorous fairy-poem on which he was engaged about this time appears to me to have originated in that occupation. He has stated, in a previous passage, that he still kept enough of his old tastes to prefer reading Chaucer to Ariosto, and the delightful vagaries of the master of Italian fancy would probably not have had so much effect on him but for Mr. Brown's intimate acquaintance with, and intense enjoyment of, those frailer charms of southern song. When, in aftertimes, Mr. Brown himself retired to Italy, he hardly ever passed a day without translating some portion of that school of Italian poetry, and he has left behind him a complete and admirable version of the first five cantos of Bojardo's *Orlando Innamorato*.

Keats had a notion of publishing this fanciful poem under a feigned name, and that of "Lucy Vaughan Lloyd" suggested itself to him from some untraceable association. He never had even made up his mind what title to give it; the *Cap and Bells* and *The Jealousies* were two he spoke of: I give here all that was written, not only because it exhibits his versatility of talent, but because it presents him, almost for the first time, in the light of a humorous writer, just at the moment of his existence when real anxieties were pressing most threateningly upon him, when the struggle between his ever-growing passion and the miserable circumstances of his daily life was beating down his spirit, and when disease was advancing with stealthy, but not altogether unperceived, advances, to consummate by a cruel and lingering death the hard conditions of his mortal being. There is nothing in this combination which will surprise those who understand the poetic, or even the literary, nature, but I know few stronger instances of a moral phenomenon which the Hamlets of the world are for ever exhibiting to an audience that can only resolve the problem by doubting the reality of the one or the other feeling, of the mirth or of the misery.

I am unwilling to leave this, the last of Keats's literary labours, without a word of defence against the objection that might with some reason be raised against the originality of his genius, from the circumstance that it is easy to refer almost every poem he wrote to some suggestion of style and manner derived from preceding writers. From the Spenserian *Endymion*, to these Ariosto-like stanzas, you can always see reflected in the mirror of his intellect the great works he is studying at the time. This is so generally the case with verse-writers, and the test has been so severely and successfully applied to many of the most noted authors of our time, that I should not have alluded to it had I not been desirous to claim for Keats an access to that inmost penetralium of Fame which is solely consecrated to original genius. The early English chronicle-dramas supplied Shakespeare with many materials and outlines for his historical plays, and the *Adamo* of Andreini had indisputably a great effect on the framework of *Paradise Lost*; but everyone feels that these accidents rather resemble the suggestions of nature which every mind, however independent, receives and assimilates, than what is ordinarily meant by plagiarism or imitation. In the case of Keats, his literary studies were apparently the sources of his productions, and his variety and facility of composition certainly increases very much in proportion to his reading, thus clearly showing how much he owed to those who had preceded him. But let us not omit two considerations: first, that these resemblances of form or spirit are a reproduction, not an imitation, and that while they often are what those great masters might themselves have contentedly written, they always include something which the model has not—some additional intuitive vigour; and secondly, let us never forget, that wonderful as are the poems of Keats, yet, after all, they are rather the records of a poetical education than the accomplished work of the mature artist. This is in truth the chief interest of these pages; this is what these letters so vividly exhibit. Day by day his imagination is extended, his fancy enriched, his taste purified; every fresh acquaintance with the motive minds of past generations leads him a step onwards in knowledge and in power; the elements of ancient genius become his own; the skill of faculties long-spent revives in him; ever, like Nature herself, he gladly receives and energetically reproduces. And now we approach the consummation of this laborious work, the formation of a mind of the highest order; we hope to see the perfect fruit whose promise has been more than the perfection of noted men; we desire to sympathise with this realised idea of a great poet, from which he has ever felt himself so far, but which he yet knows he is ever approaching; we yearn to witness the full flow of this great spiritual river, whose source has long lain in the heart of the earth, and to which the streams of a thousand hills have ministered.

One night, about eleven o'clock, Keats returned home in a state of strange physical excitement—it might have appeared to those who did not know him one of fierce intoxication. He told his friend he had been outside the stage-coach, had received a severe chill, was a little fevered, but added, "I don't feel it now." He was easily persuaded to go to bed, and as he leaped into the cold sheets, before his head was on the pillow, he slightly coughed and said, "That is blood from my mouth; bring me the candle; let me see this blood." He gazed steadfastly for some moments at the ruddy stain, and then looking in his friend's face with an expression of sudden calmness never to be forgotten, said, "I know the colour of that blood—it is arterial blood—I cannot be deceived in that colour; that drop is my death-warrant. I must die."

A surgeon was immediately called in, and, after being bled, Keats fell into a quiet sleep. The medical man declared his lungs to be uninjured, and the rupture not important, but he himself was of a different opinion, and with the frequent self-prescience of disease, added to his scientific knowledge, he was not to be persuaded out of his forebodings. At times, however, the love of life, inherent in active natures, got the better of his gloom. "If you would have me recover," he said to his devoted friend and constant attendant, Mr. Brown, "flatter me with a hope of happiness when I shall be well, for I am now so weak that I can be flattered into hope." "Look at my hand," he said, another day, "it is that of a man of fifty."

The advancing year brought with it such an improvement in his health and strength, as in the estimation of many almost amounted to recovery. Gleams of his old cheerfulness returned, as the following letters evince. His own handwriting was always so clear and good as to be almost clerkly, and thus he can afford to joke at the exhibitions of his friends in that unimportant particular. In the case of Mr. Dilke, the long and useful career of that able and independent critic has been most intelligible in print to a generation of his fellow-countrymen, and his cordial appreciation and care of Keats will only add to his reputation for generosity and benevolence.

Wentworth Place,
16 *February*, 1820.

My Dear Rice,

I have not been well enough to make any tolerable rejoinder to your kind letter. I will, as you advise, be very chary of my health and spirits. I am sorry to hear of your relapse and hypochondriac symptoms attending it. Let us hope for the best, as you say. I shall follow your example in looking to the future good rather than brooding upon the present ill. I have not been so worn with lengthened illnesses as you have, therefore cannot answer you on your own ground with respect to those haunting and deformed thoughts and feelings you speak of. When I have been, or supposed myself in health, I have had my share of them, especially within the last year. I may say that for six months before I was taken ill I had not passed a tranquil day. Either that gloom overspread me, or I was suffering under some passionate feeling, or if I turned to versify, that acerbated the poison of either sensation. The beauties of Nature had lost their power over me. How astonishingly (here I must premise that illness, as far as I can judge in so short a time, has relieved my mind of a load of deceptive thoughts and images, and makes me perceive things in a truer light)—how astonishingly does the chance of leaving the world impress a sense of its natural beauties upon us! Like poor Falstaff, though I do not "babble," I think of green fields; I muse with the greatest affection on every flower

I have known from my infancy—their shapes and colours are as new to me as if I had just created them with a superhuman fancy. It is because they are connected with the most thoughtless and the happiest moments of our lives. I have seen foreign flowers in hothouses, of the most beautiful nature, but I do not care a straw for them. The simple flowers of our Spring are what I want to see again.

Brown has left the inventive and taken to the imitative art. He is doing his forte, which is copying Hogarth's heads. He has just made a purchase of the Methodist Meeting picture, which gave me a horrid dream a few nights ago. I hope I shall sit under the trees with you again in some such place as the Isle of Wight. I do not mind a game of cards in a saw-pit or waggon, but if ever you catch me on a stage-coach in the winter full against the wind, bring me down with a brace of bullets, and I promise not to 'peach. Remember me to Reynolds, and say how much I should like to hear from him; that Brown returned immediately after he went on Sunday, and that I was vexed at forgetting to ask him to lunch; for as he went towards the gate, I saw he was fatigued and hungry.

> I am, my dear Rice,
> Ever most sincerely yours,
> JOHN KEATS.

I have broken this open to let you know I was surprised at seeing it on the table this morning, thinking it had gone long ago.

[Postmark, HAMPSTEAD, 4 *March*, 1820.]

MY DEAR DILKE,

Since I saw you I have been gradually, too gradually perhaps, improving; and, though under an interdict with respect to animal food, living upon pseudo-victuals, Brown says I have picked up a little flesh lately. If I can keep off inflammation for the next six weeks, I trust I shall do very well. Reynolds is going to sail on the salt seas. Brown has been mightily progressing with his Hogarth. A damn'd melancholy picture it is, and during the first week of my illness it gave me a psalm-singing nightmare that made me almost faint away in my sleep. I know I am better, for I can bear the picture. I have experienced a specimen of great politeness from Mr. Barry Cornwall. He has sent me his books. Some time ago he had given his first published book to Hunt, for me;

Hunt forgot to give it, and Barry Cornwall, thinking I had received it, must have thought me a very neglectful fellow. Notwithstanding, he sent me his second book, and on my explaining that I had not received his first, he sent me that also. I shall not expect Mrs. Dilke at Hampstead next week unless the weather changes for the warmer. It is better to run no chance of a supernumerary cold in March. As for you, you must come. You must improve in your penmanship; your writing is like the speaking of a child of three years old—very understandable to its father, but to no one else. The worst is, it looks well—no, that is not the worst—the worst is, it is worse than Bailey's. Bailey's looks illegible and may perchance be read; yours looks very legible, and may perchance not be read. I would endeavour to give you a fac-simile of your word "Thistlewood" if I were not minded on the instant that Lord Chesterfield has done some such thing to his son. Now I would not bathe in the same river with Lord C., though I had the upper hand of the stream. I am grieved that in writing and speaking, it is necessary to make use of the same particles as he did. Cobbett is expected to come in. O! that I had two double plumpers for him. The ministry is not so inimical to him, but it would like to put him into Coventry. Casting my eye on the other side I see a long word written in a most vile manner, unbecoming a critic. You must recollect I have served no apprenticeship to old plays. If the only copies of the Greek and Latin authors had been made by you, Bailey, and Haydon, they were as good as lost. It has been said that the character of a man may be known by his handwriting; if the character of the age may be known by the average goodness of ours, what a slovenly age we live in. Look at Queen Elizabeth's Latin exercises and blush. Look at Milton's hand: I can't say a word for Shakspeare.

Your sincere friend,
JOHN KEATS.

Towards the end of the spring Keats's outward health was so much better that the physician recommended him to take another tour in Scotland. Mr. Brown, however, thinking him quite unfit to cope with the chance hardships of such an expedition, generously dissuaded him, though he was so far from anticipating any rapid change in Keats's constitution that he determined to go alone and return to his friend in a few weeks. On the seventh of May the two friends parted at Gravesend, and never met again.

Keats went to lodge at Kentish Town to be near his friend Leigh Hunt, but soon returned to Hampstead, where he remained with the family of the lady to whom he was attached. In these latter letters the catastrophe of mortal sickness, accompanied by the dread of poverty, is seen gradually coming on, and the publication of his new volume hardly relieves the general gloom of the picture.

My Dear Dilke,

As Brown is not to be a fixture at Hampstead, I have at last made up my mind to send home all lent books. I should have seen you before this, but my mind has been at work all over the world to find out what to do. I have my choice of three things, or, at least, two—South America, or surgeon to an Indiaman; which last, I think, will be my fate. I shall resolve in a few days. Remember me to Mrs. D. and Charles, and your father and mother.

Ever truly yours,

John Keats.

My Dear Taylor,   11 *June.*

In reading over the proof of *St. Agnes' Eve* since I left Fleet Street, I was struck with what appears to me an alteration in the seventh stanza very much for the worse. The passage I mean stands thus:

> her maiden eyes incline
> Still on the floor, while many a sweeping train
> Pass by.

'Twas originally written:

> her maiden **eyes** divine
> Fix'd on the floor, saw many a sweeping train
> Pass by.

My meaning is quite destroyed in the alteration. I do not use *train* for *concourse of passers by*, but for *skirts* sweeping along the floor.

In the first stanza my copy reads, second line:

> bitter *chill* it was,

to avoid the echo cold in the second line.

Ever yours sincerely,

John Keats

My Dear Brown,

I have only been to ———'s once since you left, when ——— could not find your letters. Now this is bad of me. I should, in this instance, conquer the great aversion to breaking up my regular habits, which grows upon me more and more. True, I have an excuse in the weather, which drives one from shelter to shelter in any little excursion. I have not heard from George. My book [1] is coming out with very low hopes, though not spirits, on my part. This shall be my last trial; not succeeding, I shall try what I can do in the apothecary line. When you hear from or see ——— it is probable you will hear some complaints against me, which this notice is not intended to forestall. The fact is, I did behave badly; but it is to be attributed to my health, spirits, and the disadvantageous ground I stand on in society. I could go and accommodate matters if I were not too weary of the world. I know that they are more happy and comfortable than I am; therefore why should I trouble myself about it? I foresee I shall know very few people in the course of a year or two. Men get such different habits that they become as oil and vinegar to one another. Thus far I have a consciousness of having been pretty dull and heavy, both in subject and phrase; I might add, enigmatical. I am in the wrong, and the world is in the right, I have no doubt. Fact is, I have had so many kindnesses done me by so many people, that I am cheveaux-de-frised with benefits, which I must jump over or break down. I met ——— in town, a few days ago, who invited me to supper to meet Wordsworth, Southey, Lamb, Haydon, and some more; I was too careful of my health to risk being out at night. Talking of that, I continue to improve slowly, but, I think, surely. There is a famous exhibition in Pall Mall of the old English portraits by Vandyck and Holbein, Sir Peter Lely, and the great Sir Godfrey. Pleasant countenances predominate; so I will mention two or three unpleasant ones. There is James the First, whose appearance would disgrace a "Society for the Suppression of Women"; so very squalid and subdued to nothing he looks. Then, there is old Lord Burleigh, the high-priest of economy, the political save-all, who has the appearance of a Pharisee just rebuffed by a Gospel *bon-mot*. Then, there is George the Second, very like an unintellectual Voltaire, troubled with the gout and a bad temper. Then, there is young

[1] *Lamia, Isabella, and other Poems.*

Devereux, the favourite, with every appearance of as slang a boxer as any in the Court; his face is cast in the mould of blackguardism with jockey-plaster. I shall soon begin upon *Lucy Vaughan Lloyd*. I do not begin composition yet, being willing, in case of a relapse, to have nothing to reproach myself with. I hope the weather will give you the slip; let it show itself and steal out of your company. When I have sent off this, I shall write another to some place about fifty miles in advance of you.

Good morning to you.

Yours ever sincerely,

JOHN KEATS.

MY DEAR BROWN,

You may not have heard from ——, or ——, or in any way, that an attack of spitting of blood, and all its weakening consequences, has prevented me from writing for so long a time. I have matter now for a very long letter, but not news; so I must cut everything short. I shall make some confession, which you will be the only person, for many reasons, I shall trust with. A winter in England would, I have not a doubt, kill me; so I have resolved to go to Italy, either by sea or land. Not that I have any great hopes of that, for, I think, there is a core of disease in me not easy to pull out. I shall be obliged to set off in less than a month. Do not, my dear Brown, tease yourself about me. You must fill up your time as well as you can, and as happily. You must think of my faults as lightly as you can. When I have health I will bring up the long arrears of letters I owe you. My book has had good success among the literary people, and I believe has a moderate sale. I have seen very few people we know. —— has visited me more than anyone. I would go to —— and make some inquiries after you, if I could with any bearable sensation; but a person I am not quite used to causes an oppression on my chest. Last week I received a letter from Shelley, at Pisa, of a very kind nature, asking me to pass the winter with him. Hunt has behaved very kindly to me. You shall hear from me again shortly.

Your affectionate friend,

JOHN KEATS.

HAMPSTEAD,
Mrs. ——'s, Wentworth Place.

MY DEAR HAYDON,

I am much better this morning than I was when I wrote

you the note; that is, my hopes and spirits are better, which are generally at a very low ebb, from such a protracted illness. I shall be here for a little time, and at home all every day. A journey to Italy is recommended me, which I have resolved upon, and am beginning to prepare for. Hoping to see you shortly,

                    I remain your affectionate friend,
                                        JOHN KEATS.

Mr. Haydon has recorded in his journal the terrible impression of this visit: the very colouring of the scene struck forcibly on the painter's imagination; the white curtains, the white sheets, the white shirt, and the white skin of his friend, all contrasted with the bright hectic flush on his cheek and heightened the sinister effect: he went away hardly hoping.

                              WENTWORTH PLACE,
                                  [14 *August*, 1820.]
MY DEAR TAYLOR,
    My chest is in such a nervous state, that anything extra, such as speaking to an unaccustomed person, or writing a note, half suffocates me. This journey to Italy wakes me at daylight every morning, and haunts me horribly. I shall endeavour to go, though it be with the sensation of marching up against a battery. The first step towards it is to know the expense of a journey and a year's residence, which if you will ascertain for me, and let me know early, you will greatly serve me. I have more to say, but must desist, for every line I write increases the tightness of my chest, and I have many more to do. I am convinced that this sort of thing does not continue for nothing. If you can come, with any of our friends, do.

                        Your sincere friend,
                                        JOHN KEATS.
MY DEAR BROWN,
    I ought to be off at the end of this week, as the cold winds begin to blow towards evening—but I will wait till I have your answer to this. I am to be introduced, before I set out, to a Dr. Clark, a physician settled at Rome, who promises to befriend me in every way there. The sale of my book is very slow, though it has been very highly rated. One of the causes, I understand from different quarters, of the unpopu-

larity of this new book, is the offence the ladies take at me. On thinking that matter over, I am certain that I have said nothing in a spirit to displease any woman I could care to please; but still there is a tendency to class women in my books with roses and sweetmeats—they never see themselves dominant. I will say no more, but, waiting in anxiety for your answer, doff my hat, and make a purse as long as I can.

Your affectionate friend,

JOHN KEATS.

The acquaintance between Keats and Mr. Severn the artist had begun about the end of 1817, and a similarity of general tastes soon led to a most agreeable interchange of their reciprocal abilities. To Severn the poetical faculty of Keats was an ever-flowing source of enjoyment and inspiration—to Keats the double talent of Severn for painting and music imparted the principles and mechanical processes of Art. Keats himself had a taste for painting that might have been cultivated into skill, and he could produce a pleasing musical effect, though possessing hardly any voice. He would sit by for hours while Severn was playing, following the air with a low kind of recitative. "I delight in Haydn's symphonies," he one day said; "he is like a child, there's no knowing what he will do next." *Shakespeare's Songs*, such as

Full fathom five thy father lies,

and

The rain it raineth every day,

set to music by Purcell, were great favourites with him.

Mr. Severn had had the gratification, from the commencement of their acquaintance, of bringing Keats into communion with the great masters of painting. A notable instance of the impression made on that susceptible nature by those achievements is manifest as early as the Hymn in the fourth book of the *Endymion*, which is, in fact, the "Bacchus and Ariadne" of Titian, now in our National Gallery, translated into verse. Take these images as examples:

And as I sat, over the light blue hills
There came a noise of revellers; the rills
Into the wide stream came of purple hue—
'Twas Bacchus and his crew!

The earnest trumpet spake, and silver thrills
From kissing cymbals made a merry din—
    'Twas Bacchus and his kin!
Like to a moving vintage down they came,
Crowned with green leaves, and faces all on flame.

   .   .   .

Within his car, aloft, young Bacchus stood,
Trifling his ivy-dart, in dancing mood,
    With sidelong laughing;
And near him rode Silenus on his ass,
Pelted with flowers as he on did pass
    Tipsily quaffing.

   .   .   .

Mounted on panthers' furs and lions' manes,
From rear to van they scour about the plains;
A three-days' journey in a moment done;
And always, at the rising of the sun,
About the wilds they hunt with spear and horn,
    On spleenful unicorn.

At the period occupied by this narrative, the gold medal to be adjudged by the Royal Academy for the best historical painting had not been given for the last twelve years, no work having been produced which the judges regarded as deserving so high an acknowledgment of merit. When, therefore, it was given to Mr. Severn for his painting of Spenser's "Cave of Despair" there burst out a chorus of long-hoarded discontents, which fell severely on the successful candidate. Severn had long worked at the picture in secret—Keats watching its progress with the greatest interest. I have already mentioned one instance in which the poet passionately defended his friend when attacked, and now the time was come when that and similar proofs of attachment were to receive abundant compensation. Entirely regardless of his future prospects, and ready to abandon all the advantages of the position he had won, Mr. Severn at once offered to accompany Keats to Italy. For the change of climate now remained the only chance of prolonging a life so dear both to genius and to friendship, and a long and lonely voyage, and solitary transportation to a foreign land, must, with such a sympathetic and affectionate nature, neutralise all outward advantages, to say nothing of the miserable condition in which he would be reduced in case the disease did not give way to the alteration of scene and temperature. Such a companionship, therefore, as this which was proposed was everything to him, and though he reproached himself on his death-bed with permitting Severn to make the sacrifice, it no doubt afforded all the alleviation of which his sad condition was capable.

During a pedestrian tour, occasional delays in the delivery of letters are inevitable. Thus Mr. Brown walked on disappointed from one post-office to another, till, on the ninth of September, he received at Dunkeld the above alarming intelligence. He lost no time in embarking at Dundee, and arrived in London only one day too late. Unknown to each, the vessels containing these two anxious friends lay a whole night side by side at Gravesend, and by an additional irony of fate, when Keats's ship was driven back into Portsmouth by stress of weather, Mr. Brown was staying in the neighbourhood within ten miles when Keats landed and spent a day on shore. Nothing was left to him but to make his preparations for following Keats as speedily as possible, and remaining with him in Italy, if it turned out that a southern climate was necessary for the preservation of his life.

The voyage began under tolerably prosperous auspices. "Keats," wrote Mr. Severn on 20 September, "looks very happy; for myself, I would not change with anyone." One of his companions in the vessel was a young lady afflicted with the same malady as himself, and whose illness often diverted his thoughts from his own. Yet there are in the following letter deep tones of moral and physical suffering, which perhaps only found utterance in communion with the friend from whom he was almost conscious he was parting for ever. He landed once more in England, on the Dorchester coast, after a weary fortnight spent in beating about the Channel: the bright beauty of the day and the scene revived for a moment the poet's drooping heart, and the inspiration remained on him for some time even after his return to the ship. It was then that he composed that sonnet of solemn tenderness:

Bright star! would I were stedfast as thou art, etc.[1]

and wrote it out in a copy of Shakespeare's Poems he had given to Severn a few days before. I know of nothing written afterwards.

[1] See the *Literary Remains*.

My Dear Brown,

The time has not yet come for a pleasant letter from me.
I have delayed writing to you from time to time, because
I felt how impossible it was to enliven you with one heartening
hope of my recovery. This morning in bed the matter struck
me in a different manner; I thought I would write "while
I was in some liking," or I might become too ill to write at
all; and then, if the desire to have written should become
strong, it would be a great affliction to me. I have many more
letters to write, and I bless my stars that I have begun, for
time seems to press. This may be my best opportunity. We
are in a calm, and I am easy enough this morning. If my
spirits seem too low you may in some degree impute it to our
having been at sea a fortnight without making any way. I was
very disappointed at Bedhampton, and was much provoked
at the thought of your being at Chichester to-day. I should
have delighted in setting off for London for the sensation
merely, for what should I do there? I could not leave my
lungs or stomach, or other worse things behind me. I wish to
write on subjects that will not agitate me much. There is one
I must mention and have done with it. Even if my body
would recover of itself, this would prevent it. The very thing
which I want to live most for will be a great occasion of my
death. I cannot help it. Who can help it? Were I in health
it would make me ill, and how can I bear it in my state?
I dare say you will be able to guess on what subject I am
harping—you know what was my greatest pain during the
first part of my illness at your house. I wish for death every
day and night to deliver me from these pains, and then
I wish death away, for death would destroy even those pains,
which are better than nothing. Land and sea, weakness and
decline, are great separators, but Death is the great divorcer
for ever. When the pang of this thought has passed through
my mind, I may say the bitterness of death is passed. I often
wish for you, that you might flatter me with the best. I think,
without my mentioning it, for my sake, you would be a friend
to Miss —— when I am dead. You think she has many faults,
but for my sake think she has not one. If there is anything
you can do for her by word or deed I know you will do it.
I am in a state at present in which woman, merely as woman,

can have no more power over me than stocks and stones, and yet the difference of my sensations with respect to Miss —— and my sister is amazing—the one seems to absorb the other to a degree incredible. I seldom think of my brother and sister in America; the thought of leaving Miss —— is beyond everything horrible—the sense of darkness coming over me—I eternally see her figure eternally vanishing; some of the phrases she was in the habit of using during my last nursing at Wentworth Place ring in my ears. Is there another life? Shall I awake and find all this a dream? There must be, we cannot be created for this sort of suffering. The receiving this letter is to be one of yours—I will say nothing about our friendship, or rather yours to me, more than that, as you deserve to escape, you will never be so unhappy as I am. I should think of you in my last moments. I shall endeavour to write to Miss ——, if possible, to-day. A sudden stop to my life in the middle of one of these letters would be no bad thing, for it keeps one in a sort of fever awhile; though fatigued with a letter longer than any I have written for a long while, it would be better to go on for ever than awake to a sense of contrary winds. We expect to put into Portland Roads to-night. The captain, the crew, and the passengers, are all ill-tempered and weary. I shall write to Dilke. I feel as if I was closing my last letter to you, my dear Brown.

Your affectionate friend,
JOHN KEATS.

A violent storm in the Bay of Biscay lasted for thirty hours, and exposed the voyagers to considerable danger. "What awful music!" cried Severn, as the waves raged against the vessel. "Yes," said Keats, as a sudden lurch inundated the cabin, "Water parted from the sea." After the tempest had subsided, Keats was reading the description of the storm in *Don Juan*, and cast the book on the floor in a transport of indignation. "How horrible an example of human nature," he cried, "is this man, who has no pleasure left him but to gloat over and jeer at the most awful incidents of life. Oh! this is a paltry originality, which consists in making solemn things gay, and gay things solemn, and yet it will fascinate thousands, by the very diabolical outrage of their sympathies. Byron's perverted education makes him assume to feel, and try to impart to others, those depraved sensations which the want of any education excites in many."

The invalid's sufferings increased during the latter part of the voyage and a ten-days' miserable quarantine at Naples. But, when once fairly landed and in comfortable quarters, his spirits appeared somewhat to revive, and the glorious scenery to bring back, at moments, his old sense of delight. But these transitory gleams, which the hopeful heart of Severn caught and stored up, were in truth only remarkable as contrasted with the chronic gloom that overcame all things, even his love. What other words can tell the story like his own? What fiction could colour more deeply this picture of all that is most precious in existence becoming most painful and destructive? What profounder pathos can the world of tragedy exhibit than this expression of all that is good and great in nature writhing impotent in the grasp of an implacable destiny?

NAPLES,
1 *November* [1820].

MY DEAR BROWN,

Yesterday we were let out of quarantine, during which my health suffered more from bad air and the stifled cabin than it had done the whole voyage. The fresh air revived me a little, and I hope I am well enough this morning to write to you a short calm letter—if that can be called one, in which I am afraid to speak of what I would fainest dwell upon. As I have gone thus far into it, I must go on a little—perhaps it may relieve the load of *wretchedness* which presses upon me. The persuasion that I shall see her no more will kill me. My dear Brown, I should have had her when I was in health, and I should have remained well. I can bear to die—I cannot bear to leave her. Oh, God! God! God! Everything I have in my trunks that reminds me of her goes through me like a spear. The silk lining she put in my travelling cap scalds my head. My imagination is horribly vivid about her—I see her—I hear her. There is nothing in the world of sufficient interest to divert me from her a moment. This was the case when I was in England; I cannot recollect, without shuddering, the time that I was a prisoner at Hunt's, and used to keep my eyes fixed on Hampstead all day. Then there was a good hope of seeing her again.—Now!—O, that I could be buried near where she lives! I am afraid to write to her—to receive a letter from her—to see her handwriting would break my heart—even to hear of her anyhow, to see her name written, would be more than I can bear. My dear Brown, what am I to do? Where can I look for consolation or ease? If I had any chance of recovery, this passion would kill me. Indeed, through the whole of my illness, both at your house and at Kentish Town, this fever has never ceased wearing me out. When you write to me, which you will do immediately, write to Rome (*poste restante*)—if she is well and happy, put a mark thus + ; if——

Remember me to all. I will endeavour to bear my miseries patiently. A person in my state of health should not have such miseries to bear. Write a short note to my sister, saying you have heard from me. Severn is very well. If I were in better health I would urge your coming to Rome. I fear there is no one can give me any comfort. Is there any news of George? O, that something fortunate had ever happened to me or my brothers!—then I might hope—but despair is forced upon me as a habit. My dear Brown, for my sake, be her advocate for ever. I cannot say a word about Naples; I do not feel at all concerned in the thousand novelties around me. I am afraid to write to her. I should like her to know that I do not forget her. Oh, Brown, I have coals of fire in my breast. It surprises me that the human heart is capable of containing and bearing so much misery. Was I born for this end? God bless her, and her mother, and my sister, and George, and his wife, and you, and all!

Your ever affectionate friend,

JOHN KEATS.

Thursday.—I was a day too early for the Courier. He sets out now. I have been more calm to-day, though in a half dread of not continuing so. I said nothing of my health; I know nothing of it; you will hear Severn's account, from ——. I must leave off. You bring my thoughts too near to ——. God bless you!

Little things, that at other times might have been well passed over, now struck his susceptible imagination with intense disgust. He could not bear to go to the opera, on account of the sentinels who stood constantly on the stage, and whom he at first took for parts of the scenic effect.

"We will go at once to Rome," he said; "I know my end approaches, and the continual visible tyranny of this government prevents me from having any peace of mind. I could not lie quietly here. I will not leave even my bones in the midst of this despotism."

He had received at Naples a most kind letter from Mr. Shelley, anxiously inquiring about his health, offering him advice as to the adaptation of diet to the climate, and concluding with an urgent invitation to Pisa, where he could ensure him every comfort and attention. But for one circumstance, it is unfortunate that this offer was not accepted, as it might have spared at least some annoyances to the sufferer, and much painful responsibility, extreme anxiety, and unrelieved distress to his friend.

On arriving at Rome, he delivered the letter of introduction, already mentioned, to Dr. (Sir James) Clark, at that time rising into high repute as a physician. The circumstances of the young patient were such as to ensure compassion from any person of feeling, and perhaps sympathy and attention from superior minds. But the attention he here received was that of all the skill and knowledge that science could confer, and the sympathy was of the kind which discharges the weight of obligation for gratuitous service, and substitutes affection for benevolence and gratitude. All that wise solicitude and delicate thoughtfulness could do to light up the dark passages of mortal sickness and soothe the pillow of the forlorn stranger was done, and, if that was little, the effort was not the less. In the history of most professional men this incident might be remarkable, but it is an ordinary sample of the daily life of this distinguished physician, who seems to have felt it a moral duty to make his own scientific eminence the measure of his devotion to the relief and solace of all men of intellectual pursuits, and to have applied his beneficence the most effectually to those whose nervous susceptibility renders them the least fit to endure that physical suffering to which, above all men, they are constantly exposed.

The only other introduction Keats had with him, was from Sir T. Lawrence to Canova, but the time was gone by when even Art could please, and his shattered nerves refused to convey to his intelligence the impressions by which a few months before he would have been rapt in ecstasy. Dr. Clark procured Keats a lodging in the Piazza di Spagna, opposite to his own abode; it was in the first house on your right hand as you ascend the steps of the "Trinità del Monte." Rome, at that time, was far from affording the comforts to the stranger that are now so abundant, and the violent Italian superstitions respecting the infection of all dangerous disease, rendered the circumstances of an invalid most harassing and painful. Suspicion tracked him as he grew worse, and countenances darkened round as the world narrowed about him; ill-will increased just when sympathy was most wanted, and the essential loneliness of the death-bed was increased by the alienation of all other men; the last grasp of the swimmer for life was ruthlessly cast off by his stronger comrade, and the affections that are wont to survive the body were crushed down in one common dissolution. At least from this desolation Keats was saved by the love and care of Mr. Severn and Dr. Clark.

I have now to give the last letter of Keats in my possession; probably the last he wrote. One phrase in the commencement of it became frequent with him; he would continually ask Dr. Clark, "When will this posthumous life of mine come to an end?" Yet when this was written, hope was evidently not extinguished within him, and it does appear not unlikely that if the soothing influences of climate had been sooner brought to bear on his constitution, and his nervous irritability from other causes been diminished, his life might have been saved, or at least, considerably prolonged.

ROME,
30 *November*, 1820.

MY DEAR BROWN,

'Tis the most difficult thing in the world to me to write a letter. My stomach continues so bad, that I feel it worse on opening any book—yet I am much better than I was in quarantine. Then I am afraid to encounter the pro-ing and con-ing of anything interesting to me in England. I have an habitual feeling of my real life having passed, and that I am leading a posthumous existence. God knows how it would have been—

but it appears to me—however, I will not speak of that subject. I must have been at Bedhampton nearly at the time you were writing to me from Chichester—how unfortunate— and to pass on the river too! There was my star predominant! I cannot answer anything in your letter, which followed me from Naples to Rome, because I am afraid to look it over again. I am so weak (in mind) that I cannot bear the sight of any handwriting of a friend I love so much as I do you. Yet I ride the little horse, and, at my worst, even in quarantine, summoned up more puns, in a sort of desperation, in one week than in any year of my life. There is one thought enough to kill me; I have been well, healthy, alert, etc., walking with her, and now—the knowledge of contrast, feeling for light and shade, all that information (primitive sense) necessary for a poem, are great enemies to the recovery of the stomach. There, you rogue, I put you to the torture; but you must bring your philosophy to bear, as I do mine, really, or how should I be able to live? Dr. Clark is very attentive to me; he says there is very little the matter with my lungs, but my stomach, he says, is very bad. I am well disappointed in hearing good news from George, for it runs in my head we shall all die young. I have not written to Reynolds yet, which he must think very neglectful; being anxious to send him a good account of my health, I have delayed it from week to week. If I recover, I will do all in my power to correct the mistakes made during sickness; and if I should not, all my faults will be forgiven. Severn is very well, though he leads so dull a life with me. Remember me to all friends, and tell Haslam I should not have left London without taking leave of him, but from being so low in body and mind. Write to George as soon as you receive this, and tell him how I am, as far as you can guess; and also a note to my sister—who walks about my imagination like a ghost—she is so like Tom. I can scarcely bid you good-bye, even in a letter. I always made an awkward bow.

God bless you!

JOHN KEATS.

After such words as these, the comments or the description of any mere biographer must indeed jar upon every mind duly impressed with the reality of this sad history. The voice, which we have followed so long in all its varying, yet ever-true, modulations of mirth and melancholy, of wonder and of wit, of activity and anguish, and which has conferred on this volume whatever value it may possess, is now silent, and will not be heard on earth again. The earnest utterances of the devoted friend, who transmitted to other listening affections the details of those weary hours, and who followed to the very last the ebb and flow of that wave of fickle life, remain the fittest substitute for those sincere revelations which can come to us no more. It is left to passages from the letters of Mr. Severn to express in their energetic simplicity the final accidents of the hard catastrophe of so much that only asked for healthy life to be fruitful, useful, powerful and happy. Mr. Severn wrote from Rome:

Dec. 14*th.*—I fear poor Keats is at his worst. A most unlooked-for relapse has confined him to his bed with every chance against him. It has been so sudden upon what I thought convalescence, and without any seeming cause, that I cannot calculate on the next change. I dread it, for his suffering is so great, so continued, and his fortitude so completely gone, that any further change must make him delirious. This is the fifth day, and I see him get worse.

Dec. 17*th,* 4 *a.m.*—Not a moment can I be from him. I sit by his bed and read all day, and at night I humour him in all his wanderings. He has just fallen asleep, the first sleep for eight nights, and now from mere exhaustion. I hope he will not wake till I have written, for I am anxious you should know the truth; yet I dare not let him see I think his state dangerous. On the morning of this attack he was going on in good spirits, quite merrily, when, in an instant, a cough seized him, and he vomited two cupfulls of blood. In a moment I got Dr. Clark, who took eight ounces of blood from his arm —it was black and thick. Keats was much alarmed and dejected. What a sorrowful day I had with him! He rushed out of bed and said, "This day shall be my last"; and but for me most certainly it would. The blood broke forth in similar quantity the next morning, and he was bled again. I was afterwards so fortunate as to talk him into a little calmness, and he soon became quite patient. Now the blood has come up in coughing five times. Not a single thing will he digest, yet he keeps on craving for food. Every day he raves he will die from hunger, and I've been obliged to give him more than was allowed. His imagination and memory present every thought to him in horror; the recollection of "his good friend Brown," of "his four happy weeks spent under *her* care," of his sister and brother. O! he will mourn over all to me whilst I cool his burning forehead, till I tremble for his intellects. How can he be "Keats" again after all this? Yet I may see it too gloomy, since each coming night I sit up adds its dismal contents to my mind.

Dr. Clark will not say much; although there are no bounds to his attention, yet he can with little success "administer to a mind diseased." All that can be done he does most kindly, while his lady, like himself in refined feeling, prepares all that poor Keats takes, for in this wilderness of a place, for an invalid, there was no alternative. Yesterday Dr. Clark went all over Rome for a certain kind of fish, and just as I received it carefully dressed, Keats was taken with spitting of blood. We have the best opinion of Dr. Clark's skill: he comes over four or five times a-day, and he has left word for us to call him up, at any moment, in case of danger. My spirits have been quite pulled down. These wretched Romans have no idea of comfort. I am obliged to do everything for him. I wish you were here.

I have just looked at him. This will be a good night.

Jan. 15th, 1821, *half-past eleven.* — Poor Keats has just fallen asleep. I have watched him and read to him to his very last wink; he has been saying to me, "Severn, I can see under your quiet look immense contention—you don't know what you are reading. You are enduring for me more than I would have you. O! that my last hour was come!" He is sinking daily; perhaps another three weeks may lose him to me for ever! I made sure of his recovery when we set out. I was selfish: I thought of his value to me; I made my own public success to depend on his candour to me.

Torlonia, the banker, has refused us any more money; the bill is returned unaccepted, and to-morrow I must pay my last crown for this cursed lodging-place: and what is more, if he dies, all the beds and furniture will be burnt and the walls scraped, and they will come on me for a hundred pounds or more! But, above all, this noble fellow lying on the bed and without the common spiritual comforts that many a rogue and fool has in his last moments! If I do break down it will be under this; but I pray that some angel of goodness may yet lead him through this dark wilderness.

If I could leave Keats every day for a time I could soon raise money by my painting, but he will not let me out of his sight, he will not bear the face of a stranger. I would rather cut my tongue out than tell him I must get the money—that would kill him at a word. You see my hopes of being kept by the Royal Academy will be cut off, unless I send a picture by the spring. I have written to Sir T. Lawrence. I have got a volume of Jeremy Taylor's works, which Keats has heard me read to-night. This is a treasure indeed, and came when I should have thought it hopeless. Why may not other good things come? I will keep myself up with such hopes. Dr. Clark is still the same, though he knows about the bill: he is afraid the next change will be to diarrhœa. Keats sees all this—his knowledge of anatomy makes every change tenfold worse: every way he is unfortunate, yet everyone offers me assistance on his account. He cannot read any letters, he has made me put them by him unopened. They tear him to pieces—he dare not look on the outside of any more: make this known.

Feb. 18*th*.—I have just got your letter of Jan. 15th. The contrast of your quiet friendly Hampstead with this lonely place and our poor suffering Keats, brings the tears into my eyes. I wish many many times that he had never left you. His recovery would have been impossible in England; but his excessive grief has made it equally so. In your care he seemed to me like an infant in its mother's arms; you would have smoothed down his pain by variety of interests, and his death would have been eased by the presence of many friends. Here, with one solitary friend, in a place savage for an invalid, he has one more pang added to his many—for I have had the hardest task in keeping from him my painful situation. I have kept him alive week after week. He has refused all food, and I have prepared his meals six times a day, till he had no excuse left. I have only dared to leave him while he slept. It is impossible to conceive what his sufferings have been: he might, in his anguish, have plunged into the grave in secret, and not a syllable been known about him: this reflection alone repays me for all I have done. Now, he is still alive and calm. He would not hear that he was better: the thought of recovery is beyond everything dreadful to him; we now dare not perceive any improvement, for the hope of death seems his only comfort. He talks of the quiet grave as the first rest he can ever have.

In the last week a great desire for books came across his mind. I got him all I could, and three days this charm lasted, but now it has gone. Yet he is very tranquil. He is more and more reconciled to his horrible misfortunes.

Feb. 14*th.* — Little or no change has taken place, except this beautiful one, that his mind is growing to great quietness and peace. I find this change has to do with the increasing weakness of his body, but to me it seems like a delightful sleep: I have been beating about in the tempest of his mind so long. To-night he has talked very much, but so easily, that he fell at last into a pleasant sleep. He seems to have happy dreams. This will bring on some change—it cannot be worse —it may be better. Among the many things he has requested of me to-night, this is the principal—that on his grave-stone shall be this inscription:

HERE LIES ONE WHOSE NAME WAS WRIT IN WATER.

You will understand this so well that I need not say a word about it.

When he first came here he purchased a copy of *Alfieri,* but put it down at the second page—being much affected at the lines

> Misera me! sollievo a me non resta,
> Altro che il pianto, *ed il pianto è delitto !*

Now that I know so much of his grief, I do not wonder at it.

Such a letter has come! I gave it to Keats supposing it to be one of yours, but it proved sadly otherwise. The glance at that letter tore him to pieces; the effects were on him for many days. He did not read it—he could not—but requested me to place it in his coffin, together with a purse and a letter (unopened) of his sister's [1]; since then he has told me *not* to place that letter in his coffin, only his sister's purse and letter, and some hair. I, however, persuaded him to think otherwise on this point. In his most irritable state he sees a friendless world about him, with everything that his life presents, and especially the kindness of others, tending to his melancholy death.

[1] Miss Keats shortly after married Señor Llanos, a Spanish gentleman of liberal politics and much accomplishment, the author of *Don Esteban, Sandoval the Freemason,* and other spirited illustrations of the modern history of the Peninsula.

I have got an English nurse to come two hours every other day, so that I am quite recovering my health. Keats seems to like her, but she has been taken ill to-day and cannot come. In a little back-room I get chalking out a picture; this, with swallowing a little Italian every day, helps to keep me up. The Doctor is delighted with your kindness to Keats[1]; he thinks him worse; his lungs are in a dreadful state; his stomach has lost all its power. Keats knew from the first little drop of blood that he must die; no common chance of living was left him.

Feb. 22nd. — O! how anxious I am to hear from you! [Mr. Haslam.] I have nothing to break this dreadful solitude but letters. Day after day, night after night, here I am by our poor dying friend. My spirits, my intellect, and my health are breaking down. I can get no one to change with me—no one to relieve me. All run away, and even if they did not, Keats would not do without me.

Last night I thought he was going; I could hear the phlegm in his throat; he bade me lift him up in the bed or he would die with pain. I watched him all night, expecting him to be suffocated at every cough. This morning, by the pale daylight, the change in him frightened me: he has sunk in the last three days to a most ghastly look. Though Dr. Clark has prepared me for the worst, I shall be ill able to bear it. I cannot bear to be set free even from this my horrible situation by the loss of him.

I am still quite precluded from painting: which may be of consequence to me. Poor Keats has me ever by him, and shadows out the form of one solitary friend: he opens his eyes in great doubt and horror, but when they fall upon me, they close gently, open quietly and close again, till he sinks to sleep. This thought alone would keep me by him till he dies: and why did I say I was losing my time? The advantages I have gained by knowing John Keats are double and treble any I could have won by any other occupation. Farewell.

Feb. 27th. — He is gone; he died with the most perfect ease—he seemed to go to sleep. On the twenty-third, about four, the approaches of death came on. "Severn—I—lift me up —I am dying—I shall die easy; don't be frightened—be firm,

---

[1] Probably alluding to pecuniary assistance afforded by Mr. Brown. But before this the friends were helped out of their immediate difficulty by the generosity of Mr. Taylor.

and thank God it has come." I lifted him up in my arms. The phlegm seemed boiling in his throat, and increased until eleven, when he gradually sunk into death, so quiet, that I still thought he slept. I cannot say more now. I am broken down by four nights' watching, no sleep since, and my poor Keats gone. Three days since the body was opened: the lungs were completely gone. The doctors could not imagine how he had lived these two months. I followed his dear body to the grave on Monday, with many English. They take much care of me here—I must else have gone into a fever. I am better now, but still quite disabled.

The police have been. The furniture, the walls, the floor, must all be destroyed and changed, but this is well looked to by Dr. Clark.

The letters I placed in the coffin with my own hand.

This goes by the first post. Some of my kind friends would else have written before.

After the death of Keats Mr. Severn received the following letter from Mr. Leigh Hunt, in the belief that he was still alive, and that it might be communicated to him. But even while these warm words were being written in his own old home, he had already been committed to that distant grave, which has now become a place of pilgrimage to those fellow-countrymen who then knew not what they had lost, and who are ready, too late, to lavish on his name the love and admiration that might once have been very welcome.

VALE OF HEALTH, HAMPSTEAD,
DEAR SEVERN, 8 *March*, 1821.

You have concluded, of course, that I have sent no letters to Rome, because I was aware of the effect they would have on Keats's mind; and this is the principal cause—for besides what I have been told of his emotions about letters in Italy, I remember his telling me on one occasion, that, in his sick moments, he never wished to receive another letter, or ever to see another face however friendly. But still I should have written to *you* had I not been almost at death's-door myself. You will imagine how ill I have been when you hear that I have but just begun writing again for the *Examiner* and *Indicator*, after an interval of several months, during which my flesh wasted from me in sickness and melancholy. Judge how often I thought of Keats, and with what feelings. Mr. Brown tells me he is comparatively calm now, or rather quite so. If he can bear to hear of us, pray tell him—but he knows it already, and can put it in better language than any man. I hear he does not like to be told that he may get better; nor is it to be wondered at, considering his firm persuasion that he shall not recover. He can only regard it as a puerile thing, and an insinuation that he cannot bear to think he shall die. But if this persuasion should happen no longer to be so strong upon him, or if he can now put up with such attempts to console him, remind him of what I have said a thousand times, and that I still (upon my honour, Severn) think always, that I have seen too many instances of recovery from apparently desperate cases of consumption, not to indulge in hope to the very last. If he cannot bear this, tell him—tell that great poet and noble-hearted man—that we shall all bear his memory in the most precious part of our hearts, and that the world shall bow their heads to it, as our loves do. Or if this again will trouble his spirit, tell him we shall never cease to remember and love him, and, that the most sceptical of us has faith enough in the high things that Nature puts into our heads, to think that all who are of one accord in mind and heart, are journeying to one and the same place, and shall unite somehow or other again, face to face, mutually conscious, mutually delighted. Tell him he is only before us on the road, as he was in everything else; or, whether you tell him the latter or no, tell him the former, and add that we shall never forget he was so, and that we are coming after him. The tears are again in my eyes, and I must not afford to shed them. The next letter I write shall be more to yourself, and a little more refreshing to your spirits, which we are very sensible must have been greatly taxed. But whether our friend dies or not, it will not be among the least lofty of our recollections by-and-by, that you helped to smooth the sick-bed of so fine a being.

God bless you, dear Severn.

Your sincere friend,

LEIGH HUNT.

Keats was buried in the Protestant cemetery at Rome, one of the most beautiful spots on which the eye and heart of man can rest. It is a grassy slope, amid verdurous ruins

of the Honorian walls of the diminished city, and sur-
mounted by the pyramidal tomb which Petrarch attributed
to Remus, but which antiquarian truth has ascribed to the
humbler name of Caius Cestius, a tribune of the people,
only remembered by his sepulchre. In one of those mental
voyages into the past, which often precede death, Keats
had told Severn that he "thought the intensest pleasure he
had received in life was in watching the growth of flowers";
and another time, after lying a while still and peaceful, he
said, "I feel the flowers growing over me." And there they
do grow, even all the winter long—violets and daisies
mingling with the fresh herbage, and, in the words of
Shelley, "making one in love with death, to think that one
should be buried in so sweet a place."

Ten weeks after the close of his holy work of friendship
and charity, Mr. Severn wrote to Mr. Haslam:

Poor Keats has now his wish—his humble wish; he is at
peace in the quiet grave. I walked there a few days ago, and
found the daisies had grown all over it. It is in one of the
most lovely retired spots in Rome. You cannot have such a
place in England. I visit it with a delicious melancholy which
relieves my sadness. When I recollect for how long Keats had
never been one day free from ferment and torture of mind
and body, and that now he lies at rest with the flowers he so
desired above him, with no sound in the air but the tinkling
bells of a few simple sheep and goats, I feel indeed grateful
that he is here, and remember how earnestly I prayed that
his sufferings might end, and that he might be removed from
a world where no one grain of comfort remained for him.

Thus, too, in the *Adonais*, that most successful imitation
of the spirit of the Grecian elegy, devoted to the memory
of one who had restored Grecian mythology to its domain
of song, this place is consecrated.

> Go thou to Rome,—at once the Paradise,
> The grave, the city, and the wilderness:
> And where its wrecks like shattered mountains rise,
> And flowering weeds, and fragrant copses dress
> The bones of Desolation's nakedness;
> Pass, till the Spirit of the spot shall lead
> Thy footsteps to a slope of green access,
> Where, like an infant's smile, over the dead
> A light of laughing flowers along the grass is spread,

And grey walls moulder round, on which dull Time
Feeds, like slow fire upon a hoary brand;
And one keen pyramid with wedge sublime,
Pavilioning the dust of him who planned
This refuge for his memory, doth stand
Like flame transformed to marble; and beneath
A field is spread, on which a newer band
Have pitched in Heaven's smile their camp of death,
Welcoming him we lose with scarce extinguished breath.

Here pause: these graves are all too young as yet
To have outgrown the sorrow which consigned
Its charge to each; and, if the seal is set
Here, on one fountain of a mourning mind,
Break it not thou! Too surely shalt thou find
Thine own well full, if thou returnest home,
Of tears and gall. From the world's bitter wind
Seek shelter in the shadow of the tomb.
What Adonais is, why fear we to become?

And a few years after this was written, in the extended burying-ground, a little above the grave of Keats, was placed another tombstone, recording that below rested the passionate and world-worn heart of Shelley himself—"Cor Cordium." [1]

Immediately on hearing of Keats's death, Shelley expressed the profoundest sympathy and a fierce indignation against those whom he believed to have hastened it: in a few months he produced the incomparable tribute of genius to genius, which is of itself the complement of and the apology for this volume.

The first copy of the *Adonais* (printed at Pisa) was sent with the following letter to Mr. Severn, then enjoying the travelling pension of the Royal Academy, which had not been granted to any student for a considerable period. He resided for many years at Rome, illustrating the city and Campagna by his artistic fancy, and delighting all travellers who had the pleasure of his acquaintance by his talents and his worth. Nor was the self-devotion of his youth without its fruits in the estimation and respect of those who learned the circumstances of his visit to Italy, and above all, of those who loved the genius, revered the memory, and mourned the destiny of Keats.

PISA,
29 *November*, 1821

DEAR SIR,

I send you the elegy on poor Keats—and I wish it were

_____
[1] The inscription.

better worth your acceptance. You will see, by the preface, that it was written before I could obtain any particular account of his last moments; all that I still know was communicated to me by a friend who had derived his information from Colonel Finch; I have ventured to express, as I felt, the respect and admiration which *your* conduct towards him demands.

In spite of his transcendent genius, Keats never was, nor ever will be, a popular poet; and the total neglect and obscurity in which the astonishing remnants of his mind still lie, was hardly to be dissipated by a writer, who, however he may differ from Keats in more important qualities, at least resembles him in that accidental one, a want of popularity.

I have little hope, therefore, that the poem I send you will excite any attention, nor do I feel assured that a critical notice of his writings would find a single reader. But for these considerations, it had been my intention to have collected the remnants of his compositions, and to have published them with a Life and Criticism. Has he left any poems or writings of whatsoever kind, and in whose possession are they? Perhaps you would oblige me by information on this point.

Many thanks for the picture you promise me: I shall consider it among the most sacred relics of the past. For my part, I little expected, when I last saw Keats at my friend Leigh Hunt's, that I should survive him.

Should you ever pass through Pisa, I hope to have the pleasure of seeing you, and of cultivating an acquaintance into something pleasant, begun under such melancholy auspices.

Accept, my dear sir, the assurance of my highest esteem, and believe me,

Your most sincere and faithful servant,

PERCY B. SHELLEY.

The last few pages have attempted to awaken a personal interest in the story of Keats almost apart from his literary character—a personal interest founded on events that might easily have occurred to a man of inferior ability, and rather affecting from their moral than intellectual bearing. But now

He has outsoared the shadow of our night;
Envy and calumny, and hate and pain,
And that unrest which men miscall delight,
Can touch him not and torture not again;

From the contagion of the world's slow stain
He is secure, and now can never mourn
A heart grown cold, a head grown grey in vain;
Nor, when the spirit's self has ceased to burn,
With sparkless ashes load an unlamented urn:

and, ere we close altogether these memorials of his short earthly being, let us revert to the great distinctive peculiarities which singled him out from his fellow-men and gave him his rightful place among "the inheritors of unfulfilled renown."

Let any man of literary accomplishment, though without the habit of writing poetry, or even much taste for reading it, open *Endymion* at random (to say nothing of the later and more perfect poems), and examine the characteristics of the page before him, and I shall be surprised if he does not feel that the whole range of literature hardly supplies a parallel phenomenon. As a psychological curiosity, perhaps Chatterton is more wonderful; but in him the immediate ability displayed is rather the full comprehension of an identification with the old model, than the effluence of creative genius. In Keats, on the contrary, the originality in the use of his scanty materials, his expansion of them to the proportions of his own imagination, and above all, his field of diction and expression extending so far beyond his knowledge of literature, is quite inexplicable by any of the ordinary processes of mental education. If his classical learning had been deeper, his seizure of the full spirit of Grecian beauty would have been less surprising; if his English reading had been more extensive, his inexhaustible vocabulary of picturesque and mimetic words could more easily be accounted for; but here is a surgeon's apprentice, with the ordinary culture of the middle classes, rivalling in æsthetic perceptions of antique life and thought the most careful scholars of his time and country, and reproducing these impressions in a phraseology as complete and unconventional as if he had mastered the whole history and the frequent variations of the English tongue, and elaborated a mode of utterance commensurate with his vast ideas.

The artistic absence of moral purpose may offend many readers, and the just harmony of the colouring may appear to others a displeasing monotony, but I think it impossible to lay the book down without feeling that almost every line of it contains solid gold enough to be beaten out, by common literary manufacturers, into a poem of itself. Concentration of imagery, the hitting off a picture at a stroke, the clear decisive word that brings the thing before you and will not let it go, are the rarest distinctions of the early exercise of the faculties. So much more is usually known than digested by sensitive youth, so much more felt than understood, so much more perceived than methodised, that diffusion is fairly permitted in the earlier stages of authorship, and it is held to be one of the advantages, amid some losses, of maturer intelligence, that it learns to fix and hold the beauty it apprehends, and to crystallise the dew of its morning. Such examples to the contrary, as the *Windsor Forest* of Pope, are rather scholastic exercises of men who afterwards became great, than the first-fruits of such genius, while all Keats's poems are early productions, and there is nothing beyond them but the thought of what he might have become. Truncated as is this intellectual life, it is still a substantive whole, and the complete statue, of which such a fragment is revealed to us, stands perhaps solely in the temple of the imagination. There is, indeed, progress, continual and visible, in the works of Keats, but it is towards his own ideal of a poet, not towards any defined and tangible model. All that we can do is to transfer that ideal to ourselves, and to believe that if Keats had lived, that is what he would have been.

Contrary to the expectation of Shelley, the appreciation of Keats by men of thought and sensibility gradually rose after his death, until he attained the place he now holds among the poets of his country. By his side, too, the fame of this his friend and eulogist ascended, and now they rest together, associated in the history of the achievements of the human imagination; twin-stars, very cheering to the mental mariner tossed on the rough ocean of practical life and blown about by the gusts of calumny and misrepresentation, but who, remembering what they have undergone, forgets not that he also is divine.

Nor has Keats been without his direct influence on the poetical literature that succeeded him. The most noted, and perhaps the most original, of present poets, bears more analogy to him than to any other writer, and their brotherhood has been well recognised, in the words of a critic, himself a man of redundant fancy, and of the widest perception of what is true and beautiful, lately cut off from life by a destiny as mysterious as that which has been here recounted. Mr. Sterling writes:

> Lately, I have been reading again some of Alfred Tennyson's second volume, and with profound admiration of his truly lyric and idyllic genius. There seems to me to have been more epic power in Keats, that fiery beautiful meteor; but they are two most true and great poets. When we think of the amount of the recognition they have received, one may well bless God that poetry is in itself strength and joy, whether it be crowned by all mankind, or left alone in its own magic heritage.[1]

And this is in truth the moral of the tale. In the life which here lies before us, as plainly as a child's, the action of the poetic faculty is most clearly visible: it long sustains in vigour and delight a temperament naturally melancholy, and which, under such adverse circumstances, might well have degenerated into angry discontent: it imparts a wise temper and a courageous hope to a physical constitution doomed to early decay,[2] and it confines within manly affections and generous passion a nature so impressible that sensual pleasures and sentimental tenderness might easily have enervated and debased it. There is no defect in the picture which the exercise of this power does not go far to remedy, and no excellence which it does not elevate and extend.

One still graver lesson remains to be noted. Let no man, who is in anything above his fellows, claim, as of right, to be valued or understood: the vulgar great are comprehended and adored, because they are in reality on the same moral plane with those who admire; but he who deserves the higher reverence must himself convert the

---

[1] Sterling's *Essays and Tales*, p. clxviii.
[2] Coleridge, in page 89, vol. ii., of his *Table Talk*, asserts that, when Keats (whom he describes as "a loose, slack, not well-dressed youth") met him in a lane near Highgate, and they shook hands, he said to Mr. Hunt, "There is death in that hand." This was at the period when Keats first knew Mr. Hunt, and was, apparently, in perfect health.

worshipper. The pure and lofty life; the generous and tender use of the rare creative faculty; the brave endurance of neglect and ridicule; the strange and cruel end of so much genius and so much virtue; these are the lessons by which the sympathies of mankind must be interested, and their faculties educated, up to the love of such a character and the comprehension of such an intelligence. Still the lovers and scholars will be few: still the rewards of fame will be scanty and ill-proportioned: no accumulation of knowledge or series of experiences can teach the meaning of genius to those who look for it in additions and results, any more than the numbers studded round a planet's orbit could approach near infinity than a single unit. The world of thought must remain apart from the world of action, for, if they once coincided, the problem of Life would be solved, and the hope, which we call heaven, would be realised on earth. And therefore men

> Are cradled into poetry by wrong:
> They learn in suffering what they teach in song.

FINIS

EVERYMAN'S LIBRARY: A Selected List

BIOGRAPHY

ESSAYS AND CRITICISM

FICTION